Because It Is So Beautiful

BECAUSE IT IS SO BEAUTIFUL

UNRAVELING THE MYSTIQUE
OF THE AMERICAN WEST

A NONFICTION COLLECTION BY

ROBERT LEONARD REID

COUNTERPOINT
BERKELEY, CALIFORNIA

Library of Congress Cataloging-in-Publication Data Is Available

Jacket design by Jen Heuer
Book design by www.DominiDragoone.com

ISBN 978-1-61902-929-3

Counterpoint Press
2560 Ninth Street, Suite 318
Berkeley, CA 94710
www.counterpointpress.com

Printed in the United States of America
Distributed by Publishers Group West

10 9 8 7 6 5 4 3 2 1
6104 2379 8/17

FOR
DAVID HERTZ

All the wild world is beautiful,
and it matters but little where we go,
to highlands or lowlands, woods or plains,
on the sea or land or down among the crystals of waves
or high in a balloon in the sky;
through all the climates, hot or cold, storms and calms,
everywhere and always we are in God's eternal beauty and love.
So universally true is this, the spot where we chance to be always seems
    the best.

—JOHN MUIR

CONTENTS

AUTHOR'S NOTE

The title of this collection originates in a comment made by the writer Barry Lopez at the conclusion of a talk he gave many years ago in Sacramento. I detail the circumstances of that talk, and its relevance to this collection, in the book's opening selection, "To Live One's Life."

"Intruders on a Lifeless Ridge," "The Fire and the Rose," and "Ling-Ling Has Killed Another Baby" are published here for the first time. Each of the remaining pieces appeared earlier in one of my nonfiction books (*Mountains of the Great Blue Dream, Arctic Circle,* or *America, New Mexico*) or in some other publication (see the acknowledgments for credits). I've added material to "Decrescendo" and "The Condor's Last Flight" to document changes in the statuses of wolves and California condors as of 2017. Lastly, I've made minor changes to a few of the pieces to reflect the passage of time and smoothed out some clumsy constructions that somehow found their way into the selections the first time around.

A native Pennsylvanian, I discovered the majesty and wonder of the American West as a teenager, during two month-long summer sojourns with my parents. The first took us to New Mexico and Arizona, the second to the Pacific Northwest. After college, I taught mathematics in New York City private schools for a few years. Then, no longer able to resist the call that had beckoned since my two summer awakenings, I went west. I've been here forty years—twelve in California, eight in New Mexico, twenty in what I intend to be my last stop, northwestern Nevada. During those years I've traveled widely and written extensively about the West, the darkness no less than the light. So it is that the pieces in this collection document the astonishing journey of the Porcupine caribou herd across northern Alaska and Yukon and the Long Walk of the Navajo from Arizona to eastern New Mexico; the sublime beauty of California's High Sierra shoulder-to-shoulder with the plight of the homeless in Santa Fe. Forty years ago I set out to find the West. The pieces in this collection are the record of my quest.

ROBERT LEONARD REID
CARSON CITY
WINTER 2016

Because It Is So Beautiful

TO LIVE ONE'S LIFE

The writer's lonely, harrowing struggle to give shape to his or her elusive vision of the world—to complete a book, to discover among the fragments of a thought or a dream the precise image needed to breathe life into a poem—is a familiar chapter in the annals of pain and grief. So, too, are the equally daunting tasks the writer faces once the project has been completed—finding a market, pocketing a few bucks (maybe) in order to repeat the whole grim process again as quickly as possible. As Philip Roth explains, hilariously, in *The Ghost Writer*:

> *I turn sentences around. That's my life. I write a sentence and then I turn it around. Then I look at it and I turn it around again. Then I have lunch. Then I come back in and write another sentence. Then I have tea and turn the new sentence around. Then I read the two sentences over and turn them both around. Then I lie down on my sofa and think. Then I get up and throw them out and start from the beginning.*

Writers are the modern-day equivalent of medieval monks: They spend their lives in solitary confinement inscribing manuscripts at turtle speed while flogging themselves dutifully. If someone were to open their cell doors and offer to set them free, they'd decline. That's why you'll never see a writer at the Elks

Club or Republican Party headquarters: Writer's aren't joiners. That, too, is why writers' unions have never been successful. It's not that publishers can't be dragged to the bargaining table; some will come, albeit reluctantly. Writers, on the other hand, will never show up. They don't want to unite. They're too busy turning sentences around.

Of the several unfortunate effects that the writing life engenders, perhaps the least remarked-upon is the distancing it accomplishes, one writer from the other. Unlike members of many professions, writers don't relax by, say, playing softball in Thursday-after-work leagues, and they don't hang around water coolers trading stories with their colleagues. While everyone else is having a good time, writers are staring at the walls of their darkened rooms, or teaching dreadful nineteenth-century novels to bored college students, or going to the library to research hamster mating rituals, all solitarily. If they do meet other writers, it's usually as panel members at conferences, from which they flee as soon as the panels are adjourned in order to return as quickly as possible to their darkened rooms.

In the empty quarter of the West, this distancing effect is especially pronounced. In northwest Nevada, where I reside, many writers choose to live apart not only from other writers but from nearly everyone else, too. I know of poets and novelists who make their homes in hamlets named Virginia City, Dayton, Sierraville, Truckee, Glenbrook—places that make my own port of call, Carson City, seem practically metropolitan.

However non-communal the writing profession may be, it has spawned a vital *community* of writers, self-contradictory though this may seem. Forced by circumstances into their cheerless gulags, writers recognize in one another their common struggles and the costs they exact; the battle scars forge sentiments of mutual admiration and respect, and friendships that are lasting and strong.

Writers blurb each other's books (imagine Coke plugging Pepsi: "Monumental! Haunting! One of the truly great colas!"), exchange forewords and dedications ("For our friends at Coke, with profound gratitude"). Even writers at the top of their profession stay in touch with those below, taking on protégés, showing up in small towns to read and field questions at the local bookstore or to offer words of encouragement to students at the community college, answering letters from their fans. (Among a handful of thank-you letters I've collected from celebrated writers is a reply from E.B. White that includes this vintage White locution: "I'm not writing much anymore, being seventy-seven, but am still busy throwing books together in order to create a commotion around the house.") Many teach, and while a few are famed for their ruthless criticism (Denise Levertov comes to mind), many more follow the lead of Raymond Carver, who always had a kind word for even the most ham-fisted effort. (Novelist Jay McInerney tells of an aspiring writer in one of Carver's classes who read a bizarre story in which a young couple meets, falls in love, marries, and opens a restaurant, the opening night of which is marred by a band of submachine-gun-toting terrorists who burst in and kill everyone in the restaurant. End of story. Aghast, the other students in the class crucified the writer, then turned to Carver. Clearly at a loss, he paused, then said softly, "Well, sometimes a story needs a submachine gun.") In what other field are the great and the ungreat so closely allied?

(For the record, writers are no less competitive than members of other professions. Rivalries are fierce, competition for contracts and grants can be ugly, and bickering and sniping sometimes foul the air, especially the air around the few who command the big dollars. Murder is, for the most part, unknown. What I'm trying to say here is that there is another side to the story.)

Lately, prompted by recollections of a book festival that took place in Reno a decade ago, I've been thinking about this paradox—the physical distance that separates writers measured against what might be called the spiritual closeness of the breed. It seems to me that, having achieved its laudable results—bringing readers and writers together, retailing oodles of books, raising and hashing over issues of serious literary import, energizing the city—the festival settled into the consciousness of its participants as a symbol of the strength and diversity of the local community of writers, and of their connection to the national and international communities.

The event featured a sparkling array of activities, nearly all of which brought writers together to talk, to read, or to comment on the world of writing. The stars of the show were out-of-towners Annie Proulx, Anne Lamott, and Barry Lopez; a distinguished group, but, as I saw it, no more so than the staunch band of local writers who also participated and who, daily, provided bedrock for the Great Basin's appropriately vast cultural landscape—the Ash Canyon Poets, the one-hundred-strong Unnamed Writers' Group, participants in the Piñon Poetry Festival and the "Voces de la Vida Latina" writing contest. Over several days, the many literary streams represented by these writers met and joined into a river of considerable power and grace.

My own involvement with the festival provides an example of the phenomenon I've been describing, the spiritual link between writers that transcends physical separation—in my case, separation between writers who do not even know each other. Along with Scott Slovic, then the director of the Center for Environmental Arts and Humanities at the University of Nevada, I had the honor of introducing Barry Lopez when he delivered his keynote address at the University of Nevada's Nightingale Hall. In my remarks I told of how Lopez had indirectly opened the way for me into the community of writers during another talk he had given some twenty years before.

The bare outline of the story is this: On a winter weekend in 1979 or 1980, I joined several hundred rock climbers, river runners, backpackers, and other like-minded folk at a conference in Sacramento to consider the question: How can we save the wilderness? Some deeply committed people attended the gathering, and they proposed some drastic answers. Among us, to cite one example, was Mark DuBois, an almost mythic river rafter who, a few months earlier, had chained himself to a rock in California's Stanislaus Canyon in an (ultimately futile) attempt to halt the waters rising behind the New Melones Dam.

I was a mountain climber whose affection for the high peaks had evolved gradually into political commitment to the cause of preservation. I was, too, a fledgling writer searching for direction. I knew the importance of craft, experience, doggedness, and the other familiar requisites for literary success, but I lacked vision— an understanding of my relationship to the world.

In his talk, Lopez spoke with humor, passion, and almost frightening eloquence about bears and Eskimos, stories and spirit, connection and disconnection. So electrifying were his words that I can still remember precisely where I sat in the auditorium and the slant of light that illuminated the stage.

Lopez could not have known the effect he was having on one impressionable member of the audience. Yet I believe he established a connection with me that evening—a thin strand in the elaborate web that is community—by describing a path that was utterly new to me, and by suggesting that, as others had walked that path, it was safe for me to do so as well. This all happened in the space of a few seconds, as he mulled over the central question plaguing the men and women at the conference, namely: How could we convince lawmakers to pass laws to protect wilderness? Lopez argued that wilderness activists will never achieve the success they seek until they can go before a panel of legislators and testify that a certain river or butterfly or mountain or tree must be saved, not because of its economic importance, not because it has recreational or historical or scientific value, but *because it is so beautiful.*

His words struck a chord in me. I left the room a changed person, one who suddenly knew exactly what he wanted to do and how to do it. I had known that love is a powerful weapon, but until that moment I had not understood how to use it. What I learned on that long-ago evening, and what I have counted on ever since, is that to save a wilderness, or to be a writer or a cab driver or a homemaker—*to live one's life*—one must reach deep into one's heart and find what is there, then speak it plainly and without shame.

I didn't meet Lopez at the Sacramento conference, or any time afterward, until the evening of his address at the book festival. As I came off the stage following my introductory remarks, he embraced me warmly and mentioned something he remembered from his talk twenty years before. I felt suddenly that we were old friends—a confirmation both of the power of language and of the threads that joined us as writers.

Then he walked to the podium. Consistent with the spirit of the festival—and with his own instincts, I think—he began his presentation by mentioning another writer: the poet Francisco Alarcón, who was also a guest at the festival. "I received a copy of Francisco's latest book today," Lopez said in a tone of admiration. "I'd like to begin tonight by reading three of his poems . . ."

WEST, TO THE FUTURE

I live on the last street in the southwest corner of an unincorpo-
rated district south of Carson City called Indian Hills. Sweeping
west from my house, first in a series of low hills carpeted in sagebrush, then in steep, thickly forested mountainsides, are the foothills of the Sierra Nevada. The view from my front yard is hardly
different from what one might have seen from the same spot a
thousand years ago.

In the opposite direction, the view could not be more dissimi-
lar. Home Depot and Target crown a hill; beside them, a freshly
minted golf course opens the way to Carson Valley, a ferociously
growing portion of the fastest-growing state in America. Highway
395 bisects the scene, providing at any hour a crush of cars and
trucks. New homes spring up overnight, some on land where
magnificent, century-old farms stood until recently. At night the
Johnson Lane area looks like a small city. Ten years, my neighbor
predicts: Ten years till the valley is choked with houses and shopping malls, for ten miles, all the way to Minden.

Perhaps he is right. And yet, something about Nevada gives
me hope that it is the view west from my house, not east, that provides the ultimate glimpse into the future. One or two evenings
a week, just before retiring for the night, I step outside into my
front yard. Moments after I close the door behind me, the great
Nevada wilderness sweeps me into its arms. Inscrutable mountains

rise up around me, a coyote cries, the beguiling odor of sage fills the air, undocumented breezes report in from distant lands. In the transcendent quiet of a vast Nevada night, I'm rocked by a perception that sometimes eludes me during pedestrian daylight hours, a perception not of a withering landscape under final assault by land movers, pavers, and fast-food restaurants, but of a vibrant, tolerant, and infinitely strong omnipresence waiting patiently for the world to come to its senses.

The idea of an invincible wilderness just beyond my doorstep is a new one for me. Before emigrating to Nevada twenty years ago, I viewed the wild as an exotic, fragile place to which I traveled after months of dreaming and planning—the Tetons, where I went to climb summer after summer, the Bugaboos, Shasta, the High Sierra. I'd load up my backpack and my climbing gear and drive two or three days and then: Hooray! Wilderness!

In Nevada, where we're understocked in Top 10 thrills like the Tetons and the Bugaboos but crammed to the rafters with the grandeur of the everyday, I've come to understand wilderness not as the stuff of *Arizona Highways* photographs but as the world I live in; not as spectacle but as air and sky and earth—the taste and feel of Tuesday evening in my front yard. Here the veneer of civilization lies lightly over the landscape. On a sidewalk near the capitol building, indomitable desert plants press upward between the cracks. Ten minutes from my house, I watch a team of badgers excavating an unlucky ground squirrel from its den. My friend in Jacks Valley returns home at the end of the day to find a pair of bald eagles perched on the roof of his house. In many parts of the country, civilization is crowding in on eagles. In Nevada, it's sometimes the other way around.

A Nevadan has an easy time understanding Robinson Jeffers's confidence in the steadfastness of nature. "It has all time," reflected the brooding poet of the Pacific:

It knows the people are a tide
That swells and in time will ebb, and all
    Their works dissolve. Meanwhile the image of the
        pristine beauty
    Lives in the very grain of the granite.

The people are a tide. For Jeffers, humans were the problem—all humans. Enraged by profit-driven development, he made the mistake of confusing the ravenous few with everyone else and became an intolerable misanthrope. I wish he had known a few of the men and women who live on my street, who are not destroyers. Working-class one and all, they provide healthy antidotes to the bitterness and disengagement that come with living alone on a privileged rock, as Jeffers did, and also a firm refutation of his thesis. They like unspoiled nature. They're kind to it. They walk their dogs in it. They fish it and hike it and swim it and picnic it. They turn off their porch lights at night and then go out and smell it. I don't deny that my neighbors want their toys, their TVs, and their Burger Kings; so do I. Americans, all of us, want and use too much. We need to work on this.

Meanwhile, it's time to trust each other again. Most Nevadans don't want to crush wild things. Wild things are in our hair and in our nostrils and in our dreams. Why should we want to crush them? A few years ago, wildlife biologists in the Netherlands freed some European beavers whose forebears had lived in zoos for more than half a century. Scores of generations of the species had known only confinement behind iron bars; none had gnawed a tree or swum a stream. Yet, delivered into a forest, the newly liberated animals set to work at once building a dam. Their wildness could not be defeated; it lived in their genes, in their cultural memories, and perhaps in their spirits—as surely and as vividly as the view west from my house lives in my own.

I'm not sure what the mechanism of freeing ourselves from our own confinement will be. But I do believe that the future is in free-running rivers and snowy mountains and deserts so wide and graceful they bring tears to your eyes. If I'm right, the purpose of Nevada, where the wild and the beautiful are as familiar as day and night, may be to remind the world of the primacy and goodness of wilderness as a moral principle, and of the will of the people to live in it and to glory in it. The future is here.

REBUILDING THE CLOUDS

FROM *AMERICA, NEW MEXICO*

The deepest words
of the wise men teach us
the same as the whistle of the wind when it blows,
or the sound of the water when it is flowing.
—ANTONIO MACHADO, "REBIRTH"

In this wondrous scientific age, with its astonishing discoveries that life is biology, the stars chemistry, the atom physics, and the mind a set of crisp instructions analyzable on a laptop computer, John Greenleaf Whittier's belief that nature speaks in symbols and signs ought to seem as quaint as a husking bee. Strangely, it does not. Perhaps the most amazing thing about modern science is not the startling new view of the world it has given us but rather its failure to efface the old view. Church attendance and horoscope readings are up, psychics and channelers are doing brisk and lucrative business, afternoon television resounds with tales of near-death and out-of-body experiences, and a recent poll reveals that one out of five Americans not only do not understand that the sun is a thermonuclear reaction nearly a million miles in diameter, but they believe that the sun revolves around the earth. "When has astrology not been popular?" Robertson Davies inquires. "When has the heart of man given a damn for science?"

Experts tell us that the science gap is one more lamentable consequence of our failed education system. As an avid reader of nature's symbols and signs, I'm not so sure. The science gap may reveal as much about the poverty of science as it does about the failure of our schools. Recently, a friend whom I know to be intelligent, informed, and sane described to me an encounter he had had with a coyote on sagebrush flats near Cuba, New Mexico. My friend called the incident "magical." For a few seconds he and the coyote stood no more than thirty feet apart, gazing into one another's eyes. In that brief moment, my friend believes, a message of kinship, mutual respect, and goodwill passed between the two creatures. Then they nodded to each other and the coyote trotted off. Science would have a hard time explaining the language of that remarkable communiqué or the manner of its transmission. John Greenleaf Whittier would not.

Not long ago I saw a dolphin leaping in the northern sky. The figure was a slim and muscular storm cloud a contrail in length. It leapt like a rainbow, its curve exactly matching that of the sky. In color, the creature was hurricane gray with a swash of tangerine splashed across its dorsal fin by the soft bristles of the late afternoon sun.

Far below, the month was April and springtime was in flood. Deep in thought, I tramped about in my backyard reconnoitering for tender shoots and sprouts, even as I crunched beneath my feet the pale remains of last year's greenery, brittle as old bones. As I crunched, I wondered over a mysterious illness which for more than a year had kept my wife in a state of constant and steadily worsening pain. In vain Carol had trudged from one practitioner to the next, collecting a steady stream of confident and expensive diagnoses, each one contradicting the last. We still didn't even have a name for the demon that had turned our lives upside-down, never mind a cure. I was weary and afraid—which is to say, a perfect candidate for a message from the sky.

When I glanced up and saw that graceful dolphin cavorting in the celestial sea, I knew its meaning at once. A meteorologist might have seen an altocumulus cloud and understood that rain was imminent; I saw a kind smile where the dolphin's mouth would have been and understood that there is a benevolent force in the universe and that it has the power to heal.

One's interpretation of the world is a function of the language one speaks, and on this worrisome day, my language was religion, a common tongue in lands of wide skies and yawning spaces like New Mexico. Historian Roderick Nash wrote of the Chinese Taoists of the fifth century BC, who sought in wilderness glimpses of the unity and rhythm of the universe. He located the beginnings of the Jewish and Christian traditions of seeking God in big empty country in the Israelites' forty years of wandering in the desert. Before that, wilderness had been anathema to the Hebrews, but in the Sinai Desert, wrote Nash, "wild country came to signify the environment in which to find and draw close to God."

The backcountry traveler in New Mexico finds an environment that has been put to just this purpose. Scattered throughout the state are mountains, mesas, and remote hideaways that are sacred to New Mexico's Native Americans. In hidden valleys, at bends in lonely roads, one stumbles upon Benedictine monasteries, Buddhist retreat centers, Tibetan *stupas*, Catholic churches of crumbling adobe. In sublime Chaco Canyon, the organizers of the 1987 Harmonic Convergence discovered one of the earth's cardinal energy points, a place to which they attributed enormous spiritual significance. Religions old and new have found a home in New Mexico, and even nonhumans seem to benefit from the rarefied surroundings. Contemplating the crows over The Monastery of Christ in the Desert near Abiquiu, Thomas Merton decided that the birds flew "at a greater psychic altitude, in a different realm" than other crows.

~

PARADOXICALLY, NEW MEXICO has another side that is the antithesis of the one I have been describing. During the past eighty-five years, this land of sacred mountains and adobe churches has evolved into one of the U.S. military's most spirited and devout partners. There has always been a taste for war here, of course, but it was usually small in scale, waged first with rocks and spears, later with grapeshot and Colt .45s. The state's weapons upgrade to Patriot missiles and stealth bombers began in 1930 with the arrival in the town of Roswell of rocketry pioneer Robert Goddard. Booted out of Massachusetts as a fire hazard and dismissed by the army as a crank, Goddard discovered on New Mexico's parched southeastern plains the ideal laboratory for perfecting the science of liquid fuel. In the deep skies over Roswell there was cushion enough to absorb Goddard's occasional miscalculations, space enough to encourage even the myopic to envision a new and deadlier manner of war. The army came to its senses at last, and Goddard's flying pipe bombs became Pershing missiles and multiple independently targeted reentry vehicles.

World War II brought the Manhattan Project and the challenge of building an atomic bomb to New Mexico. The intricate network of connections between Washington and New Mexico that evolved during that period became the basis of a new economy. Following the war, military-based employment in the state skyrocketed. Today, the Los Alamos and Sandia national laboratories employ some twenty thousand New Mexicans. Several thousand more labor at the state's three military bases. One in four jobs in the state is defense related.

Whatever its spiritual heritage, New Mexico has never been a reluctant partner in its alliance with the military. During World War II, New Mexico suffered the highest casualty rate of any state, including some nine hundred deaths during the Bataan Death March and subsequent imprisonments. Car license plates are officially stamped with highlights of the driver's military career: "Purple Heart," "Ex-Prisoner of War," "Pearl Harbor Survivor," "Congressional Medal of Honor." Sonic booms are as common in Albuquerque as chile overdoses and are tolerated without complaint. A popular bumper sticker explains the public's forbearance: "Jet Noise—The Sound of Freedom." For many New Mexicans, those six words define the state's purpose. They view this mission as no less important than that of serving as the spiritual capital of America.

New Mexico's military-based economy has paid off handsomely. Huge numbers of jobs and no small amount of capital have been created in exchange for a few minor inconveniences. The latter include the Kirtland Underground Munitions Storage Complex, the world's largest nuclear weapons storage facility. Albuquerque has maintained the stockpile since 1992. Residents of San Francisco or Boston might balk at such an arrangement; for Albuquerqueans, a cellar full of B-83 and B-61 gravity bombs is no more troublesome than jet noise—offering the occasionally queasy feeling of freedom.

Only once has New Mexico come close to paying more than it bargained for in its partnership with the Pentagon. That was on May 22, 1957, when a B-36 bomber crew accidentally dropped a hydrogen bomb on Albuquerque. The weapon was called the Mark 17, and it was one of the nastiest ever built, packing about six hundred times the punch of the Hiroshima bomb. As we know, Albuquerque was not destroyed, so the Air Force simply pretended that the incident had never occurred and said nothing about it. Nearly thirty years passed before reporters from the *Albuquerque Journal* finally unearthed the story.

Looking back, the crew member who accidentally pulled the wrong lever readily admitted that he'd been a little careless, but, hey, the thing didn't go off, right, so what's all the fuss? Seeing Old

Scratch slip from his moorings and take to the air over land owned by the University of New Mexico in southeastern Albuquerque, an excited crewmember shouted, "Bombs away!" The twenty-one-ton weapon plunged thrillingly through New Mexico's famed azure skies, singled out a nice open field for itself, made its potentially historic approach, and landed on a cow, killing it severely.

Fortunately for the city, the crew had been as negligent with the Mark 17's arming device as it had been with the plane's bomb-bay doors. Conventional explosives on the weapon blasted out a small crater, but nothing you couldn't create just as easily by dropping a locomotive out of an airplane. The crew flew back to base, an Air Force team cleaned up the crater, and the citizens of Albuquerque went on with their lives, unaware of how close they had come to celebrity.

∿

WHITE SANDS MISSILE Range, a thirty-two-hundred-square-mile slice of south-central New Mexico, is America's largest military installation. Practically everything that flies and has an acronym for a name is tested at White Sands. Here modern warfare was invented, essentially antiquating bloody battles between ground troops and replacing them with desperate face-offs between electrical engineers. Inside range control, a computer jockey squeezing a Coke can in one hand and a joystick in the other zeroes in on a blip on a screen and fires. Another blip—the missile of the moment—streaks across the screen toward the first blip, usually a tank or a drone out on the range but occasionally a herd of sheep or a carport on a ranch adjacent to White Sands. The blips square off and the kill is made—or not, depending on the adequacy of congressional funding. And White Sands reloads for another test.

Most of the time, the secrecy of these pocket wars and the dangers they present to observers keep the gates to White Sands tightly locked to outsiders. But two days each year—the first Saturdays in April and October—the military grounds its missiles, clamps a lid on its secrets, and opens its doors to the public. Several thousand visitors come to pay homage to the spot of the most famous test ever conducted at White Sands: Trinity Site, where the first atomic bomb was exploded on July 16, 1945.

It would be difficult to overemphasize the importance of that test to the future course of events in New Mexico. Were the drop at Trinity to have fizzled and the Manhattan Project team to have been thwarted in their efforts to correct the problem, New Mexico's spectacular growth since the war would never have occurred. The state's reputation sullied, its name forever after uttered in scientific circles with derision, this briefly glamorous and up-to-date place would have slunk quickly, quietly, and permanently back into the Dark Ages.

At first glance, the army's decision to build the bomb here may appear to have been misguided. Of New Mexico's notable resources in 1942—peaceful isolation, heart-thumping beauty, and an old and distinguished culture—only the first was an obvious asset to the Manhattan Project team. But there were plenty of equally remote places where the bomb could have been built. Why, then, New Mexico? The answer was furnished by project director J. Robert Oppenheimer, and it turned on those very resources of beauty and culture that New Mexico had in such abundance.

Oppenheimer was a New Mexico kind of character: understated, rugged, sophisticated, an outdoorsman drawn to grand vistas and soul-searching ruminations. He did exquisite physics, he read Hindu philosophy, and he wore cowboy boots. He knew and loved New Mexico, having summered here for twenty years. With his brother he owned a ranch in the Pecos Valley, not far from Los Alamos. Sizing up potential sites for project headquarters, Oppenheimer was naturally drawn to New Mexico, not only because of his personal experience of the state, but also because he knew that it offered aesthetic rewards that might sweeten ever so slightly the arduous work of the elite scientists and engineers who would be giving up several years of their lives to work here.

Oppenheimer was largely responsible for the choice of Los Alamos as headquarters for the Manhattan Project. Something of a Shangri-La set on the forested Pajarito Plateau among the graceful, rounded peaks of the Jemez Range, Los Alamos looks out on the bare, brown, deeply scarred floodplain of the Rio Grande, an Old Testament backdrop for Oppenheimer's mystic Hindu texts. Beyond the floodplain rise New Testament peaks: the Sangre de Cristos, mountains of the blood of Christ. Six centuries ago, aeries in nearby cliff-sides provided homes for the long-vanished Anasazi. Backcountry hikers still stumble upon pre-Columbian statuary and ancient petroglyphs depicting deer, eagles, and the wonderful hunchbacked flautist Kokopelli.

In many aspects of their culture, Santa Clara and San Ildefonso residents, whose pueblos border on Los Alamos, still marked the hours by Anasazi time. The day began with the sun; the night was lit by the moon. Music and dance were as essential to life as water and food. The calendar was a cycle of cosmic reminders. The people worshipped in secret but celebrated in public, and soon after Oppenheimer and his people arrived in New Mexico, white faces from the labs began appearing in the crowds attending the Puye ceremonial dances at Santa Clara and the Buffalo, Comanche, and Corn Dances at San Ildefonso. Some of the Manhattan Project team discovered New Mexican arts—pueblo pottery, especially the stunning black pots by the renowned Maria Martinez at San Ildefonso, the woodcarvings of the master Hispanic carvers of nearby Cordova, and the weavings of Chimayo. In the evening a physicist could step outside his lab and smell provocations of piñon and juniper, hear Tewa lullabies rising just beyond a smoky ridge of evergreen, and, in the cold and glassy night, see the lights of

Albuquerque sixty miles distant, as cheerful and steady as camp-fires. Spring brought warm winds from the valley, summer mild, easy days. In winter there was skiing in deep powder on Pajarito Mountain. Most afternoons brought cottony clouds to solve along with differential equations.

Even today, seventy years after the Manhattan Project, the vast research labs that sprawl over the plateau remain overshadowed by the grandeur of their setting. My friend who once worked at Los Alamos spoke of browsing deer and dark mountainsides beyond his office window, and blissful noontime runs on roller-coaster trails lined with ponderosa pine. Oppenheimer understood the importance to his team of amenities such as these. They could spell the difference between failure and success.

Seen in retrospect, work on the atomic bomb appears to have been driven by an irresistible moral and intellectual force. Success seems to have been assured from the start. And yet the success of the Manhattan Project was anything but inevitable. The technical problems presented by Fat Man and Little Boy were fiendishly difficult. Solving them required a new breed of weapons designer. Before Los Alamos, bomb builders were anonymous underpaid technicians who rode subways and slaved away in dimly lit basements. Their job, crudely put, was to figure out new ways to cram more and more dynamite into smaller and smaller spaces.

By contrast, Manhattan Project team members were celebrated, princely. They collected Nobel Prizes, appointments to presidential commissions, tenured university positions. They played cellos and wrote poetry. Together they constituted perhaps the brainiest, most accomplished group of people ever joined in common cause. They brought a new aesthetic to the theretofore somewhat distasteful business of weapons design. Old-time bomb builders were tinkerers, plodders, pyromaniacs. Bomb builders on the Pajarito Plateau were artists.

For obvious reasons, there is a sizable danger in allowing such people to write their own press releases. On the day of Trinity, the Manhattan Project team created not only a bomb but a cloak for the bomb as well, an almost impenetrable linguistic cloud concealing the true nature of their invention. Physics and engineering became prayers and incantations; New Mexico once again became big, empty, God-fearing country. Here is J. Robert Oppenheimer quoting the Bhagavad Gita as the fireball lit up the New Mexico dawn: "Now I am become death, the destroyer of worlds." Another source gives him this line: "If the radiance of a thousand suns were to burst forth at once in the sky, that would be like the splendor of the Mighty One." (We are not told whether Oppenheimer lowered his voice for this reading or embellished it with primitive dance steps.) Said physicist Isidor Rabi: "It was a vision which was seen with more than one eye. It was seen to last forever." Said physicist Robert Serber: "The grandeur and magnitude of the phenomenon were completely breathtaking." Said chemist George Kistiakowsky: "I am sure that at the end of the world, in the last millisecond of the earth's existence, man will see what we have just seen."

And on and on. What the poets of Los Alamos observed was glorious, terrible, uncanny, unearthly, apocalyptic—anything but more dynamite in a smaller space. The bomb was pure science, but the idiom of the bomb was religious to its plutonium core. It was as if the true nature of New Mexico could not be destroyed, not even by a nuclear weapon. At exactly the moment when spirit appeared doomed, it revealed itself more clearly than ever.

The Kyries of Trinity are truly soul-stirring. Given their suspect origins, however, one is well advised to treat them as warily as one might treat a physics text by Robert Lowell or calculus theorems by Allen Ginsberg. As guides to understanding the events at Trinity, they are too riddled with ecstasy to be trusted. Add the oversimplifications of a fawning and thoroughly addled press attempting to whittle the bomb down to column size: Inevitably, the Manhattan Project team was said to have "unlocked the secrets of nature." Factor in the workaday obfuscations of the military: General Thomas Farrell, an observer at Trinity, said, "The effects could well be called unprecedented, magnificent, beautiful, stupendous, and terrifying."

The result is a mythology as profound, as sweeping, and as grand as Wagner's Ring Cycle. It was only a bomb, but one would have thought it the Holy Grail. One might as well come to know Trinity through these hosannas as study the history of Germany by attending a performance of *Parsifal* at Bayreuth. On the wide and fearful desert of New Mexico, the sands are white and J. Robert Oppenheimer is a Heldentenor in cowboy boots. Behind the chorus, a black and terrible cloud rises toward the heavens, and we raise our opera glasses to see . . .

∽

ON THE ROAD to Trinity, I resolved to stay sober. I would indulge in no ornamentation, no reflection—just the facts. The setting was not ideal for attempting such a stunt. From the town of San Antonio, the highway struck east into a vertiginous scrubland that pitched and rolled like a choppy sea. Low on the horizon floated the Oscura Mountains, bare and sullen as tramp steamers. The sky was weary, the wind mean. At a dip in the road I came upon a textbook dust devil, a complete meteorological event scrunched into a space the size of a barnyard. The twister lurched to and fro drunkenly, dust and debris flying about like squabbling chickens. At every turn the landscape conspired toward mindscape, and I feared that before long I would be seeing a mushroom cloud rising over the Oscuras.

But I resolved to stay sober. Here, barely expanded, are the notes I made during the remainder of my journey.

⌣

SAN ANTONIO, A dusty crossroads but nonetheless home of three internationally famous celebrities—the Owl Café, the world's finest green chile cheeseburger, and, somehow, Conrad Hilton. Drive twelve miles east on Highway 380 to the White Stallion turnoff. Take a right.

White Sands Missile Range.

A couple of cars ahead of me, one behind. Straight south over Jornada del Muerto, the dead man's march. I'm on the military base now, technically, though there's no way of telling by looking around. Nothing military about it. Looks like a big ranch. No sand, certainly no white sand. The white sand of the name is gypsum, and it's eighty miles from here, at the south end of the range. Here it's dirt and rocks. Big, wide, scrubby—nothing. It's easy to see why they chose this place.

Pickup truck ahead of me, family in a van ahead of the truck. It still looks like a ranch, but now things are changing. Low hills. Tracking dishes. Little backyard observatories, little Palomars, a whole hill of them. Trailers, Quonset huts, army-green vehicles zipping around like jackrabbits. A huge plateau, like a Chinese military base in Tibet.

Check-in at a kind of tollbooth or border-crossing station. The M.P. is formal but friendly. He smiles and hands me a sheet of regulations: no photography, no demonstrations, no picketing, no sit-ins, no protest marches, no political speeches, no weapons of any kind (I read this one twice), no alcohol, no drugs, no wandering about in a silly manner, no taking of souvenirs, no motorcycle riding without a protective helmet.

Pretty much nothing.

I ask for directions.

"Thirteen miles south, hang a left and another four."

In a minute I'm doing eighty; it doesn't say "no doing eighty." Vegetation tearing across the road, tumbleweeds, UFOs. Wind blazing like retro-burners, clouds chugging like freight trains. Surroundings dreadful, nothing but yucca, black, cracked, sucked dry. Van half a mile ahead. Not much to see except twenty miles of not much to see. Patches of mesquite. More yucca. Wretched mountains. The scenery is Neptune without the fun.

Sign: high-explosive test area.

Sign: missile impact area. Do not enter without permission.

A line from Loren Eiseley comes to me: "Certain coasts are set apart for shipwreck."

More cars. Hang a left. Here's where the road comes in from the town of Alamogordo. More cars. More cars. Military buses full of visitors. People all over the place. Ahead, straight-topped and striated, a low wall of mountains. The road readies, aims, fires straight at 'em.

M.P.s, male and female. The parking lot is full of cars, hundreds of them. At one end stands a row of buses. Visitors mill about in the parking lot. I park and join the crowd. There's a feeling of tension and excitement, as though we're on our way to a ballgame. Churning winds, thickening clouds. Somehow it's as bright as hell.

Near the entrance, vendors hawk books, hot dogs, T-shirts. The crowd drifts by: Lots of retired folks and families with kids. I hear German and French. I pass a party of Japanese.

A dirt path leads two hundred yards to GROUND ZERO. The wind is cold and nasty. Sheets of dirt fly parallel to the ground, forcing me to squint even behind sunglasses. People on the path walk slowly, talk in undertones. Everyone has a camera, despite the regulation. What brought them here? I'm nervous, sick to my stomach. Warning: THE USE OF EATING, DRINKING, CHEWING AND SMOKING MATERIALS AND THE APPLICATION OF COSMETICS IS PROHIBITED WITHIN THIS FENCED AREA, PER AMC REGULATION 385-25. There's an

M.P. answering questions. There's a woman with a Geiger counter. There's a man with a Lhasa Apso.

～

OPPENHEIMER WAS AT S-10000, a concrete-and-earth-covered wooden shelter ten thousand yards south of the test site. General Leslie Groves, the military director of the Manhattan Project, was ten miles southwest. Most of the witnesses were twenty miles northwest at a place called Compañia Hill. During the night there was thunder and lightning. Groves and Oppenheimer considered calling off the test. Groves threatened the project meteorologist, who promised a break in the weather at dawn.

The rain stopped at 3:15 A.M. Groves phoned the governor of New Mexico and told him to prepare to declare martial law. At 3:45 breakfast was served at the ten-mile shelter. At 4:00 the wind shifted and observers could see the stars. At 5:09:45 the automatic timing sequence was started at T-minus-2.0. At T-minus-1 Oppenheimer said: "Lord, these affairs are hard on the heart."

～

END OF THE path. On July 16, 1945, no one was here, of course— no pounding pulses.

Come in, come in!

I expect a crater but there is none, not even a saucer. The area is as flat as the surrounding countryside. The blast scooped out a hole eight feet deep, but afterward a mop-up crew filled it to keep down the radiation.

Fenced area the size of a skating rink. Still some radioactivity here, but not enough to hurt: a whole-body exposure of half a milliroentgen per hour, about what you get during a coast-to-coast jetliner flight. Even so, ten times the amount of natural background radiation, after fifty years.

Silver-green grass. Yellow twisted blades. Mats of dead and trampled gray. Flecks of glassy Trinitite, Coke-bottle green, a compound of blast-fused sand. Shadowy mountains, dark clouds in a sky rapidly going bad. Small clusters of people scattered throughout the enclosure. A cold wind. A bookstore hush. A scent of dry, baked, barren earth. A mangled section of one leg of the tower, all that was left. A hideous monument of black lava. A Japanese woman. A sound of weeping.

TRINITY SITE, WHERE THE WORLD'S FIRST NUCLEAR DEVICE WAS EXPLODED ON JULY 16, 1945.

Carol is sick. Please, God.

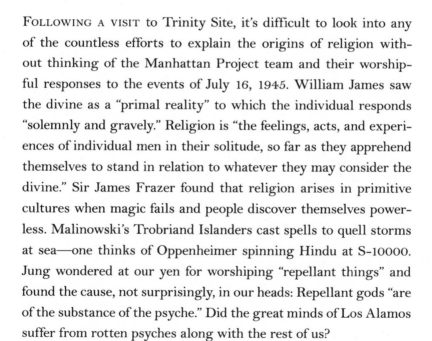

FOLLOWING A VISIT to Trinity Site, it's difficult to look into any of the countless efforts to explain the origins of religion without thinking of the Manhattan Project team and their worshipful responses to the events of July 16, 1945. William James saw the divine as a "primal reality" to which the individual responds "solemnly and gravely." Religion is "the feelings, acts, and experiences of individual men in their solitude, so far as they apprehend themselves to stand in relation to whatever they may consider the divine." Sir James Frazer found that religion arises in primitive cultures when magic fails and people discover themselves powerless. Malinowski's Trobriand Islanders cast spells to quell storms at sea—one thinks of Oppenheimer spinning Hindu at S-10000. Jung wondered at our yen for worshiping "repellant things" and found the cause, not surprisingly, in our heads: Repellant gods "are of the substance of the psyche." Did the great minds of Los Alamos suffer from rotten psyches along with the rest of us?

Then there is this sentence, which leaps out from Huston Smith's introduction to his grand survey, *The Religions of Man*: "Authentic religion is the clearest opening though which the inexhaustible energies of the cosmos can pour into human existence." Clearly, Smith was not thinking of the atom, but his observation may help to explain our reverence for the bomb and our difficulty in renouncing it—a difficulty that has often led Americans to denounce as heretics those who oppose nuclear weapons.

Earlier I observed that the fenced enclosure at Trinity Site has the area of a skating rink and, during my visit, the hush of a bookstore. Perhaps I should have said that the confine has the size and stillness of a cathedral. Like the classic cathedrals of medieval Europe, Trinity Site is laid out along an east-west axis. Entering by the south door, one traverses the south transept to the crossing, the intersection of the transept and the nave. To the right stands the detonation point, exactly where the altar would be. Most visitors begin here, then in respectful silence pay homage to the statues and relics located elsewhere in the interior—the tower footing, a bomb casing like that of the Nagasaki bomb, beads of Trinitite sparkling beneath the glass of a shelter erected to protect a small section of the original crater floor.

Along the north fence hang several dozen historical photographs—Stations of the Cross. In a long solemn line, visitors file past. Base Camp. Assembling the bomb. Hoisting the bomb into the tower. A copy of the Santa Fe *New Mexican*, dated August 6, 1945, which reveals what had been going on up on the plateau: "Los Alamos Secret Disclosed by Truman," "Atomic Bomb Drop on Japan," "Deadliest Weapons in World's History, Made in Santa Fe Vicinity." Hiroshima, one learns, was "an important Japanese army base." There is no mention of suffering or death; there are no photos of charred bodies. (Nor at Chartres are there depictions of the dead of Constantinople, Dalmatia, or Jerusalem.)

The display ends with a series of photographs of the blast itself. Like all such photos, they are failures. The light is too brilliant, the silver nitrate too worldly to record the unearthly transfiguration.

One sees a flat, featureless, bloated cloud—a horrible egg, or a massive tumor, or the grotesque distended belly of a fish brought up from the black depths of the sea. So ghastly are the images that they evoke terror in an instant—not the terror of death by vaporization, for it is nothing to die in a microsecond, but nuclear terror, the terror of slow, silent, helpless, wretched death by radiation poisoning. The vomiting, the creeping blindness, the snapping off of the skin like tree bark. The kind of terror only a god could devise. An Old Testament terror, delivered by the wrathful God of the Seventh Plague.

The deity created in New Mexico moves by clouds and kills by shadows. For years it has been omnipresent yet, amazingly, almost totally unseen, for not one in a thousand of us has witnessed a nuclear explosion. Like the god of the medieval mystic, it is a cloud of unknowing. Created in secrecy on the Pajarito Plateau, shrouded in metaphor, photographed surreally, venerated in prayer, understood abstractly or not at all, tested beneath the ground, stored in hollowed-out mountains, denied by those who make it and those who guard it, the bomb has ascended Christ-like into a heaven of incomprehension—not as the big, ugly, glorified stick of dynamite that it is but as the central theological mystery of our time. Not communism, not totalitarianism, not terrorism, not even the peerless joy of making a buck can explain the permanent state of war that has existed in the United States since nuclear weapons were invented; only nuclear religion can account for the condition. We have a president, whether Republican or Democrat, whose powers are truly papal, allowing him or her to mount crusades against demons real or imagined, openly or clandestinely, with or without the consent of Congress. We accumulate state secrets faster than Abraham and Jeremiah accumulated wisdom and truth; only the Word of God could mount with such fury. Our arms salesmen venture to the ends of the earth, spreading the gospel of weaponry

with the zeal of missionaries. Meanwhile, at the doors to the
Pentagon, obedient members of the fourth estate stand watch with
the solemnity of Swiss guards at the Vatican, heralding fabulous
press releases as though they were encyclicals.

Like archangels we discover infidels worthy of our awe-
some power. Before World War II, our enemies were treacher-
ous or villainous or detestable, but they were rarely evil or mad.
Beginning with Hitler, they have been nothing but: Stalin, Mao,
Ho Chi Minh, Qaddafi the mad Libyan. Khomeini, quite mad; bin
Laden, evil. Mugabe. Assad. Hussein. Kim Jong-il, evil and mad.
Like Christian soldiers, we slay the dragon and march on, oblivious to the silent dead, the shattered lives, the burning flesh—the
human faces behind the cloud. No souvenir photos of Nagasaki or
Baghdad or Afghanistan adorn our fences. War is hell or evil or
shadow or madness or hypothesis or God or blips on a screen. But
it is not something we believe ourselves capable of understanding,
so we do not even try.

The mystery of Trinity clouds our view of the world; it is
an element of the "awful smog" of which Daniel Berrigan spoke.
Berrigan challenged us to see through the veil, through "a duplici-
tous leadership, an inert Congress, a morally cloudy church, and
the jingoistic media." Even today, decades after the blast, something unnamed and powerful conspires to obscure the events at
Trinity Site. Tramping back and forth over that tiny circle of earth,
my emotions conflicted, my thoughts confused, I could make no
sense of what I saw or felt. It was as though I were trying to understand the Virgin Birth.

Utterly defeated, I was about to return to my car when on a
hunch I decided to visit the wall of photos one last time. There my
perseverance paid off and I found the piece of the puzzle that had
been missing. The key photo shows not the blast, not the front
page of the *New Mexican*, but J. Robert Oppenheimer, sometime

after the event, standing at ground zero inspecting the mangled strut of the tower.

I gazed at the familiar figure—pale, skinny, almost emaciated—and the baggy clothing, and the signature porkpie hat. Behind him runs a long low shape of mountains. Looking more closely at the shape, I realized I had seen it before. I studied the photo, memorized the angles and shadows behind Oppenheimer. Then I set out toward the spot where the photographer must have stood. As I moved, I trained my eye on the fluid geography of the horizon. With each step I took, the shape changed minutely, melting toward the profile of mountains I had memorized from the photo. After I moved a few more steps, the two slipped together: a perfect fit. Those old dusty hills became my link to Trinity. They were there to witness the events of July 16, 1945, and they were there for me half a century later, to see with my own eyes. Before me stood the project director—a physicist, not a priest. I understood that a great scientific experiment had taken place on this spot, and that what lit up the New Mexico desert that July morning was not a thousand suns or the splendor of the Mighty One or a vision of the last millisecond of the earth's existence: it was an explosion triggered by the compression of a subcritical mass of plutonium into a high-density supercritical mass.

～

A HEALER—I DON'T remember whether it was the neurologist or the Tibetan lama—divined a diagnosis, and to Carol it seemed right. Another cloud began to lift. As it did, we read of the appearance of nuclear weapons in more and more alarming places. The world is full of Fat Men, Little Boys, and their jolly obese cousins, it seems, along with potentates ready to employ them.

But there is another, hopeful part of the story. Some of those obese weapons are being disarmed. Not since 1992 has either the

United States or Russia tested a nuclear device. Redirected weapons-grade uranium and plutonium from nuclear warheads now fuels nearly one-fifth of the world's civil nuclear power requirements. At Los Alamos there is work for people like plutonium chemist Joe Marz, who spends much of his time working on problems of disarmament. Through the haze we see the faint outlines of the faces of individual men, women, and children again. And we begin to wonder if the god may be false, or mortal at least—a silly wizard pressing buttons behind a curtain.

Through seventy years of war, the fundamental peaceableness of New Mexico, its habit of addressing the deepest concerns of people through the language of mountains and deserts, has not vanished; it has merely been overshadowed. Many New Mexicans remain committed to the old-time religion, and in every community there are churches to serve them: the Albuquerque Center for Peace and Justice, the New Mexico Peace Alliance, Veterans for Peace, the Society of Friends. There is a long list of such organizations.

It's argued by some that we have come too far, that the bomb is here to stay and that history cannot be reversed. Nonsense. Ridding the world of nuclear weapons presents an enormous challenge, but so did building the first atomic bomb. Eliminating its descendants will require men and women with the intellect, the determination, and the poetic vision of the team that J. Robert Oppenheimer gathered around him at Los Alamos. Such men and women exist in great numbers. I picture a day when the brightest and best of them will be brought in secret to some lofty and beautiful spot in New Mexico, and there put to work on this urgent and difficult problem. And a morning, perhaps years later, when we will witness the shining success of their efforts rising in the east—not a thousand suns but one, the old and good and best one, sign and symbol of the human capacity to light the world..

JOURNEYS THROUGH
SPACE AND TIME

FROM *AMERICA, NEW MEXICO*

*The Creating Power gave the people the pipe. "Live by it" he said.
He named this land the Turtle Continent because it was there that the
turtle came up with the mud out of which the third world was made.
"Someday there might be a fourth world" the Creating Power thought.
Then he rested.*
—LEONARD CROW DOG, BRULE SIOUX LEGEND

ong after dark one blustery evening in early March, I found
myself in Gallup, New Mexico. It was still winter there, at
an elevation of nearly seven thousand feet in the heart of New
Mexico's geological rust belt, the sprawling landscape of shattered red rock and worn-out hogbacks and buttes that composes
the state's northwest corner. The temperature was 18 degrees.
A surly wind kicked a pair of sickly-yellow food wrappers along
old Route 66, the long, grim fantasy in neon that is Gallup's signature after dark. G.K. Chesterton observed of Times Square
after dark that a man who couldn't read might think he was in
paradise. The strip in Gallup is a long way from paradise: fast-
food joints, pawn shops, dilapidated motels ("No train noise"),
food marts dealing cigs at the cash register for a quarter apiece,
saloons, liquor stores, more saloons, more liquor stores. No, the

rhinestone fantasy is closer to hell for anyone unlucky enough to land here on a cold winter night.

I parked near Fourth Street, zipped up my jacket, stepped into the wind. In spite of the cold there was a brisk trade at a liquor store half a block away. A steady stream of customers, most of them Navajo—or Diné ("the People"), as many prefer to be known—passed through the door in both directions. Outside, a group of young men, hatless, coal-black hair shining eerily in the amber light, huddled near the curb. They were smashed—struck down in midsentence. Silent and immobile, they appeared to be frozen in time.

Two women paced nearby. They complained hoarsely, waved their arms. A male friend approached. The women turned on him, scolding him angrily. Then the three stepped smartly into the store.

Propped against the door of my car, I observed from twenty yards away. No one seemed to notice or to care. The scene unfolded with ghastly proficiency, too carefully scripted to admit a new player. Smiles were desperate, laughter uncontrolled. Drinking is serious business in Gallup. Binges can last for days. On this night it was Coors and Richard's Wild Irish Rose. On Sunday when liquor sales are banned, drinkers will turn to hairspray and household cleaner.

A few steps from the door stood a tall, frail, ghostly figure, a Diné. He was framed by a wide window hung with an assortment of frayed ads for cheap beer and wine. The man was alone, limned in a silver glow from inside the store. He wore a blue watch cap, a brown, tattered, thigh-length belted jacket, jeans, and brown leather shoes. His gaunt frame curved in a smooth thin line from head to foot—a crescent moon fast slipping toward the horizon. He appeared to be in his sixties, though he could have been much younger. His face was long and bony, his eyes unfocused.

He was floating.

Several minutes passed. The old man turned and shuffled to a new spot a little farther from the door. To propel himself along he clenched his fists, raised his forearms parallel to the ground, and swung his arms jerkily, like rusted pendulums. When he settled into his new position, his eyes were nearly closed. His face was contorted as though he was in pain.

Patrons came and went, oblivious to the man by the window. Beside the building stood an empty lot, a pissing-and-puking place littered with paper and broken glass. A bare bulb high on the wall cast a septic glow over the area. The old man shuffled into the middle of the lot, then turned to face the street. He appeared lost, a lonely figure adrift in an immensity of space. For a few seconds he struggled for balance. He reached up and adjusted his watch cap, as if to anchor himself more securely to the ground. Briefly moored, he opened his eyes wide, and for a long moment he seemed to be at peace.

Raptly watching the old man, I failed to hear the police van pull up in front of the store. There was a sudden commotion as the men and women on the sidewalk scattered in all directions. The dreadful, earsplitting sound of a bullhorn rent the night.

"ALL RIGHT, GET A MOVE ON!"

An expression of alarm crossed the old man's face. Curiously, he made no effort to escape. Instead, he broke into a slow-motion trot toward the van. An officer stepped out to greet him. The Diné smiled self-consciously, his eyes lusterless. Then he lifted his hand slightly, index finger extended, as though he were hailing a waiter.

The officer stepped to the rear of the van and threw open the door. The man attempted to step up gracefully but missed his footing. With a huge effort, the officer seized him like a side of beef and hoisted him through the opening.

I was ten yards behind, gazing into the dark interior of the van. On either side there was a long seat, the seats facing each other separated by a narrow aisle. The old man was on his hands and knees in the aisle; above him on both sides hung drooping heads. The officer stepped back, and for a moment the vehicle appeared to be stuffed with corpses. Then the door slammed and the van sped off into the night.

~

LIKE MANY OF New Mexico's cities, Gallup resists easy classification, for it has two sides: one handsome and inviting, the other almost unbearably repellent. By day it is a bright and agreeable place, a leathery, upbeat community of some twenty thousand, steeped in the history, culture, and feel of the Old West. Set in a valley of enormous beauty, the city is a natural destination for travelers. Navajo, Zuni, and Hopi reservations are nearby. This favored location has made Gallup one of the nation's premier trading centers for Native American arts and crafts. For the nature-oriented visitor seeking gems of another kind, Gallup is the perfect jumping-off point for excursions to iridescent deserts, ornamented canyons and mesas, turquoise lakes, black-rock volcanoes collapsed in huge, glittering heaps, and those jewels of Anasazi culture, cliff dwellings set like diamonds in stone.

At night, however, the allure disappears, and the city's downtown area is transformed into a bleak and joyless place. Gallup is the county seat of McKinley County, the poorest county in one of the poorest states in America. Thirty-six percent of the county's residents, most of them Native Americans, live below the poverty line. For children under the age of eighteen, the poverty rate is 43 percent. Liquor is not sold on the nearby reservations, so men and women who want to drink come into Gallup to do so. Local police lock up scores of them each night. McKinley County's highways are among the nation's most dangerous, largely because of alcohol. Prudent New Mexicans steer clear of the area, especially at night and on weekends and holidays.

The state's Native Americans are not always among the prudent. Their slaughter on New Mexico's highways proceeds with a kind of historical inevitability. Some die conventionally in car accidents. Others are hit as they stagger along streets or country roads. In 2014, a total of seventeen were struck and killed by vehicles. Ten more were found in fields or alleys, dead from exposure. Age is not a factor, and some Gallup residents grow misty-eyed at the mention of Shannon Garnenez, a Diné girl found frozen to death in a ditch behind a Gallup grocery store a week before Christmas in 1989. She was thirteen.

During the early 1990s, widespread publicity about Gallup's alcohol-related problems led a coalition of community and Native American leaders to take remedial steps. Prevention programs were implemented in schools, new treatment centers were opened, drive-up liquor windows were shut down, and DWI patrols and arrests were beefed up. Early indications gave cause for hope: Alcohol-related deaths dropped markedly. But most of the gains were soon reversed, and old patterns returned.

What is the cause of this distressing state of affairs? In New Mexico, whose Native American population as a fraction of its total population is second only to Alaska, one hears a multitude of answers. Some theorists postulate a defective gene that makes certain individuals unusually susceptible to alcoholism, though a major study at the University of Arizona, published in 2016, casts serious doubts on that theory. Others argue that joblessness and poverty are to blame, still others credit a broken spirit. A few—ignorant and surely broken in spirit themselves—say that this is the best that Native Americans can do.

I had my own theory. To test it, I drove three hundred miles from beleaguered Gallup in New Mexico's tumbledown red-rock badlands to placid Fort Sumner on the state's lyrical eastern plains. As closely as roads would allow, I followed the route of the Long

Walk, the forced march that in 1864 took the vast majority of the Diné from their ancestral homelands in Arizona and New Mexico and into captivity at a place called Bosque Redondo. In 1863, following years of hostilities between Diné and the encroaching white population, General James H. Carleton had issued an ultimatum to the Diné: Surrender or die. Those who turned themselves in would be resettled and converted to the white man's ways.

Like many of his contemporaries, Carleton had a simplistic notion of the ease with which such a transformation could be achieved. The Diné were savages, he reasoned, but like naughty children, they could be taught to behave. Take them far from their homes, Christianize them, show them the superiority of the life of the gentleman farmer to their own uncivilized ways, administer a little encouragement as necessary, and all would soon be well.

To implement his plan, which would serve as a prototype for the Native American reservation system, Carleton oversaw the construction of Fort Sumner on the banks of the Pecos River, at a spot known as Bosque Redondo—"round grove of cottonwoods." A scanty oasis in the midst of expansive plains, haunted by wolves, coyotes, and marauding parties of Comanches and Kiowas, the spot was fearfully isolated and almost comically ill-contrived for teaching the joys of farming. Nevertheless, Carleton pronounced it "a fine reservation." There, "old Navajos would soon die off, and carry with them all the latent longings for murdering and robbing; the young ones would take their places without these longings; and thus, little by little, the Navajos would become a happy and contented people, and Navajo wars would be remembered only as something that belongs entirely to the past." Not incidentally, Carleton had a second motive in wanting to remove the Diné to Fort Sumner: Like many before him, he believed that the tribe's homelands were storehouses of vast amounts of mineral wealth. Carleton dreamed of seizing the Diné's lands and opening them to plunder by whites.

Few Diné turned themselves in. When the deadline passed, Carleton attacked with every weapon in his arsenal. Army troops invaded Diné lands, determined to bring the renegades to their knees. Methodically moving from one habitation to the next, soldiers burned fields, slaughtered sheep and horses, and destroyed homes. Diné who refused to submit were slain or captured and released quietly for the slave trade that flourished in New Mexico at the time. (Some five hundred Diné slaves served white owners in Santa Fe alone.)

The Diné resisted with tenacity and courage, but they were hopelessly outgunned. When brutal snows hit late in 1863 and food supplies gave out, the game was up. The majority of the people, many of them starving, stumbled into Fort Defiance and Fort Wingate, army outposts near today's city of Gallup. There they were told to say goodbye to the land where they had resided for centuries, where their creation story affirmed that their ancestors had emerged from beneath the ground, and where tradition held that their world was bounded by a circle of sacred mountains. Early in 1864 in deep snow and freezing cold, tribal members set out in several huge contingents for Bosque Redondo, accompanied by officers of the First New Mexico Cavalry.

Most of the Diné were clothed in rags. They slept in the open and subsisted on brutally low rations. They were issued white flour they had never before seen and had no idea how to use; some tried to eat it raw, and others made a paste of it with water. Many doubled up with cramps and were unable to walk. Hundreds of Diné died of dysentery, exposure, and starvation. Those who could not keep up were shot.

Eight thousand Diné walked across New Mexico to Fort Sumner. There, General Carleton determined, they would learn prosperity and peace.

And there I found confirmation of my theory. It lay not in hard science or in masses of carefully marshaled sociological data, but in legend, which—along with chiles and sunsets—is one of New Mexico's finest products. Science and data give us facts, which are useful in establishing truth; legend gives us melody, redolence, and hue, which are essential to that end.

New Mexico is bursting with such resources. Before Carol and I thought of moving there from California, she visited a friend in Albuquerque. The two spent an afternoon at the pueblo of Acoma, and there Carol experienced what she and I have come to understand as an enchantment: an awakening to a vivid transcendental truth that lay beyond the grasp of reason—hers or anyone else's. When she returned home, she managed to convey to me the fact if not the nature of her encounter; a short while later we emigrated to New Mexico.

The catalyst for her inexplicable apprehension was a metaphysical thread in the warp and weft of the everyday that is brighter in New Mexico than anywhere else I know. It is the central and overwhelming affective resource of the state. I'm speaking not simply of the richness of the native culture or the splendid achievements of New Mexico's native peoples, though those are parts of it. But more importantly, New Mexico (a state with a greater concentration of scientists, engineers, and other no-nonsense rationalists than any other) bears witness at every turn to a critical wisdom preserved doggedly by its native peoples in the face of massive denial by whites: The world has a mystical, spiritual nature that is absolutely inaccessible to reason.

"The facts may help us to feel sure about our control of circumstances," observes nature writer John Hay, "but they are a poor substitute for the deeper equations of earth and human life. The American Indian saw the Word behind all manifested things, the primal, creative power." That sovereign intuition, I am convinced, is essential to our survival as a nation. Today the native peoples of this continent hold it in trust for us all. I hope that one day we will thank them for their trouble.

As a man who once earned a degree in mathematics (by the skin of my teeth, I should admit), I for a long time looked at unexplained phenomena as something like genial trout lollygagging in the sun and waiting patiently for some passing logician to throw in a line and haul them out. Today I suspect I was only about half right. Climbing mountains for a quarter century softened me up by introducing me to the melodies and hues of the natural world; opening my heart to the enchantments of the American West finished the job. I do not argue for a rejection of reason in favor of transcendence, rather for an incorporation of both into any effort to understand the world. Surely scientists should strive to answer every question that presents itself to them. They would be well-advised, too, to read self-help manuals on how to handle disappointment and failure, to prepare themselves for the day when they complete their grand explication of the universe and discover that half of its pages are still blank.

In America, only the native peoples have consistently shown a keen understanding of the duality of nature. The great Lakota warrior Tȟašúŋke Witkó—Crazy Horse—provides a fascinating example of a man who not only understood this duality but learned to control it and to use it for his own ends. Crazy Horse believed that we live in a shadow world, a sort of limbo parallel to another more fully realized abode. His genius was that he learned to pass from one world to the other, perhaps through the use of meditation techniques similar to those employed by Buddhist masters and other mystics. His powers enabled him to achieve what Thomas Merton, referring to the ultimate goal of Buddhism, called a "metaphysical intuition."

Crazy Horse took his horse with him into the parallel, fully realized world. The animal was happy there. It danced and leapt about in a very undignified fashion, and that was why Crazy Horse took the name that he did. He was in that parallel world, too, at the Battle of Little Bighorn, and he was there fifteen months later at Fort Robinson when he was arrested. As Dee Brown tells the story in that essential volume of American history *Bury My Heart at Wounded Knee*, Crazy Horse stood outside the jail and looked into the shadows behind the bars where men were chained like dogs, where all was madness, and he knew he could never go inside. He chose the freedom of the fully realized world, and for that he was killed.

We have photographs of every great Native American leader from the mid-nineteenth century onward, save one: There are no photographs of Crazy Horse. Perhaps the science of photography is inadequate for capturing certain images.

In the mountains and deserts of New Mexico, it is possible to see a world no photograph can depict (leave your camera at home). It is a world oblivious to comment, interpretation, judgment, or conclusion—Thomas Merton's obstacles to metaphysical intuition—a world inaccessible to those whose antennae are unresponsive to enchantments. Cautions Annie Dillard: That we are much informed does not mean that we are well informed.

To the much-informed, New Mexico proclaims, unplug your computers, toss out your guidebooks, and retune your antennae for some truly eye-opening information.

~

AN HOUR FROM Gallup, I left the interstate and rambled up to Acoma. I'd been there at least a dozen times, never tiring of the place. Residents call it Sky City, because the pueblo is built atop a tall mesa that overlooks a broad, peaceable valley of indescribable splendor. From the streets of Sky City one looks down, as if from the sky, on the woebegone rest of the world. The pueblo is well over a thousand years old—some say it's the oldest continuously inhabited settlement in North America. Information like that might get you to Acoma, but what will bring you back are the tumbling, juniper-scented wind and the sensation of lusty adventure the place invariably imparts, dizzy and mysterious, like a kiss from a beautiful stranger.

Not far from the village stands a formation called Enchanted Mesa. Its walls are vertical; there is no safe or easy route to the summit. According to legend, the Acoma once lived atop Enchanted Mesa. Then a storm arose, destroying the stairway carved into the rock. Villagers who were stranded at the top died of starvation.

Historians say that there is no evidence to substantiate this legend. Geologists tell us that the mesa is built of Dakota sandstone. Surveyors have calculated that it is 430 feet tall. Guidebooks point out that it is nearly three times the height of the Statue of Liberty.

A swirling wind surrounded me as I stood beneath the mesa, utterly alone, struck both by the poverty of the facts and the richness of the legend. I had no doubt that what I was observing was a 430-foot-tall chunk of Dakota sandstone. But it was equally clear to me that as a means for understanding the mesa—for grasping its essential nature—the facts are hilariously inadequate. In the cry of the wind I picked out an anguished call for help floating down from the hidden recesses far above me. I listened, then searched the forbidding walls for signs of vanished stairs.

~

AT CORREO I turned southeast toward the town of Belen and made for Abo Pass, the cut in the Manzano Mountains that opens the way to the tenacious plains. I was following a route sketched on an old map but without much confidence that the line on the map marked the exact route of the Long Walk. The official U.S. Army record of the walk is almost nonexistent. Several dozen military personnel accompanied their Diné captives on each of the marches to Bosque Redondo, but few left details of their several weeks on the trail. Almost everything we know from the army's point of view stems from a single long letter, dated May 12, 1864, written by Captain Francis McCabe, the leader of one of the marches.

Most narratives of the walk are based on McCabe's letter. But a rich storehouse of little-known material can be found in the stories passed down from the Diné who were there. In the 1970s, students in the Navajo and Indian Studies Program at Navajo Community College in Tsaile, Arizona, under the direction of coordinator Ruth Roessel, collected many of these stories from older Diné, who had heard them from their parents and grandparents. The recollections were published by Navajo Community College Press under the title *Navajo Stories of the Long Walk Period*. The book will provide vivid and compelling reading for anyone accustomed to bloodless bureaucratic and academic history.

Said Howard W. Gorman, seventy-three, born into the Bitter Water Clan:

> *On the journey the Navajos went through all kinds of hard-ships, like tiredness and having injuries. And, when those things happened, the people would hear gunshots in the rear. But they couldn't do anything about it. They just felt sorry for the ones being shot. Sometimes they would plead with the soldiers to let them go back and do something, but they were refused. This is how the story was told by my ancestors. It was said that those ancestors were on the Long Walk with their daughter, who was pregnant and about to give birth. Somewhere beyond K'aalogii Dzil (Butterfly Mountain) on this side of Bilín (Belen), as it is called, south of Albuquerque, the daughter got tired and weak and couldn't keep up with the others or go any farther because of her condition. So my ancestors asked the Army to hold up for a while and to let the woman give birth. But the soldiers wouldn't do it. They forced my people to move on, saying that they were getting behind*

*the others. The soldiers told the parents that they had to leave
their daughter behind. "Your daughter is not going to survive,
anyway; sooner or later she is going to die," they said in their
own language.*

*"Go ahead," the daughter said to her parents, "things
might come out all right with me." But the poor thing was
mistaken, my grandparents used to say. Not long after they
had moved on, they heard a gunshot from where they had been
a short time ago.*

*"Maybe we should go back and do something, or at least
cover the body with dirt," one of them said.*

*By that time one of the soldiers came riding up from the
direction of the sound. He must have shot her to death. That's
the way the story goes.*

Gorman's story and others in the book preserve human feelings, a critical component of history ignored or downplayed by many historians. Gorman is regarded as an unreliable source, not only because he heard his story secondhand but because he is emotionally engaged in it.

Yet Captain McCabe was engaged in the story too (and who could have avoided becoming engaged?), and he brought his own biases to his report. Nevertheless, because of his putatively superior status, he has become the source of nearly all that we "know" about the Long Walk. Here, then, is a dose of supposed truth from McCabe:

*On the 29th I reached Fort Wingate where I obtained a fresh
supply of rations for the indians [sic]; but only in the proportion of half a pound of flour, and half a pound of beef to each.
Apprehensive that this unexpected diminution of their rations
would have the effect of shaking their faith in the government,*

*and of creating mistrust and suspicion which if not promptly
removed might lead to serious consequences I called the principal chiefs and warriors together, and told them that I believed
they would receive their full amount of rations at Los Pinos;
and that the present diminution was but a temporary arrangement occassioned [sic] by the scarcity of provisions. This
seemed to satisfy them, and they assured me that they would
travel forward to the reservation cheerfully; and that they had
every confidence in the word of the Genl. Comdg. Department,
and in the Justice of the Government. They further remarked
that their minds were now firmly settled and that on arriving at the reservation they were determined to go diligently
to work, and with the assistance of the Government establish
themselves and their descendants forever in that location—
which they regarded of all others peculiarly adapted to their
present and future condition.*

The wide, easy miles leading to Abo Pass revealed New
Mexico at its most beguiling. Bright vagabond spring had arrived,
the sun was soft, the slightly frayed countryside was a tattered
picnic blanket waiting for customers. Above the evergreen-dotted
foothills, Manzano Peak gleamed in a feathering of fresh snow.
The road jogged left and right, sprang from one rounded destination to the next. It was midmorning in midweek in early March
in New Mexico; the brooks were dawdling, the roadrunners were
walking, there wasn't a cloud in the sky, and I was poking along
at forty miles an hour with the windows wide open and the road
to myself.

In scruffy fields beside the road slept more than the usual portion of those melancholy New Mexico staples: crumbling adobe
walls, sad foundations, burned-out Chevies and Fords, great plans
gone to seed. At Salinas National Monument, more of the same.

Here one can mourn the centuries-old ruins of once-grand pueblos and the long-abandoned Spanish structures that replaced them. Among the latter is the church of San Gregorio de Abo, which dates from 1629.

I passed with a wave. No sackcloth today, thank you. Beside a bridge over the Santa Fe Railroad tracks I parked the car and hiked to mid-span to await a freight train sweating toward the pass. Five awful engines thundered beneath me like an earthquake, shaking the bridge so hard I wondered if it was going to collapse along with everything else around here. I leaned over the railing and exchanged greetings with the engineer. After him, appearing one by one from between a pair of dusty hills, pounded a steady rhythm of boxcars bound for the pass. I was listening to the train, but I was thinking of lost homes and the rigid, unavoidable plains.

⌇

THE CIRCLE OF sacred mountains passes through parts of New Mexico, Arizona, and Colorado. Traditional Diné believe it is wrong and even hazardous to travel beyond the perimeter. To go to Bosque Redondo in 1864—even today for some Diné to journey to Albuquerque or Phoenix to see friends or to look for jobs—is to violate profoundly held religious beliefs.

It is unlikely that James Carleton knew of this proscription or, if he knew of it, that he gave it any importance. Utterly convinced of the rightness of his mission, he saw himself as the savior not only of New Mexico's whites but of the Diné as well. He would never have allowed the niggling concerns of a people he deemed inferior to himself—and pagan to boot—to interfere with his designs.

Carleton's supreme self-assurance illustrates a problem that has perennially plagued conversations between whites and Native Americans: the disinclination of whites to listen quietly and respectfully, to hear what is said, and to act on it. New Mexico in particular suffers from this syndrome, perhaps because of its large Native American population. During the 1980s, the federal government proposed the creation of a national monument on some hauntingly beautiful volcanic badlands which happen to include grounds that residents of Acoma Pueblo have used for religious purposes for hundreds of years. The Acoma protested. Hearings were held. The Interior Department accused the pueblo leaders of stalling, obfuscating, negotiating in bad faith—everything but what they were doing, which was stating clearly and explicitly that they wanted to retain exclusive rights to their traditional worship sites. At one point the Acoma were told that they would be permitted to worship on the lands and that they would need only to apply to the park superintendent for a pass when they wanted to do so. One Acoma wondered how the superintendent would feel if he needed only to apply to tribal leaders for permission to attend church on Sunday.

In the end, El Malpais National Monument was created on lands that include the traditional religious sites. The Acoma may visit the sites without the superintendent's permission. But because their locations are a closely guarded secret, when the Acoma arrive they may find campers or sightseers already in possession of the sites.

At its most inexcusable and most easily rectified, white misunderstanding of Native Americans stems from mere ignorance or laziness. A newspaper column by the late Andy Rooney is a notable but far from atypical example. "American Indians were never subjected to the same kind of racial bias that blacks were," Rooney wrote. "The impact on the world of their culture has been slight. There are no great American Indian novels, no poetry. There's no memorable music. There's no American Indian art, except for some good craft work." About religion, Rooney had this to say: "They hang on to remnants of their religion and superstitions that may have been useful to savages 500 years ago, but which are meaningless [today]."

One hesitates to respond to such a statement for fear of honoring it. But I cannot help quoting the distinguished art historian Vincent Scully, who, unlike Rooney, came to the Southwest to observe and to listen, and to study indigenous cultures. Scully was deeply impressed by what he found. Of Pueblo dance, he wrote: "The dances themselves I believe to be the most profound works of art yet produced on the American continent."

As for novels, Rooney could no more demand of Native Americans great examples of this recent Western European innovation in order to establish their cultural credentials than the Japanese can demand great Kabuki of the Irish to establish theirs. Poetry, music, art, *House Made of Dawn* (the 1969 Pulitzer Prize–winning novel by the Kiowa N. Scott Momaday), Pueblo myth, the Diné Blessing Way, the Corn Dance at Cochiti, the Fiesta de San Geronimo at Taos: It simply makes no sense to trivialize such achievements.

At their most intractable, misunderstandings involve clashes between wildly differing views of such concepts as space, time, and, as I have already mentioned, nature, which whites and Native Americans perceive in markedly differing ways. As cultural anthropologist Edward T. Hall has amply documented, whites often take such disparities as evidence of inferiority or defectiveness, rather than as merely different points of view.

As part of General Carleton's plan to bring down the Diné, army troops under the command of the legendary Kit Carson destroyed some five thousand peach trees on Diné lands. Before the conflict began, Carson had been a longtime friend of the tribe. Dee Brown states that of all the atrocities committed by Carson against his old friends, the one act for which they never forgave him was the destruction of their peach trees. To Carson, the trees

were simply a component of the Diné economy—one that, ironi-
cally, had been introduced to the Diné by European settlers. To
the Diné, for whom the origin of the acquisition mattered less than
its essential nature, the trees were sacred. Lupita Johnson, a Diné
of the Towering House Clan and a ranger in Arizona's Canyon
de Chelly, where the peach trees were destroyed, turns to white
legend for a comparison to what her people suffered when they
lost their trees, their land, and their way of life. It was, she says,
the equivalent of Adam and Eve being expelled from the Garden
of Eden.

More than a century later, the divergent viewpoints are little
changed. To many whites, the destruction of the peach trees is a
subject of historical and perhaps anthropological interest. To many
Diné, it remains an unforgettable blasphemy. Prayer books tossed
into a cesspool. Communion wafers fed to pigs.

∽

BELOW ABO PASS, through a stratum of old snow, the town of
Mountainair popped up beside the road like a bed of crocuses. Ahead
lay a new world: the Great Plains, a world of emptiness and space.

Few of the Diné could ever have seen such a thing. The monstrous upending of convention, even for a people intimate with the
huge scales of the West, must have amazed and disturbed them.
Bosque Redondo lay dead ahead, a hundred miles in the interior of
that strange and forbidding country.

I don't do space well. Does anyone? As close as the sounds
and smells of breakfast, as common as small talk, space is invisible
and impalpable—void of the kind of data we're good at processing.
And so it remains unreal. The surest proof of our insensibility to
space is that we tend to think of it as something far away, when in
fact it is everywhere. The greatest loss we suffer in our ignorance
is knowledge of the space around us, surely our most intimate and

constant companion. Unknown, it becomes an obscuring envelope that clouds our view of the world. Perhaps it is the mysterious nature of this envelope that makes it so difficult for human beings to see one another as they really are.

Of all the wonders of the plains, surpassing even its length and width and textures and always-springtime odors, the greatest wonder is the opportunity it affords us to sense our extended architecture—to see and feel the tiny room in which we live. Somewhere near the Lucy Ranch, the road and the land suddenly abandon the horizontal and tilt upward a few degrees. This was a major event, and great consequences ensued. Around me lay a pale dash of snow on the land. Ahead loomed a wispy white sky. As I rocketed upward, the whites of snow and wisp met and melted together and became one.

I stopped and stood by the road. And there alone, suspended in a fullness of white, I suddenly got it. The sky isn't *up there*, it's down here, all around me. I live in it. That stuff beside me and in front of me: It's sky.

"Before me is beauty, I am walking," sing the Diné, even as they sang while walking to Bosque Redondo. "Behind me is beauty, I am walking." What power that refrain conveys, its tidings of the earthly heaven that surrounds us, its celebration of the nexus between Mother Earth and Father Sky that is life.

And time. As we know from Einstein, that old trickster, it is as baffling as space. Near a shallow salt pond where paleo–New Mexicans gathered spice for their banquets, time was a grand white horse. He was alone, magnificent, side-lit into ivory, patient as the dark earth awaiting spring. Does another creature know the hours so well? As I made my way across a tawny esplanade dotted with mesquite, the animal looked on in silence. Not a muscle moved.

Then, with a magic I couldn't fathom, he took us both into a new world, one that was all peacefulness and light. He shifted his weight and tossed his head, and then he began to dance. Stepping forward, he cocked his ears in a gesture of barely contained glee.

In the clear sky we were friends at once. I stroked his long nose, rubbed the miraculous softness where he took in the wind. He mesmerized me with his pleasure and his heart. As I gazed eastward toward my destination, my view unobstructed by mountains or trees, my timepiece an animal unhurried by plans or concerns, time and landscape seemed suddenly to melt away. That distant moment when my ancestors wagoned west and for the first time came face to face with the people who called the mountains sacred no longer seemed so remote. The grove of cottonwoods beside the Pecos suddenly seemed close enough to touch.

Said Curly Tso of the Many Goats Clan:

> *A majority of the Navajos didn't know the reason why they were being rounded up, and different stories went around among the people. There were reasons like: The government in Washington had ordered that all Navajos be rounded up and bunched together at Tsehootsooi [Fort Defiance] and then taken to Hwééldi [Fort Sumner] where they could be put to death eventually—killing them by means of subjecting them to different diseases, starvation and exposure, as well as using every other possible way to kill all of them. The government's reason seemed to be that the white people, coming this way, needed more land, and Navajos were scattered out too far and lived on some of the best lands; so, in order to give the white people the land, plans were made by the government to kill most of the Navajos and send the rest to Halgai Hatéél [Wide Plains or Oklahoma], or, perhaps, to round them up and force them to live close together like the Hopis.*
>
> *Personally, I often wondered, after I became aware of white men's laws, why our ancestors were treated so unjustly. White*

*men make and preach about all kinds of laws, laws that protect
individual rights; and where were these laws then? At the time,
the Navajo people were ignorant of the fact that if an individual
does something wrong that individual is punished according to
the laws for his wrong doings, but the laws do not say to place
blame and have innocent people suffer the consequences; and such
was the case that the Navajo people went through.*

A group of Diné chiefs met with General Carleton at Fort
Sumner. They reported that he had fierce eyes and the mouth of
a man without humor. He was also fatally bullheaded. His plan to
"civilize" the Diné was a disaster. Despite warnings from the field
that he had vastly underestimated the number of Diné who would
be coming in, he readied the fort for five thousand prisoners. To
count the captives, soldiers regularly lined them up, and then, jab-
bing them with bayonets, sent them running through a gate like
sheep. In the late fall of 1864 the tally showed 8,354 Diné, plus
405 Apaches whom Carleton had rounded up in the further conceit that he could smooth relations between these long-standing
enemies. Before the experiment ended, more than nine thousand
Diné would be quartered at Fort Sumner.

Few of them had adequate shelter. For twenty miles up and
down the Pecos, most lived in holes in the ground covered with
woven grass or discarded sections of tent. The Pecos itself was
alkaline; many prisoners became ill from drinking the water. Fort
Sumner was so far from army supply lines that there was never
enough food to eat or material for improving living conditions.
Diné and Apache subsisted on constantly low rations. Barefoot and
in tattered clothing, they set to work building several miles of irrigation ditches. Carleton could come up with only fifty spades and
a few hoes, so most of the workers were forced to dig with rocks or
sticks or their bare hands.

Despite the hardships, the Diné brought in three thousand acres of corn, wheat, and beans the first year. Within weeks, cutworms destroyed the corn; floods and tornado-like winds finished off most of the rest. Rations were further reduced. Deaths mounted from starvation, pneumonia, and tuberculosis. Venereal disease spread as desperate Diné women sold themselves to soldiers for food. Nighttime Comanche and Kiowa raids against the defenseless prisoners became common. Firewood gave out. Near the end, captives were walking twenty miles to find mesquite to burn. When the branches were gone, the Diné unearthed the roots with their fingers.

Despite the dangers of setting out onto the open plains alone, captives began slipping away. On the night of November 3, 1865, almost the entire Apache contingent escaped. With the Civil War ended, Congress began looking into the huge cost of interning nine thousand Diné at Fort Sumner. General William Tecumseh Sherman quipped that the government could save a great deal of money by putting the prisoners up in New York City hotels.

White New Mexicans who only a few years earlier had seen Carleton as their savior began to have second thoughts. Cattle and sheep interests looked covetously on the Pecos bottomlands. Citizens who merely coveted safety recognized that the vast majority of the Diné who had been rounded up by Carleton were peaceful; the tribe's few troublemakers were still at large. A call went out for Carleton's ousting. As for the Diné, most New Mexicans favored sending them to Arizona.

Carleton was relieved of command in the fall of 1866. Two years of controversy ensued. The Diné remained at Bosque Redondo. Costs mounted; the suffering continued. On June 15, 1867, the principal Diné chief, Herraro Grande, spoke to A. Baldwin Norton, the superintendent of Fort Sumner:

*I am thinking more about my old country than ever before,
because there I could secure myself from my enemies; here we
have not that chance . . . We are all the time thinking of our
old country, and we believe if the government will put us back,
they could have us the same there as here.*

*Notwithstanding the cold and heat we have worked and
we will work, but as poor as we are we would rather go back
to our country. What does the government want us to do—
more than we have done? Or more than we are doing?*

*I think in the world, the earth, and in the heavens we are
all equal and we have all been born by the same mother—what
we want is to be sent back to our own country. Even if we
starve there, we will have no complaints to make.*

A year passed. Peace talks began between the Diné and the
United States government.

The Diné chief Barboncito said: "I hope to God you will not
ask us to go to any other country except our own. It might turn out
another Bosque Redondo. They told us this was a good place when
we came here, but it is not."

The Diné chief Ganado Mucho said:

*Let us go home to our mountains. Let us see our flocks feed-
ing in the valleys, and let us ride again where we can smell
the sage and know of hidden hogans by the smell of pinion
smoke. Let us go where we can build our homes in solitude and
privacy and live again as men, not animals. Let us be free to
build a better way of life and learn to live in peace where the
red buttes rise from the desert sands, and eagles sweep across
the sky. Let us go home. We have learned not to kill and not
to steal from the flocks of others. Here we have nothing. Our
children grow up in ugliness and death. Let us go home.*

The town of Fort Sumner stands by the Pecos at the edge of the Llano Estacado—"the staked plain"—the high, dry, treeless tableland that connects New Mexico geographically with the Texas panhandle. On his search for Quivira in 1541, Coronado crossed the Pecos a short distance to the north.

"It is impossible to find tracks in this country," wrote Coronado's chronicler Castaneda, "because the grass straightened up again as soon as it was trodden down. In 250 leagues was seen not a hillock which was three times as high as a man. The country is like a bowl, so that when a man sits down, the horizon surrounds him all around at the distance of a musket shot."

Not exactly a ringing endorsement, but much has changed since Coronado passed this way. On the balmy spring afternoon when I reached Fort Sumner, the countryside appeared gentle and giving. Green fields bordering on the east and broad cottonwoods crowding the river's edge provided a luxuriant setting for the town. Cattle grazed beside narrow lanes emanating from the river. A light breeze drifted in off the plains. Fort Sumner seemed more like a Midwestern town than any other place I had visited in New Mexico.

I drove south a few miles to Fort Sumner State Monument. Practically nothing remains of what scornful post–Civil War New Mexicans began calling "Fair Carletonia." Most of the fort was washed away by floods in 1932 and 1941. The visitor will find a few markers, a foundation, some artifacts. Perhaps understandably, the town plays down this chapter in its history. It's Billy the Kid who gets the notices around here, providing a cottage industry for purveyors of Wild West souvenirs and plenty of work for painters of garish signs. The notorious outlaw was killed at Fort Sumner in 1881. Local residents insist he is buried here, though some historians and champions for a competing site dispute that claim.

The tranquil Pecos, in March just a wisp of a stream, snaked north and south out of town. I pushed through the dense vegetation lining the river and jumped down a steep bank to the water's edge. Like many New Mexican rivers during the sensible, sober months leading up to the spring blowout, the Pecos is easy to take personally. The far side isn't far—two quick skips of a flat-backed stone. The water is so shallow it's mostly sandbars; long and fat, they stuff the river like a herd of hippos. The Pecos tiptoes around them carefully, as though it's afraid of waking them up.

Under a slow and peaceful midafternoon sun, I started downstream, tracing a zigzag path. It was quiet enough to hear the whispers of the rivulets beside me. A red-winged blackbird called from a nearby bush, then catapulted across the river like a rock, scarcely lifting its wings. The muddy flats were stamped with hand-sized asterisks—duck prints, as I quickly made out. The Pecos is a major flyway for migratory birds. Herons, snow geese, sandhill cranes, and now and then a rare whooping crane hotrod it up this old highway. My approach startled a party of ducks snacking in ankle-deep water; they were airborne at once, wings pumping like pistons. The birds leveled off at ten feet, deployed as meticulously as navy jets, banked left, filtered through the bony arms of a scrawny cottonwood.

I padded along, suddenly suffused in melancholy. At a bend in the stream, I knelt and dipped my hand into the water. The inexorable Pecos parted and trickled on.

Like the creation stories of most North American Indian peoples, that of New Mexico's Jicarilla Apaches tells us that in the beginning the earth was covered with water. The Jicarilla say that great storms rolled back the waters in each direction to form oceans at the edge of the world. To preserve water in the middle for people to drink, the beaver built a dam, creating a lake. The Jicarilla visited each of the oceans in turn but decided to return to the lake at the center of the world, near Taos, and there they remained.

The creation story of science tells us that the waters of the earth are formed from hydrogen and oxygen. Two atoms of hydrogen and one of oxygen combine to create every molecule of water. So vast is the number of molecules in even a drop of water, and so thorough is the blending of the world's waters over time, that it is likely that a few of those washing over my hand each second entered Alexander the Great in the last drink of water he ever took, and a few bathed each hoof of Coronado's mount when he forded the Pecos in 1541, and a few helped clear the throat of Barboncito in 1868 when he said, "After we get back to our country it will brighten up again, and the Navajos will be as happy and peaceful as the land."

In the clear waters of the Pecos, one can read both legend and fact. But which is which, and which shall we believe?

In the shimmering mirror, I studied the face of the man staring back at me, the sun a flickering fire on his shoulder. The stern eyes, the straight mouth . . . the two possessed a familiarity that reached far beyond self-knowledge. In my face I saw the face of James H. Carleton, the face of my people—tough, practical, and supremely self-assured.

～

IN 2015, THE median income of American Indian families in the United States was 60 percent that of white families. The poverty and unemployment rates more than doubled those of whites. On a few reservations, unemployment topped 50 percent. The suicide rate for adolescents and young adults was two and a half times the national average; suicide was the second-leading cause of death among adolescents and young adults, compared to the eleventh-leading cause of death nationally.

There are three dependable sources of income for American Indians today: operating gambling houses for whites, working in dangerous occupations such as uranium mining, and burying toxic wastes on their reservations. White New Age prophets ignore American Indian political struggles but rip off religious practices—drumming, dancing, sweat ceremonies, spirit quests, visions, talking circles—and then in glossy, no-effort-required packages hawk pale-faced imitations of these ancient rites to dispirited whites at get-rich-quick prices. Developers, lumber companies, and city planners plow roads across Native American religious sites without even saying hello. Justice-minded Americans greet the news that Swiss banks hold billions of dollars plundered from European Jews by the German government during World War II with a demand for the swift return of the money to the aggrieved parties or their descendants; no such demand is made for the swift return of billions of dollars in real estate to the descendants of Native Americans from whom that real estate was plundered by the United States government during the nineteenth century. Pious whites bow their heads before the majesty of the Constitution's guarantees of religious freedom, then thoughtlessly sink mine shafts into Native Americans' sacred mountains, construct ski resorts on their slopes, erect television towers on their summits. White fans of white-owned sports teams with racial slurs for names paint sacred symbols on their faces, chant sacred songs, mock sacred rituals. When Native Americans object, fans bristle in indignation: "What's the problem, for Christ's sake? It doesn't bother *me!*"

Writes Lakota Sioux Randolph G. Runs After to the editor of the *Albuquerque Journal*:

What words of encouragement can be said to the young Indian kids who see non-Indians jumping around drunk with painted

faces when they've learned that it was a sacred religious prac-
tice? Where is the pride we are supposed to feel in watching the
use of sacred Indian feathers trivialized and Indian specta-
tors showered with obscenities at Kansas City Chiefs home
games? . . . Would Catholics . . . be offended if the Lord's
Prayer was chanted by a rowdy, inebriated crowd at a New
Orleans Saints game during timeouts or if ashes were smeared
across their faces and the "holy water throw" was the norm?

"Every nation, like every individual, walks in a vain show, else it could not live with itself," remarked Rudyard Kipling, a man who was something of an expert on national vanity. "But I never got over the wonder of a people who, having extirpated the aboriginals of their continent more completely than any modern race had ever done, honestly believed that they were a godly little New England community, setting examples to brutal mankind. This wonder I used to explain to Theodore Roosevelt, who made the glass cases of Indian relics shake with his rebuttals."

The native peoples of this continent continue to confound those of us who discovered them here when we arrived. Partly our bewilderment stems from our observation, continually reaffirmed, that after all our painstaking efforts, many Native Americans, for reasons we cannot even remotely fathom, remain largely unimpressed by General Carleton's ways. Partly it originates in our continuing ignorance of alternative practices and points of view. Foolishly self-satisfied, we deprive ourselves of invaluable lessons in community, tolerance, moderation, cooperation, respect for nature, art, family values, and other matters we cannot even name—all of which we might learn from the continent's first inhabitants. A huge gulf continues to separate us, white and red. The result is that whites remain afraid of the people on the far side of the gulf, afraid of the spell they cast upon us and the power they hold over us.

Partly we are disconcerted because we know in our hearts that our victory over those people, if that is what it was, had nothing to do with moral or cultural superiority. Victory, hollow thing, was an accident of gunpowder. Invented in the Far East, introduced into Europe during the thirteenth century by a Christian friar, it came to America in the guns of the conquerors. Had it traveled instead in the opposite direction, across the Bering Strait and down the North American continent, the Queen of England might today be Sioux and the Washington Redskins might be known as the Nanticoke Savage Whites.

But mostly, I believe, we are deeply troubled because the native peoples of this land remind us of the monstrous truth in our past, which we have tried to hide behind the obscuring mists of myth and legend and which we continue to deny as vehemently as Germans and Russians until recently denied the truth of theirs. Our self-deception will continue to torment us until we bring it out into the open, make it the centerpiece of a great national discussion, seek reconciliation with the Native American, and come face-to-face at last with this long repressed but central fact of our history. The walk will be long. But it will certainly be worth taking.

I know a man, a Diné, who is succeeding brilliantly on his own scrupulously prescribed terms. He furnishes a luminous counterexample to commonly held white stereotypes about his people. Fluent in his native language, rooted deeply in Diné culture, he joins his people in ritual and dance, in all-night celebrations of the hunt, in ceremonies of marriage, healing, and death. He knows Diné who can transform themselves into bears and wolves, and he has seen eagles fly down to contribute their feathers to the work of medicine men. My friend has described these events to me, and because I know him to be an honest man, I believe that the stories are true.

This is also the man who encouraged Carol and me to attend the Santa Fe Opera soon after we arrived in New Mexico, and who gave us a quick lesson on how to behave while we were there. He is a college graduate who knows and appreciates what is good in white culture, an understanding few whites have of his own. For a time he worked as an agent representing the works of several Native American artists. Today he is a drug-and-alcohol rehabilitation counselor. He is married to an Apache woman and is nearer to the end of his walk than most of us are.

Not long ago, he had a strange experience. A radio talk-show host invited him to talk about his work with alcoholics. In the midst of the interview, as my friend struggled to describe the long and painful journey his clients must make, he suddenly heard himself blurt out a Diné word with which he was completely unfamiliar. It popped from his mouth as easily as if it had been his own name. A tribal elder later confirmed that the word was an ancient one no longer in common use, and that the startled speaker had pronounced and employed it with absolute precision. The word means "to travel back to oneself."

What a powerful fragment of neglected language my friend had discovered stranded on the distant shoals of his subconscious; what a grand journey it describes. For travelers marooned on the outer reaches of loss, it points the way home and promises that a healing place waits at the end of the road.

∼

ON JUNE 1, 1868, the principal Diné chiefs at Bosque Redondo signed a treaty of peace with the United States government. In return for their agreement to cease hostilities forever, the Diné gained freedom after more than four years in captivity. Two weeks later, a column ten miles in length comprising some seven thousand Diné waded the Pecos and began the three-hundred-mile journey home. Two thousand had died at Fort Sumner. Before the internment of these traditional shepherds, a government survey estimated their holdings at around a quarter of a million sheep. As the Diné set out across the plain, the number of sheep in their care had been reduced to under a thousand. Recalled the Diné chief Manuelito:

> *The days and nights were long before it came time for us to go to our homes. The day before we were to start we went a little way towards home, because we were so anxious to start. We came back and the Americans gave us a little stock and we thanked them for that. We told the drivers to whip the mules, we were in such a hurry. When we saw the top of the mountain from Albuquerque we wondered if it was our mountain, and we felt like talking to the ground, we loved it so, and some of the old men and women cried with joy when they reached their homes.*

Not many years ago, in a neighboring country where the earth's skin is red and where the people speak the language of mountains and rivers, there was a beautiful meadow. Each day as the sun fell toward the mountains the people went to the meadow to tell stories and play games with their families and to enjoy the beauty of descending night. Deer came to the edge of the meadow to graze in the lengthening shadows. Birds perched in the trees and sang their songs, and insects made their scratchy music in the grass. For a long time the voices of the people could be heard murmuring in that secluded place like a winding mountain brook.

One evening a group of strangers came and stood on the outskirts of the meadow. The strangers had stern expressions on their faces. They watched the goings-on without understanding. The birds flew away and the deer raced off into the forest and the insects crawled into their holes. Seeing the faces of the strangers, the people in the meadow grew afraid. They gathered their families together and returned quickly to their homes.

One man only remained behind. He was young and strong and handsome, a man greatly admired by his people. He was outfitted in traditional garb, except for a blue watch cap that he wore all the time, and of which he was very proud. He stood in the middle of the meadow without fear. And while the strangers watched, the light of the falling sun became yellow and ghostly, and the soft grass beneath the young man's feet turned to rubble. His body bent over like a crescent moon, his face became sorely wrinkled, and his eyes grew vacant and dull. Instead of going to him, the strangers watched from a distance. And the youth grew old and decrepit before their eyes, and his face contorted in pain.

He stands there yet, in New Mexico, in a city called Na'ni'zhoozhi. The strangers pass by each evening and see him and his blue cap and wonder why he is there. They do not understand that the ugly place where he stands is a beautiful meadow. They do not know that the old man is the tears they have never shed.

A SHELTER IN THE SKY

FROM *AMERICA, NEW MEXICO*

Your house is the last before the infinite,
whoever you are.
—RAINER MARIA RILKE, "INITIATION"

I

TO LONDONERS OBSERVANT of the rhythms and patterns of nature, the autumn of 1940, that stark season of witness to the fire and madness of the blitz, must have seemed a season without a soul. No drifts of golden plane-tree leaves stirred in the evening wind; no banks of chill, fine mist brooded over the Thames at dawn. The leaves burned where they hung that dreadful fall, and the mist on the river was hot and thick, the acrid residue of parachute mines and incendiary bombs. In the sky, the plaintive cry of greylag geese crossing from Iceland to their wintering grounds in southern France gave way to the drone of Heinkels and Messerschmitts rising from airfields just beyond the channel. A Londoner seeking cause for the emptiness of those soulless times might have found it in the words of Macbeth: "Now o'er the one half-world nature seems dead; and wicked dreams abuse the curtain'd sleep."

Nature was not dead. It lived, some said, in the hearts and minds of the German pilots and the men who commanded them, though I cannot accept such an allegation. Nature is baffling, but it is not cruel or evil or insane.

What was preeminently natural about the autumn of 1940 was the capacity of those beleaguered Londoners to touch us in their plight, and our irresistible need, in return, to see ourselves in their shoes. In such entanglements lies the essence of nature, which is connection from one particle to the next. Connection explains the human capacity for reaching out to the oppressed and seeking common ground with them. It explains, too, why the most compelling work of art to emerge from the fearful days of the blitz was a series of drawings not of bombers or of flaming buildings but of Londoners sheltered in the tunnels of the Underground. The artist was the sculptor Henry Moore, the drawings his *Shelter Sketches*. Explicit, unsentimental, executed in dense whirlwinds of incisive strokes, they depict a people reduced to a single unifying concern: the business of being human. In our own season of fire and madness, they remind us of the majesty of innocence and the resilience of all life.

Moore later recalled that during the early days of the blitz he had paid scant attention to the news that Londoners by the thousands were crowding into the tube each night to seek protection from the bombs. One evening he and his wife, Irina, found themselves without a ride after dining with friends in the West End. They returned home by Underground, exiting at Belsize Park. There they discovered that an air attack had begun. Because of the hostilities, they were unable to ascend to the surface.

"I spent the time looking at the rows of people sleeping on the platforms," Moore later wrote. "I had never seen so many reclining figures, and even the train tunnels seemed to be like the holes in my sculpture. Amid the grim tension, I noticed groups of strangers formed together into intimate groups and children asleep within feet of the passing trains."

In the nights that followed, Moore began haunting the Underground. He carried a notebook with him on his rounds, jotting down brief descriptions of scenes to flesh out later in his studio. Those scenes possessed him. In an uncanny example of life imitating art, they mirrored his own prewar sculptures: helpless, sprawling, bloated figures (Moore's subjects lay shrouded in blankets and sleeping bags), all horribly transfigured by their circumstances.

But there was a second and equally important reason for Moore's nightly visits to the underworld. Those huddled thousands, packed, as he said, like slaves in a ship bound from Africa to America, possessed a monumental quality. However nightmarish their circumstances, however powerless the innocents to affect their fates, they bore their condition staunchly and with dignity. In squalid shelters beneath the streets of a devastated city, the measures of life continued unabated: kindness, tolerance, selfishness and generosity, anger and amiability, community, heroism, love. Moore's sketches show a people not beaten down by hardship but lifted up by it. As the site of a grand epic of human survival, the Underground became a hallowed sanctuary, consecrated by the sacrament of suffering within. To go down into that hellish place was to enshrine oneself in human history at the highest level. It was to be ennobled.

That an artist could find grandeur in such baseness should not surprise us, for shelters have always had the capacity to raise up those who inhabit them and to inspire those who look on. Think of Robert Scott and his party in their pathetic tent on the endless Antarctic ice, of Anne Frank in her secret annex, of the battered wife sleeping peacefully at last in a safe house with no address. The quality that touches us in these scenes arises from the poignancy of human confinement, often undeserved, sometimes defenseless, amid the menacing tentacles of peril. However timorous the act of taking shelter may seem, it has about it something of the intrepid and the defiant. Whether it is the house in which we live, our own familiar and essential refuge, or a storm-tossed raft at sea, a shelter is a place where gallantry reigns, where the human spirit takes wing.

A prominent and troubling exception mars this otherwise stirring history: Far from the hallowed sanctuary of a Robert Scott or an Anne Frank, the homeless shelter has today descended to an ignoble level, a refuge unspeakable from blitzes unmentionable for the most detested among us. The homeless have come to represent our unfinished and perhaps unfinishable business as a society, and because they persist like a spot on the lungs, we regard them not with admiration for their dauntlessness but with loathing and rage. Recently I remarked on a ragged family of four camped on an Albuquerque streetside in attitudes that in a different era might have inspired a Henry Moore to great art. A well-meaning friend assured me that the homeless did not in fact want permanent dwellings, that surveys showed they preferred—what, refrigerator cartons in picturesque alleyways with expansive views of garbage cans and graffiti-fouled walls? Against all of our experience and better judgment, this astounding discovery supposedly held for children as well, two of whom hunched somewhat dazedly beside their parents in their grand parlor over the gutter.

As though entering upon one of the stages of death, we cope with the doctor's bad news by denying it. The homeless become the worthy victims of their own supposedly grossly mismanaged lives. And because they are to blame for their wretched predicaments, we irritably, piously, and apparently with clean hands consign them to street corners or dank shelters on the wrong side of town, like parents sending naughty children to their rooms. The word "shelter," uttered with a hint of scorn, becomes a wedge to drive between ourselves and the homeless, to shield us from them and from the disquieting knowledge that only a thin line may separate their fate from our own. Weighted down in that way, the word describes a place that is neither ennobling nor inspiring but humiliating and degrading.

Whether we can recover a full measure of respect for these sojourners on America's streets and alleys without actually joining them in their pasteboard boxes, I don't know. I think we can make at least a beginning in that direction by recognizing that theirs is not a lonely quest but one they undertake with us all. To seek shelter is an elemental instinct, one which neither war nor arctic winds nor a ravaged economy is necessary to excite. A nagging fear, an aching heart, a failure of nerve can be enough. Shelters are safe harbors from personal storms, places that allow us fleeting moments of conviction that we matter, and we seek them through-out our lives. When we cannot find them in the world beyond, we create them within ourselves, homespun sanctuaries that prom-ise escape and peace of mind. Within, we pray, we daydream, we delude ourselves. A porch swing becomes a stronghold against an uncaring world; an old rocking chair becomes a beacon in the night. I have turned often to such refuges. One was a cramped room with bare walls and an out-of-tune upright piano to which I retired often during a period of utter failure while I was in college. Another was a dimly lit hall in New York City's American Museum of Natural History. There, among scenes of the great mountains and deserts of the American West, I overcame the despair I felt as a city dweller, found renewal and a settled heart.

I escape to such a place sometimes today. It is not a building or a room, not even an enclosed space, but a simple clearing by the road in the radiant upper reaches of Santa Fe. My shelter is open to the world, an unshackling place: the floor earth, the roof sky, the walls history, culture, and the roughcast masonry of nature. The route of the old Santa Fe Trail rambles by, still echoing with the creak of buckboards and wagon springs. The Sangre de Cristo Mountains tower to the north, while westward the horizon tumbles to infinity with the peaks and mesas of the Jemez range—gray, weary things beaten down by a million years of trouble.

At the foot of the Jemez Mountains, slicing a stark twenty-mile-wide plain, flows the Rio Grande, the lifeblood of New Mexico: mainstay, dream maker, signifier, keeper of the faith, master of ceremonies, soul brother number one. Usually it wanders the landscape with a kind of jovial and majestic forbearance. But when the hour is late and the sun cooperative, the river sometimes catches the low-angled light, and I see a ribbon of water ignite, leap up, and race over the plain like wildfire—south through the valley of the conquistadors, south to Albuquerque and beyond, to the curving earth and the era before armies and before names. It is all there to see from my shelter, a panorama that I call the Great History. It is a vista of untold centuries, measured first in miles, then leagues, then cycles of the moon.

And just below, checkering a slanting esplanade of piñon and juniper, are the flat roofs of Santa Fe, surely one of the world's most welcoming and beguiling places. Santa Fe is advertised as America's oldest capital city, but aficionados are more likely to describe it as a feeling, a bedazzlement in the clouds. Wrote D. H. Lawrence: "The moment I saw the brilliant, proud morning shine high up over the deserts of Santa Fe, something stood still in my soul and I started to attend." Writer Paul Horgan called the city "intoxicating." Santa Fe literature is full of such commendations. To me, none captures the essence of the city better than this by a friend of mine: "When I think of Santa Fe, I think of kissing a beautiful woman in the snow."

For those not given to such romantic sentiments, there is no shortage of more practical reasons for visiting Santa Fe. It is a city with perhaps more to see and to do (and to buy), block for block— more music and art to enjoy, more history to absorb, more games to play, more beauty to admire, more sensual pleasures to indulge in—than any other city I know. Santa Fe is a fiesta for hedonists. I visit several times a year and never fail to fall utterly under its spell. Who needs shelter in such a place!

Yet sometime during each visit I'm overcome by a feeling of stark oppression among the dark adobe walls and narrow streets of this ancient city. Gracious though Santa Fe may be, it carries a burden of history—a concentration of experience—that can be overwhelming. Visitors to Florence sometimes succumb to a malady called Stendhal syndrome, an illness characterized by dizziness, depression, sometimes even paranoia. The cause is art poisoning, the cure a quiet day in the country beyond the inhuman demands of Ghiberti and Michelangelo. As a nexus of history, culture, and natural beauty matched by few other places, Santa Fe is capable of inducing a similar malaise that can be crushing. For me it begins as a vague feeling of unease and descends quickly to a deep and lingering despair—for Santa Fe, for New Mexico, for the condition of the world.

To gain relief, I make my way upward out of the shadows into the evergreen-studded foothills rising to the east. At each intersection the sky widens and brightens, the vista expands, the patient's condition improves. In a short time I'm stationed in my shelter, my clearing by the road, immersed in an envelope of mountain air lucid and resonant as wind chimes. An exquisite silence, the silence of daybreak, meets my ears. The Great History opens before my eyes. The sorrow of an unhappy world disappears behind the sheltering walls. In my grand refuge overarched by a vault of fathomless blue, I remember myself and my place and rekindle my belief in something Henry Moore understood well: the monumental nature of humankind. The restorative powers of the place arise in the ultimate gift of every shelter, and that is hope—which is to say, trust that beyond the madness of electrons there are ordered molecules, and beyond them rivers, trees, music, poetry, and the quiet conversation of friends. And farther yet, in that epic sphere that defines, shapes, and connects us all: kindness, generosity, and the courage of the valiant, dauntless before the storm.

All of which is prelude to my purpose: on a bleak December morning, I met one of the valiant seated on a curb in a parking lot in Santa Fe. His name was Thomas, and he slept in a field with prairie dogs. In a roundabout way, what follows is my effort to find him a home.

~

II

I'M NOT THE only one to have discovered the therapeutic quali-ties of the mountainside high over Santa Fe. Hundreds of houses dot the nearby slopes. The old river's smooth flow into history, a rare entertainment for me, is for the occupants of those houses a feature of the property, a special touch located just over the garden wall.

But they pay fearfully for the privilege. A residence in the Santa Fe hills is not simply a home, but what the real estate bro-chures call "a gracious island of privacy," "a prestigious, elegant compound," "not a house but an experience." They are shelters of a sort, but what shelters! Through most of the past century an occasional destination for the bored and the splendid, and sec-ond home to a few, Santa Fe in the final decades of the twenti-eth century underwent a tumefaction in reputation that sent real estate prices soaring into the Sangre de Cristos. Money arrived in bundles, much of it in the pockets of Californians. Between 1985 and 1990 the average selling price of a home in Santa Fe doubled. By 2016 the average listing price stood at two-thirds of a million dollars. The quaint little town in the mountains of northern New Mexico, once notable merely for its beauty and its charm, is now notable as an ambition, one of America's highest.

The upgrade was not accidental, though the speed at which it happened and the completeness with which it took over the city surprised many Santa Feans and troubled not a few. At a certain moment in the early 1980s, the city's residents, smelling something in the wind, swept their sidewalks, filled their potholes, razed their headshops. A few moments later their town was brimming with clothing stores that had branches in Carmel and Aspen.

The news spread. Stories in the national press documented the wonders of "the City Different," "Sagebrush Shangri-La," "Salzburg Southwest." Breathlessly, *The Washington Post* raised Santa Fe to number one on its list of the world's most prestigious "in" spots. Local artisans once happy to see their names tacked to telephone poles suddenly found themselves approving ad copy for *The New Yorker.* By 1983 the city had squeezed a hundred art galleries into its tiny downtown area and had begun to bill itself as the nation's third largest art market. By 1984 it was possible to purchase Venetian pastries in Santa Fe. By 1985 the channelers, polarity mechanics, and psychic podiatrists—always omens of a trend—had arrived. One in fifty Santa Feans was said to be a healer of one kind or another. By 1986 a million visitors a year were choking city streets. By 1987 a logo of sorts had been created: a ridiculous coyote, usually rendered in some dizzying sunset hue. No ordinary varmint, this one craned its neck to the vertical, threw open its chops, and howled in apparent chiropractic agony. To the horror of old-timers, animal lovers, and the even modestly refined, the creature took over the city like an army of migrating toads. By 1988 the coyote with the neck brace was the ubiquitous symbol of Santa Fe, bellowing from every T-shirt, postcard, and shop window, drowning out more preferable, more tasteful images like the opera house and the Palace of the Governors.

All that remained to confirm the city's arrival as a destination as essential as Paris or Milan was a context in which to understand

it. The context was created: style. *Santa Fe Style.* Originally a tribute to traditional New Mexican motifs and manners of presentation, it quickly became a tribute to the notion that you could sell
anything if you said it was Santa Fe Style, even if it wasn't, even if it
was a clock radio. Santa Fe Style wasn't exactly High Renaissance,
but at its best it tried honestly to celebrate widely admired local
design values: simplicity, earthiness, informality, all done up in
traditional Hispanic, Native American, and Anglo garb. It generated considerable amounts of civic pride and national attention,
plus oodles of cash.

With context in place, the truly important began to arrive.
There were rumors of icons: Redford! Spielberg! One winter day I
lunched with a friend in a tony restaurant just off the main plaza.
A perfect fire of harmoniously arranged piñon logs crackled beside
us in the fireplace. Polite noises interrupted the studied quiet of
the place—snatches of civilized conversation and clinking crys-
talware, our own included, which snuggled a delightful California
chardonnay. We dined on peasant food: pinto beans, chiles, and
tortillas, deployed in such a manner as to cost $19.95. Between
bites, a shadow suddenly fell across me as an enormous figure
came between our table and the fireplace. The eclipse was caused
by a celebrity moon, common in Santa Fe—the actor Jack Palance,
as it happened, revolving grandly around the room as though he
were in orbit. No one gaped or jabbed a tablemate in the ribs. Self-
containment, too, is Santa Fe Style.

While the city prospered, a transformation equal in magnitude
but opposite in direction was taking place. The poor of Santa Fe,
always a presence in the city, grew poorer, and many joined their
ranks. Here, as in all of America, the distance between rich and
poor widened, the desire to find common ground dwindled, the
mass of the faceless society grew larger and closer to critical. In
opulent Santa Fe the transformations were merely more apparent,

as well as more ironic. As restaurants catered to more and more exclusive clientele, the line of Santa Feans waiting for groceries at the First Presbyterian Church food pantry grew longer by the month. As real estate values skyrocketed, so did the number of homeless seeking refuge in the city's shelters. Because they earned minimum wage or less, many of those on whose labors the city depended—salespeople, museum workers, restaurant and hotel employees—could not put together the several-thousand-dollar nest eggs they needed to move into apartments. (Buying homes, of course, was out of the question for those who supported the city at ground level.) Some crowded into lodgings with three or four companions. Some commuted from cheaper cities. Others, less fortunate or more resilient, found themselves sleeping in arroyos, under bridges, or in Chevies parked behind the Safeway. Competition for less and less intensified. The spirit of friendliness and community long celebrated in the city began to dissipate, replaced by a hard edge and a bitter tone. A young man hawking newspapers on a street corner put it to me this way: "The streets are the new killing fields."

III

SHELTER: IT IS a theme woven thickly into the rich tapestry of Santa Fe history, an enduring trope that explains many of the city's paradoxes and idiosyncrasies. To understand why, it helps to see Santa Fe not as it is today—cluttered with tourists and traffic and pulsating with the rhythms of a modern sophisticated city—but as it was through the first two centuries of its history, a distant outpost at the nearly forgotten end of the Spanish empire in America. Perhaps comparison with Tibet is apt, for old Santa Fe shares some of Tibet's peculiarities: frightful isolation, religious zeal, certainty of purpose. It served as the capital of the province of

Nuevo Mexico, part of the territory claimed by the Spanish, which extended from the Mississippi River to the Pacific Ocean.

Yet to see that enormous region as a province ruled by the Spanish would be a distinct mistake. A few hundred soldiers, merchants, and administrators in Santa Fe and perhaps a thousand settlers and Franciscan missionaries within a few days' journey of the capital: Such a presence in an area twice the size of Spain does not make for an all-powerful authority. From a Spanish viewpoint, the province of New Mexico was one prodigious emptiness, relieved only in a distant corner by the alluring smile of civilization.

But it is well to remember that in New Mexico there is always a second and equally persuasive point of view, and often several more. Native Americans lived here in great numbers: By one estimate some forty thousand in central New Mexico alone at the time of Coronado's expedition. In native terms, the region was hardly empty. The many firsts of which New Mexicans boast proudly today—first capital city in North America, oldest public building, oldest continuously celebrated annual festival, first epic poem—rightly deserve to be lorded over only those puny bragging rights of nearsighted East Coast historians, whose working methods proceed directly from those of Julius Caesar ("It was not certain that Britain existed until I went there"), and who have yet to grasp that a certain kind of American history, one they admire and have always pretended to command—the history of European America—began here, in Spanish America.

So much for priority. There are cities in New Mexico—Taos and Acoma, to name two—that are older than Santa Fe by centuries, annual festivals older yet, epic poems already hoary when Columbus set sail for America. Little of this is known outside the Southwest because the native peoples, who hold all the records, rarely make a fuss over such trivia. As ancient travelers of the land, they know that before Plymouth, Jamestown, Santa Fe, Taos, and Acoma, there were now-forgotten kingdoms, and before them kingdoms more, and before them the kingdom of the earth itself, the ultimate title holder.

The first Spanish attempt to gain a foothold in New Mexico failed. Founded in 1598, the settlement of San Gabriel was hot, dusty, barren, and poorly defended. Many of the settlers came seeking gold, and when they found none, they felt swindled. Only the missionaries achieved success, finding in New Mexico's thousands an almost unbelievable fortune in souls to save. The friars went to work with a vengeance.

The San Gabrielenos held on till 1609. Late that year, cheered by a fresh commitment of support from Spain, they packed their wagons and moved thirty miles south to make a fresh start.

In the new location, the settlers proved at once that they had learned from their mistakes. Santa Fe's founders chose a beneficent place for their lonely city, a cool, well-watered spot among piñons and junipers at an altitude of seven thousand feet on the western slope of the southernmost Rocky Mountains. They laid out their main plaza on the ruins of an ancient pueblo. Around and near the square, using sun-dried bricks of soil, straw, and water, they constructed an administration building, a barracks, a church, a convent, shops, and homes for a few hundred residents. With San Gabriel no doubt in mind, they erected a wall at the edge of town to protect themselves from raids by local tribes, invasion by the French or English to the north, and perils of not quite definable origin that disturbed their sleep by night and fostered rumor and suspicion by day.

Those Santa Feans were quite on their own. The nearest Spanish settlement lay fifteen hundred miles to the south in Mexico. Were an envoy from Santa Fe to have set out for help, say, at first snow in October, the winds of a different winter would have been blowing when he returned a year later with a relief party. A male child born the morning a supply caravan rolled into town might be a soldier defending the city before three more such caravans arrived. The expected invasion from the north (which, for its entertainment value at least, might have been welcomed by the citizenry) never came. Never mind armies: Not a single Anglo entered New Mexico for almost two hundred years.

Even after Mexico won its independence from Spain in 1821 and began seeking trade with the almost-as-new nation to the north, visitors from the United States were rare. The journey over the Santa Fe Trail was long and arduous, a two-month ordeal at best. In *Death Comes for the Archbishop*, Willa Cather gave her ecclesiastic Jean Marie Latour a year to reach Santa Fe from Cincinnati. That was in 1851, mind you. It is true that certain misadventures befell Latour on his journey, delaying him more than most. But there is no denying the isolation of the settlement he was striving to reach: "New Mexico lay in the middle of a dark continent," Cather wrote. "No one in Cincinnati could tell him how to get to New Mexico—no one had ever been there."

In such a place, in a tiny shelter surrounded by gut-wrenching emptiness, European New Mexico found its start. The chronicles tell us nothing of the beauty of the location, but I cannot imagine that the river, the vastness, the great mountains splitting the clouds did not sometimes stir the hearts of those brave Spanish settlers. By day they must have thought they could see clear to Mexico. At sunset the high walls to the east shimmered in a dozen shades of gold and then red. The pastel sky bent low as though alighting, then grew soft and still, like a songbird closing its eyes. And then it was night and the sky dissolved, revealing the awful infinity fastened in radiant, unreachable stars clear to the western horizon.

It was an unworldly beauty, and a terrifying one. The city's founders called their refuge La Villa Real de la Santa Fe de San

Francisco de Asis—the Royal City of the Holy Faith of Saint Francis of Assisi. However else you may judge their achievements, grant them their due: the gallantry of the intrepid, the nobility of monuments.

The choice of Francis as patron saint was both inspired and paradoxical. The home city of Christendom's perhaps best-loved saint shares much in common with Santa Fe. Assisi is hewn from the forested slope of a mountain in Umbria in central Italy. In Francis's time it was a well-fortified shelter for a people prepared to do battle at any moment with enemies real and imagined. As a young man, Francis himself went to war against the nearby city of Perugia. He was captured and spent a year in prison.

Like Santa Fe, Assisi is built on the ruins of an ancient city, the first-century B.C. Roman settlement of Asisium. At the center of town stands the plaza, the focus of civic activity. Radiating out from there are government buildings, shops, churches, and homes, all fashioned from native stone, a local rock as pink as a Santa Fe coyote.

From the plaza, steep, narrow streets wind upward, past fine homes and into the deep forests that carpet the mountainside. There in a refuge called the Hermitage, Francis retired to rest, to pray—even, it is said, to preach to the birds. It is a serene and beautiful spot, little changed today from the way it was eight centuries ago when Francis was alive, when Santa Fe was a bustling Tewa Indian village.

One can hike to the Hermitage from Assisi in an hour or so. From the road there are expansive vistas south and west across the Umbrian plain into the haze and history of the Roman Empire. Seeing the view years ago, I was reminded at once of the valley of the Rio Grande. Assisi and Santa Fe both impart a feeling of safe refuge in the sky. Saint Francis, I think, would have been happy in the city in New Mexico that bears his name.

It was perhaps inevitable that the teachings of the simple man who preached love, kindness, and tolerance would be perverted almost from the moment of his death. Married, as he said, to Lady Poverty, he could not be permitted by the Catholic church to serve as a spiritual representative of that institution, which was already married to the international banking system founded during the very years of Francis's ministry. The troublesome conviction of the once-wealthy Francesco Bernadone that wealth corrupts and peace redeems was buried quietly along with his bones and his humble domicile beneath the sumptuous basilica erected in his honor.

Four centuries later, Franciscan missionaries fanned out from Santa Fe to Christianize the native New Mexicans. In the name of the man who preached the felicity of birds, they practiced the brutality of tyrants, enslaving some fourteen thousand men, women, and children. Within a few years of Santa Fe's founding, trade caravans could be seen snaking their way south to Mexico with their Diné, Apache, and Puebloan captives in tow. Men were sent into the mines, where inhuman conditions led to early deaths for many. Women and children were forced into domestic service in the homes of the nobility. If a woman had the misfortune to be beautiful, she faced the alternatives of service in a brothel or in the bed of a nobleman. The only crime of these unfortunates was refusal to cooperate with the friars.

Through forced labor and tribute, those who remained in New Mexico became the workhorses in the province's dismal economy. Much of the small amount of capital that was generated went to line the pockets of an endless procession of corrupt officials who sat in the Governor's Palace in Santa Fe. The traditional economy was reduced to shambles, the life of the village destroyed. Franciscans had a hand in it all.

The friars saved their greatest wrath for native religion. They outlawed all traditional rites, destroyed ceremonial kivas, burned relics, profaned beliefs, condemned to death anyone who refused to submit to their teachings. In one of many such reprisals, forty Puebloans were hanged in Santa Fe in 1645 for defying the clerics. In another, twelve Acoma children were taken from their parents and sent to Mexico as slaves to pay for the bell that hangs in the tower of the pueblo church of Esteban Rey.

Today the majority of New Mexico's Native Americans are outwardly Christian. But in the sanctuaries of the reconstructed kivas, in secret hideaways hidden among the red rocks, many of the same worshippers who faithfully attend mass each Sunday invoke the ancient gods and practice rites unchanged since before the arrival of Coronado. The religion they practice is an amalgam of traditional and Christian beliefs, a blending of inviolable old and acceptable new. The shape is Christian, the spirit native. The painting behind the altar at the Church of San Jose at Laguna Pueblo shows Christ, a cross, a crown, and the Virgin Mary; above it, stretching across the ceiling, is an enormous animal hide bearing images of the sun, the moon, a rainbow, and stars—pagan symbols of a nature-oriented religion. The work is a product of the nineteenth century, when relations between missionaries and natives relaxed and tolerance found its way back into Franciscan practice. Pondering the strange and wondrous Francis, one is moved to realize that among Christians of old, perhaps only he, who numbered among his spiritual allies brother fire and sister wind, would have stood humble and exultant before the altar at the Church of San Jose.

After the final words of the liturgy at Christmas Eve mass in the mission church at San Felipe Pueblo, the Catholic priest retires to the sacristy. Suddenly the music of ancient New Mexico erupts and fills the air—children chirping on whistles tuned to the melodies of the sparrow and the meadowlark. The door of the church swings open, and from a distance comes the thunder of drums pounding in electrifying unison. The drummers come closer and closer, and as they enter the mission and march down the aisle, the old walls threaten to burst from the din.

And then the dancers sweep in from the night—women magnificent in feathers, shells, turquoise, and spruce boughs; men in antlers and robes, leaping and strutting like deer. They are celebrating the birth of the Christ child but also something more: strength, endurance, the everlasting heartbeat of the land. And something much of Christianity has never been able to abide—the wild swinging of the hips, the unbuckling of the soul strings, the unbridled passion for the here and now. It continues through the night, this Christmas of Heaven and Earth, till the first light of dawn glimmers on the horizon.

There is a power in it that the Spanish could not contain. On August 10, 1680, the northern pueblos revolted. Under the leadership of a religious leader named Popé, a plan several years in the making unfolded with mathematical precision. Masses of Puebloans swept down on the interlopers, slaying men, women, and children. Four hundred Spaniards died during the first four days of the revolution; twenty-five friars were martyred. After ransacking and burning Spanish homes, natives went into the fields and slaughtered the cattle. At the missions, the assailants gutted the interiors, tumbled the walls and bell towers, destroyed every symbol of Christianity, every reminder of the hated friars.

The Spaniards who survived the first wave took refuge in Santa Fe and Isleta Pueblo, the latter of which briefly refused to join the uprising. The insurgents laid siege to Santa Fe: sacking homes, cutting off the water supply, tightening the noose street by street.

The Spanish rallied briefly. In a fierce and unexpected counterattack they came out from their hiding places and killed some three hundred insurgents—but behind those hundreds stood thousands more. The leaders in Santa Fe and Isleta saw that their situation was hopeless. Within two weeks of the uprising, the Spanish abandoned both refuges and headed south. Watching from the surrounding hills, the Puebloans allowed them to go.

The retreating parties, comprising some two thousand Spaniards, met near Socorro and continued south together. Within a month they were in El Paso. One hundred forty years after Coronado, seventy-one years after the founding of Santa Fe, not a single Spaniard remained in what had been the province of New Mexico.

Little known beyond New Mexico's borders, sometimes omitted altogether from American history texts, the Pueblo Revolt of 1680, when it is discussed at all, is usually called the most successful uprising ever to take place on the continent. Such a characterization trivializes what was surely one of the most remarkable events of any kind in American history. Had something similar happened in Massachusetts, had the Wampanaog Metacom (King Philip) scored an equivalent victory in the war he waged at almost the same moment, every last colonist not slain by Philip would have fled to Boston harbor, dived aboard ship, and beat it back to England. So consummate a triumph was more than a successful uprising: It was a confounding of destiny.

One might expect that Popé's glittering victory would have earned him fame as a military leader of the first rank. History was written, however, not by the Pueblos but by the Spanish, who returned thirteen years later and, against little resistance, recaptured the lost province. Not unexpectedly, we learn from the conquerors that Popé was a devil and a madman, and so he disappears among the soiled footnotes of history, even in the state where he engineered his breathtaking rout. New Mexico is, after all, more Hispanic than Native American. One is not surprised to learn that the exuberant Fiesta de Santa Fe celebrated each September commemorates not the revolution of 1680 but the reconquest in 1693 by don Diego de Vargas.

Today, in an hour or so, one can complete a short course in New Mexican history since the reconquest by wandering about Santa Fe's plaza and along a few of the side streets that emanate from it. Much of the old Palace of the Governors with its massive adobe walls stands yet, stately in a grace and stillness that belie its stormy history. It served as shelter for Popé, for scores of Spanish governors after him, for rebel Texans, imperial Americans, usurping Confederate Army forces, and finally, and apparently permanently, for Union forces in 1862. The palace looks heavy and tired and past its prime, but you will not see a grander building anywhere. In its resplendent quiet, one cannot fail to hear the echoes and feel the beat of its turbulent history.

Near the altar at Saint Francis Cathedral, a block away, stands the statue of the Virgin Mary that don Diego de Vargas brought with him on his return from Mexico and to which he attributed his easy, though not bloodless, victory. Few Santa Feans care to admit it, but the prominence of the statue—she was known until recently as "La Conquistadora"—firmly establishes the cathedral as a monument to New Mexico's violent past. At the entrance to the building is a plaque noting that the state is the site of more Christian martyrdoms—thirty-eight—than any other place in the New World. It neglects to mention why.

So much for the short course. Something of the longer course in New Mexico history may be glimpsed beneath the colonnade that shambles in front of the Governor's Palace. Each morning several dozen Puebloans spread blankets on the sidewalk and lay out rows of handmade jewelry to sell. It is a thoroughly modern enterprise but one whose practitioners perfectly symbolize the continuity and changelessness of New Mexico history. Those dogged Puebloans not only threw the rascals out, if only briefly, and coopted the best parts of the imposed religion; in the important aspects of their lives, Puebloans remain substantially unchanged by the arrival of whites in America. Today they live in villages located exactly where they were five hundred years ago. Puebloans speak the ancient tongues, wear the ancient costumes, practice the traditions and rites of their fore-bears, and detect in the hard crust of this creaking land the old sure signs of affirmation and timelessness. It is no coincidence that New Mexico, home of Folsom Man (8,000 B.C.), Sandia Man (10,000 B.C.), and Orogrande Man (dated by some authorities at 25,000 B.C.), is one of the longest-running shows in the Western Hemisphere.

Drive the interstate to Santa Fe in the most up-to-date vehicle you can find and you will experience landscape overpowering mind, body, and technology. Nature, you will know, is not dead. Charles Lyell, the father of modern geology, theorized that the processes that shape the land today are the same ones that have shaped it since the beginning. He applied his theory of uniformitarianism to geological history, but I think it can be adapted to human history as well. Beyond conquest and reconquest, goes my theory of human uniformitarianism, beyond random blips on the screen, beyond style . . . it is as it was.

Read the sage and the chamisa, lift your eyes above volcanic hills and fifty miles of piñon to gray shadows on the horizon, and you will know that you have seen it before. Speed across a whole county of sunlight and gaze over two counties more into a convocation of thunderstorms, three or four of them trumpeting atop the mesas, each storm visible in its wholeness and its singularity. And you will know that you have seen it before. The sky wheels and the earth tumbles and the moon comes up so big and fast you nearly jump out of your skin; and in your fine car driving the interstate to Santa Fe, you may undergo a blinding conversion to a religion uniquely New Mexican, a dizzy synthesis of Puebloan harmony and joy and Franciscan tolerance and peace.

At the center of the plaza where following the Civil War the townspeople of Santa Fe erected a memorial to soldiers, some keeper of the faith has delivered a message. The original inscription on the side of the memorial facing the Palace of the Governors once read: "To the heroes who have fallen in the various battles with the savage Indians in the Territory of New Mexico." Armed with a chisel and the hopefulness of the shelter of Santa Fe, an unknown sculptor has excised two words and written two others in their places. The inscription now reads: "To the heroes who have fallen in the various battles with our brother Indians in the Territory of New Mexico." Perhaps it is a sentence that will one day find its way into a chapter in the Great History of New Mexico.

A few steps from this monument, foreshadowing the Santa Fe of tomorrow, stands a plaque honoring the origins of the Santa Fe of today. It marks the end of the Santa Fe Trail, the trade route that transformed Santa Fe from the city it was—languid, unpolished, enlivened only by the occasional spilling of great quantities of blood—into the city it is today, where "to buy" is the operative verb. Old-timers grumble over the supposedly recent transformation of their beloved hometown into a Destination, where, in the correct downtown parlor, ice cream may run them five dollars a scoop.

"I feel like someone peed on my Renoir," a local merchant complained to me. It was a fairly ingenuous comment, I thought, given that his metaphor fairly sang with the very aesthetic he was seeking to discredit. In the rest of New Mexico, where a five-dollar ice cream would strike most people as depraved, there is not a lot of sympathy for Santa Feans, whose rather operatic troubles seem mostly self-induced. And there is more than a little of the opinion that the city has received pretty much what it deserved. Many New Mexicans feel that in its present incarnation, Santa Fe would be better off in California, or Colorado at least, to be welcomed home when it is ready to rejoin the community of struggle and pain. Behind all the finger-wagging and tongue-clucking, of course, there is a certain amount of raw envy. Still, when they have their emotions under control, the majority of New Mexicans, I think, would agree with the message on the bumper sticker seen occasionally around the state that reads: "I don't care how they do it in Santa Fe."

What they recognize but Santa Fe's old-timers may not is that today's "City Different" is far from an aberration; it is, rather, a logical and probably inevitable outgrowth of yesterday's city. Modern Santa Fe is said to have begun in May 1981 with a cover story in *Esquire* entitled "The Right Place to Live!" ("We've found it: great women, great weather, and plenty to do. Pack your bags!") Not long after, Christine Mather and Sharon Woods wrote a book called *Santa Fe Style*. It sold a hundred thousand copies, and a movement was born. Reports soon reached New Mexico that the situation in the rest of the country was getting out of hand. People in Pittsburgh—normal people—were said to be snacking on blue corn tortillas. Stores called Santa Fe Style and Santa Fe Collection opened in Washington, D.C., and Chatham, Massachusetts. Living rooms in Des Moines blossomed overnight with sun-bleached cow skulls and Indian drum coffee tables. Georgia O'Keeffe became everyone's favorite grandmother, the one who paints.

The merriment reached an apotheosis of sorts when Bloomingdale's in New York City declared June 1990 "New Mexico: America's Spirit" month. Cheerfully offering its patrons a taste of what was happening in the Southwest—buffalo dancers, *concho* belts, broomstick skirts, green chile peanut butter—the store's proprietors conferred the coveted mantle of Nowness on the city in the sky. It was only the second time in history that the New York elite had actually acknowledged the existence of New Mexico. The first was in 1988 when *The New York Times* reported that a consortium of East Coast venture capitalists had turned down a request for backing from some New Mexico businesses because the venture capitalists "did not wish to invest in a foreign country."

With all the sudden and unaccustomed attention, few people in New Mexico knew how to behave. Albuquerque newspapers swallowed their pride and covered the Bloomingdale's triumph as though it were a cotillion. Most New Mexicans were touched by all the fuss though not certain whether it signified approval or amusement. The only complaints came from a few residents of Carlsbad, whose plan to wear bat outfits at Bloomingdale's to promote Carlsbad Caverns was vetoed at the last minute by the store's management.

The pink of fashion though it may seem, Santa Fe Style is as ancient as the city itself. Santa Fe has always been a style. The city is today what it was yesterday: a fortress against the dangers of the world, an exotic and sublime haven from reality. Place Santa Fe where Willa Cather located New Mexico—in the middle of a dark continent—and you have a perfect explanation for Santa Fe Style, past, present, and future. Style evolves in isolation as finches evolve in the Galapagos, and the strange and rare species that have found shelter in Santa Fe, continually redefining and reshaping its character, constitute a life list for students of hermetic behavior: fanatic Franciscans, venal administrators, assorted climbers, reprobates, and flatterers, trappers and traders, the unwell (asthmatics, tuberculars, depressives suffering from diseases of the spirit), artists, photographers, actors, writers, gays and lesbians, political and social refugees, prophets, misanthropes, trendsetters.

And the most exotic species of all, the old-timers themselves, who were born here or came wide-eyed and innocent and stayed because something about the place reached into them and grabbed them and wouldn't let them go, and who, however much they may protest the transmogrification of their paradise into a glorified shopping mall, happily celebrate The Look: the mountainside of identically shaped, colored, constructed, and appointed buildings that compose modern Santa Fe, investing it with a form and feel that could not be mistaken for those of any other city in the world.

The Look is the brainchild of the old-timers of 1957, who, far-sightedly and no doubt with a clear understanding of the peculiar-ity of what they were doing, adopted an ordinance that created for all time an immaculate tribute to adobe. (I say "created," not preserved, because the Santa Fe of old was never as compulsively rendered as this one.) The code, strictly enforced and tested many times in court, prohibits throughout the central section of the city construction of any building not in the ruthlessly defined Spanish-Pueblo Territorial style of architecture:

> *With rare exceptions, the buildings are of one story, few have three stories, and the characteristic effect is that the buildings are long and low. Roofs are flat with a slight slope and surrounded on at least three sides by a firewall of the same color and mate-rial as the walls or of brick. Roofs are never carried out beyond the line of the walls except to cover an enclosed portal, the outer edge of the roof being supported by wooden columns. Two-story construction is more common in the Territorial than in other substyles, and is preferably accompanied by a balcony on the level of the second story. Facades are flat, varied by inset portals, exterior portals, protecting vigas or roof beams, canales or waterspouts, flanking buttresses and wooden lintels.*

Rough-textured and earthy, the structures that have grown up under the ordinance splay with religious fervor over the foothills of the Sangre de Cristos like a field of uprooted baking potatoes. The Look is generally agreed to be charming, if Territorial-style gas stations can be charming (much less historically meaningful).

Gazing at Santa Fe from a distance, one is amazed to realize that there exists in America a city where, under penalty of law, neither lunatic nor certified public accountant—nay, not even Robert Redford himself!—may erect a gin mill or a bordello of yellow and puce sandalwood. It is a considerable irony that a city sometimes praised for its progressive social policies is home to one of the most draconian measures ever enacted in the United States. Such an instrument can have only one effect, and that is to create style, which is a self-conscious, self-shaping of culture by decree rather than by evolution. Style is paternalistic, replacing choice with determinism and creativity with imitation. It is enfeebling, as homogeneous gene pools are enfeebling. It is incestuous and oppressive. Most of all, it is boring. It transforms the singular, the personal, and the exciting into product, ripping out the heart in the process. No doubt today's version of Santa Fe Style, essentially a solemnization of shopping, is more banal than most. We may be grateful to know that before long it will give way to another, something perhaps a little more compatible with the Great History of New Mexico. Whatever happens, this much is certain: If it happens in Santa Fe, it will be style.

~

IV

ONE DECEMBER MORNING, I spent several frustrating hours chasing a man named Mr. Lucero up and down the streets of America's oldest capital city. It was windy and bitterly cold in Santa Fe that day, conditions many of my East Coast friends are unable to reconcile with their notion of Santa Fe as an upscale city smack in the middle of pitiless desert—Phoenix, say, with curbside recycling. The myth is perpetuated in an endless succession of films, television shows, and advertisements, like the magazine ad for a product called Santa Fe cologne. In sultry desert tones it depicted an L.A.

kind of couple (he shirtless and godlike, she lightly clad and dewy) reclining on a Santa Fe kind of bed, their lips locked in upscale, pitiless passion. The caption read: "It gets pretty hot in Santa Fe." Well, yes, and in Denver, Seattle, and Boston, too, all of which enjoy higher average temperatures year-round than Santa Fe.

In any case, no shirtless guys or lightly clad beauties passed me on the street that morning; the people I saw were swaddled like newborns. As for Mr. Lucero, I didn't know how he might be dressed, but I hoped to find out. He was a well-known thorn in the side of the Santa Fe City Council for his persistent lobbying efforts on behalf of the homeless, of which he was one. I wanted to track him down because I was sure he could tell me something about Santa Fe Style that I'd missed during my strolls around the plaza.

I was thwarted in my search at every turn. From the Friends Meeting House to the public library to the soup kitchen on Marcy Street, I was never more than a few steps behind my prey. At each location I was told that Mr. Lucero had been there only a few minutes earlier but had gone elsewhere. As the day wore on, Mr. Lucero came more and more to symbolize for me the faceless society I had heard so much about. I never found him, though I may have passed him a dozen times on the street.

Dashing from one dead end to the next, I suddenly thought of a man I once knew in California. Gary worked as an all-night street cleaner for the city of Palo Alto. From him I learned that until one's eyes become accustomed to the dark, one cannot see the creatures of the night. I had daytime eyes. I couldn't believe my friend's reports of old men sleeping under the freeways and kids in sleeping bags and the occasional lifeless body without papers turning up in an alley or under a clump of bushes. Gary assured me they were true. There was a huge invisible population that dwelt among us, phantoms who might be creatures from another planet except that they were human beings no different from ourselves. The only power they held over us was their invisibility.

This I realized with a start a moment after I decided reluctantly to abandon my search for Mr. Lucero. *I'll drop him a letter*, I thought. Then, of course, I realized my mistake. *And what is Mr. Lucero's address? And will it be the same in two days, when a mail carrier tries to find him?*

The deeper I dug, the clearer and more distressing the magnitude of the disaster became. Here in Santa Fe, like Palo Alto one of America's wealthiest cities, there were people sleeping on the streets. It wasn't that the residents of Santa Fe didn't care. Many did, and many were working to alleviate the problem. But here, as in most American cities, there was simply no affordable housing for people of little means. What Santa Fe had to offer was temporary shelter with room for a hundred or so guests each night.

Sometimes that wasn't enough. Imagining the usual suspects, I guessed the identities of these phantoms of the shelters—winos, spare-change artists, crazies. My eyes still weren't used to the dark. At the La Luz de Santa Fe Family Shelter, director Carol Luna told me that most of her guests were normal people down on their luck. Many had jobs, and many who did not were searching for work. Entire families were involved. During the coldest months of the year, half of the guests at La Luz were children.

And then there were those who didn't come into the shelters—those who slept in their cars, or worse. Their numbers could only be guessed at but certainly ran into the hundreds. Sometimes on a winter morning one of them was found somewhere frozen to death.

It was the ones who slept out without roofs over their heads who began to haunt me. Perhaps my several decades of mountain climbing and countless nights out in the rain and snow gave me a distant and admittedly simplistic understanding of their discomfort and a sympathy for their plight. Needless to say, there was a world of difference between their experiences and mine. Many of them were draftees, so to speak, unwilling foot soldiers in the war against the dark, while I in my goose-down sleeping bag was a cheerful volunteer.

Still, volunteers dodge bullets along with the rest of the grunts, and in at least one respect I could claim solidarity with the draftees: On many occasions I had measured the winter night moment by moment, snowflake by snowflake, and I knew its silence and its length. What I did not know was how much quieter and longer it might be were the long-awaited dawn to bring with it not a measure of hope, as it always had for me, but rather the prospect of continued night.

Or perhaps my link with the dwellers of endless night lay through Jake, my only child, at the time not yet two years old but a source of insight and understanding for me since the day he was born. Of the many rituals he, his mother, and I practiced together, none was more precious or vested in primal duty than the last: the tucking in at night. How urgent it was to ensure that his hours alone in the dark would be safe and contented ones! Did ever an evening pass when Carol or I did not look up from a book or a chore and ask: Do you think he's warm enough? Should I check to see if he's okay?

It was on Cerrillos Road, well beyond the zone of architectural correctness, in a parking lot tumbled in smoky snow and reeking of exhaust fumes, where I met the embodiment of my fears. I saw him as I walked by and immediately averted my eyes, intending to continue on.

But something told me to stop, and a moment later I was walking toward the man. He was smoking a cigarette and seated on a curb in a rich pool of sunlight that had burst over the parking lot unexpectedly. He was about forty, a thin, tired figure in a black raincoat so scanty and frayed it appeared to need him more than he needed it. The rest of his outfit was equally unsuitable for winter in Santa Fe—T-shirt, wrinkled slacks, tattered Reeboks.

I introduced myself. I told him I wanted to talk. He smiled self-consciously. Then with an exaggerated gesture he motioned for me to sit down. We shook hands, and in a gravelly voice he told me his name was Thomas.

We talked for perhaps half an hour; or, rather, he talked, for my simple invitation for him to tell me about himself seemed to open a reservoir of bottled-up need. He had the sheepish, self-deprecating manner of those who as kids failed to master the essentials like salad forks and long division and who never catch up. He had heavily lidded eyes, a small nose, and thin red hair that he combed straight back, a hedge against the possibility of finding himself without a mirror in the morning. His face was long and narrow, red as a sunset, and as ravaged as his poor raincoat.

He was from Kentucky. After graduating from high school he joined the Navy. He completed a tour of duty, then returned to Kentucky, where he took up the steam-fitting trade. During the next few years he enjoyed some success, saved a little money, allowed himself the hope of a brighter tomorrow.

But something went wrong. Something didn't work out as he had planned. Someone double-crossed him and jobs dried up and friends disappeared and family failed him and love did not come, and wisdom and prudence eluded him, and he made some mistakes.

He shook his head and chuckled. His story was short on dates and details, as though they no longer mattered. It was the broad sweep of the thing that occupied him and perplexed him—the inexplicable shape and direction of his life. If there were reasons behind any of it, he was disinterested in them or he could no longer remember them. He was like Francis Phelan, the protagonist of William Kennedy's *Ironweed*—"sure only that he lived in a world where events decided themselves, and that all a man could do was to stay one jump into their mystery." He went to school, he joined the Navy, he worked, he played. One night he found himself on a freight train headed west.

It would be hard to invent a story more different from my own. But listening to the man, I realized that the narrative line we cherish so, those bright twists of plot we brandish like trophies, are not ultimately what define or distinguish us, are not even what matter. What matters is simply that each of us is the star of an epic tale, and that every tale must be heard.

It's a useful exercise to consider the unique view of the world that each of us enjoys from birth until death, the aisle seat on the performance of our play. Mine seems to be oval-shaped, a bit wider than it is high. Glancing up now, I notice a bit of eyebrow protruding on the left; downward I see the profile of my nose. Alone in these dark theaters we spend our days and nights, observing a sometimes unruly cast of characters as they perform our curious and unpredictable lives. Here we comment secretly on the turns of plot, the botched lines, the unexpected entrances. Here we guard the secrets of our hearts.

But there is more to the exercise. It is complete only when we can see the eyes of another as observation points exactly like our own, and the darkness behind as a universe of perception as unique and precious as the ones we inhabit. V.S. Pritchett, that master of the short story, writes, "They dwell—and this to me is the moving and dramatic thing about people—in a solitude which they alone can populate."

As I listened to the man's story, I had no difficulty appreciating the gentle nudge that presses us to one side of the line or the other. Time passes, our paths diverge, and one day I am snug in my fine PolarGuard jacket while you are shivering in a raincoat of rags. The great secret—how minimal our control, how vital the cooperation of fate—goes unspoken. Before long we are strutting like ostriches, confident that we alone are responsible for our successes and our failures. It is the cornerstone of the American theology, and it is utterly false. Ours is a theology of convenience. It relieves the successful of any tiresome need to seek common ground with the failed. It is a knife in the heart of nature, for it severs connections between one elementary particle and the next.

The belief that we are masters of our fate requires, more than anything, a mountain of self-deception. A former Delaware governor campaigns for the presidency on an anti-welfare platform, declaring that a man must work if he expects to be paid. The governor is the beneficiary of a portion of one of America's great family fortunes, one he lifted not a finger to earn. (A good rule of thumb is that the louder a man bellyaches about welfare, the cushier the free ride he received from his parents.) A Supreme Court nominee, a man who claims to have pulled himself up by his own bootstraps, pours out tears of gratitude for the love and support of his grandmother. The nominee fails to notice the love and support of his grandmother woven into his bootstraps. Phil Gramm, the former Texas senator, congressman, and senior economic advisor to John McCain during the latter's 2008 presidential bid, has been a relentless purveyor of the bootstrap myth, warning that "we have gone too far in creating an entitlement society." Gramm's sentiment is echoed up and down the corridors of Congress by public servants who solemnly warn of the grave threat to the republic posed by welfare, unemployment compensation, and any other government handout the speaker is not likely to need. A little research always reveals that the same person is, in fact, hip-deep in government relief. Senator Gramm is in up to his shoulders: his expenses as a child paid for by a father on a veterans' disability pension, his tuition at the University of Georgia paid for by the War Orphans Act, his graduate education paid for by a National Defense Education Act fellowship, his salary as a professor at Texas A&M University paid for by the citizens of Texas, and as a member of the U.S. House of Representatives and Senate by the citizens of the United States.

Gramm might be faulted for being unusually shameless, but not for being unusual. Who among us does not cheerfully and unapologetically accept such bestowals as encouragement and inspiration from teachers, helping hands from friends, sympathetic ears from strangers, aid and comfort from family members? Offers to open doors, smooth paths, and cut corners from cronies, trust-fund annuities and down payments for houses from parents (and inheritances not many years later), mortgage interest deductions and tax credits from the federal government, decades of love, understanding, and forbearance from spouse and children—and then to imagine that we did it all ourselves! One is grateful for the occasional blunt statement of truth, like this from Metromedia founder John Kluge, at one time one of America's wealthiest men, on how a simple fellow goes out and makes a billion dollars: "The greatest factor in my life—and I know entrepreneurial people don't want to express it, they think it diminishes them—but luck plays a large part."

In Peru, New Guinea, and Namibia we discover men in strange hats and marvel at how different from us these people are. What should impress us is how like us they are. On Cerrillos Road on a bleak December morning, I felt a chill that had nothing to do with the weather when I began to hear my voice echoing in the voice of another man and to see the lines of my story weaving through his own.

In New Mexico, Thomas's luck failed to improve. His will began to falter. He went on the dole, drank some, drank some more, failed to find permanent work, lasting friendship, a woman to love. Not long before I met him, someone stole everything he owned. It wasn't much—a bag with some clothes and a few other belongings. But the violation shook him deeply. It seemed to be the only thing that angered him.

"I just don't see how anyone could do that," he kept repeating. "Take a man's clothes practically right off his back. That's one thing I just don't understand."

He was not even bitter over the irony of being homeless in one of America's most glittering cities.

"There's good people in Santa Fe and there's bad people in Santa Fe," he reflected with a shrug. "Just like anywhere." Earlier that morning he had heard about a job, and he intended to apply for it, though he wasn't optimistic about being hired. He smiled. "I'm not as smart as the president of IBM."

I knew he wouldn't get the job, or that if he did he wouldn't keep it, because I had met him before, scores of times, on the front porch of my childhood home in Pennsylvania. Beaten, sheepish men—we called them bums. They showed up at our house asking for handouts. My mother enjoyed a kind of celebrity in those days. Her fans, if that is what they were, came from far and wide to knock at her door. When one arrived, she plunked him down on the porch swing and handed him a magazine to read. Then she went into the kitchen and cooked up a hot meal of meat, potatoes, fresh vegetables, salad, bread, coffee, and homemade berry pie. She arranged this feast on her best china and carried it out to the porch as though she were serving a king. I think my mother fed bums as a way of nourishing her children, and I think that it nourished her, too, and that it was one of the reasons she lived a long and happy life.

I kicked at a block of cinder-encrusted snow. The sun slipped behind the gray overcast and froze. Tonight the temperature would plunge to zero. I asked Thomas where he had spent the previous night.

He glanced at me from a corner of his eye and laughed. He owned a few blankets, he said. He managed to stay warm. He pointed across the road to an open area slanting down to the Santa Fe Railroad tracks.

"Over there in the prairie dog town."

Thinking he was joking, I laughed. Then, realizing he was serious, I looked across four lanes of traffic toward the spot where he was pointing. My stomach turned.

"The cops don't usually hassle you, but the railroad don't let you have a fire. Sometimes I go to the shelters but it's embarrassing. They run them like a military operation. There's no place that's perfect."

He tugged his raincoat tighter around him. Suddenly I wanted to be gone, to be as far away from this man as possible. We talked for a few minutes more. Then, abruptly and rudely, I told him I had to leave. I stood and shook his hand, then hurried off, leaving him seated on the curb.

As quickly as I could, I returned to the center of town where I wanted to be, among the relentlessly uniform buildings of Territorial and Spanish-Pueblo Santa Fe. And there I saw the fallacy of the Historical Zoning Ordinance of 1957 and its grand vision of a perfectly unified city: Perfection cannot be achieved by proclamation, and unity cannot be built with bricks. The unity of a city arises from its people, in their ability to join together in common cause, to share hopes and dreams and at least a small degree of prosperity. The oneness of Santa Fe and, no doubt, of most American cities runs as deep as stucco siding. Paradoxically, Santa Fe's entrancing design works to destroy the very harmony it is meant to promote. It is like a magnificent painting of heartbreak, whose splendor so overshadows its subject that we fail to perceive what the painting is about—or even to care. So blinded, we drift further and further from the only true source of unity that is possible, the ability to see through buildings and walls into each other's eyes and to say: Those people are us. That child is my child. That person is me.

⌁

V

CHRISTMAS IN NEW Mexico is a vibrant and luminous holiday, a grand synthesis of delights combining the old and familiar with the new, the exotic, and the unexpected. The combination is exactly right, for it places personal experience of Christmas at the center, where it belongs, and at the same time points toward a more universal expression of the season that is paramount yet easily overlooked. For an old conservative in these matters, raised in the Lake Erie snowbelt, trained in the preeminence of the scotch pine in the living room and the blizzard at the door, I was alarmed not many years ago to find myself in New Mexico, my somewhat mysterious new home, with this most precisely defined of holidays approaching. Could a place that revered salsa music and pinto beans measure up to my exacting standards for Christmas?

I had nothing to fear. This is a state whose forests are deep and piney, whose ski areas boast some of the deepest and fluffiest snow to be found anywhere in the country. Through the winter the northern frontier towns crackle in delicious subzero temperatures that can make even the Lake Erie region seem temperate. Carol and I found a scotch pine at a local tree lot. On Christmas Eve the snow started flying, and by morning several inches of powder lay on the ground. To my surprise I felt at home, properly connected to family and friends, to childhood and memories, to the personally designed traditions that give Christmas its unique and irresistible character.

Along with the old, I found much here that was new to heighten my enjoyment of the holiday. There was, to begin with, the geography of New Mexico. Much of the state outside the northern mountains has the look and feel of the place where Christmas began. Water is scarce. The land is harsh. Traveling a back road on a gray winter day, one has an easy time imagining the howling wastes of the Old Testament. One might even see shepherds tending their flocks on the treeless expanses of the southeast or along an arroyo on Diné lands or on the intermountain park that rolls south from the town of Chama.

Through the crisp evenings leading up to Christmas, the air reels from the dreamy aromas of piñon and juniper. Then on the final night the darkness comes alive with the assembled light of untold numbers of *farolitos*. The *farolito* is a Spanish invention: a paper bag containing a few handfuls of sand and a tiny candle. Two or three *farolitos* don't amount to much, but New Mexicans set them out by the dozens in front yards, by the thousands in city plazas. Each timid glow joins the next and then the next, and soon the state where light is as essential as food and water is afire, a new star in the firmament. Planes steer by it. Satellite networks are disturbed. Lost sheep find their way home.

The Native American celebration of Christmas is an explosion of music, dance, and pageantry that lasts for days and can make visitors forget their fruitcake and their eggnog. At some of the pueblos, men fly like eagles. (This actually happens.) At San Juan, bogeymen devour naughty children. (This is only a simulation.) At several pueblos, actors perform *Los Matachines*, a four-centuries-old drama rooted partly in Aztec tradition, partly in medieval mystery play. Often, Anglos and Hispanics are invited into the homes of Native Americans to join in the feasting. To a person so invited, such an invitation, coming from one who might be forgiven for choosing selfishness over generosity, may come as a shock. Yet the practice only expresses the theme of goodwill toward all people, which under the circumstances ought not to be surprising. That it is may produce a second and even greater shock.

Paradoxically, the opening up of the boundaries of Christmas that is possible in New Mexico has a narrowing effect as well. By looking beyond one's personal definition of the holiday to other, more challenging definitions, one begins to see what is unique to each and what is common to all. The year of my Santa Fe Christmas, I caught sight of something I had forgotten long ago, an element of the holidays that is common to all traditions: an image of a poor carpenter and his wife far from home seeking shelter from the cold and the night. For the first time since my childhood, I wanted to frame that image and hang it on my Christmas tree.

At a little over a year of age, Jake was about to celebrate his first Christmas that would register as more than a glow of candlelight in his eyes. He delighted in the tree and quickly adopted a set of favorite ornaments on the lower branches. Several times a day he collected the ornaments and deposited them in his toy box. On Christmas morning he would learn that packages contain surprises, and he would learn to liberate the latter from the former, not always elegantly. Sometimes he asked Carol or me to lift him up to view the manger scene on the mantle over the fireplace. Chipped and faded, a relic of sixty Christmases past, it seemed to speak to him like a revered member of the family. He gazed at the figures one by one—the wise men, the cow with three legs, the three figures grouped at the center whom he understood to be mother, father, and child.

Late on the afternoon of Christmas Eve, as the frail winter sky shattered and fell and the grand light of the *farolitos* rose up over New Mexico, we three drove to Santa Fe. It was about an hour from our house, up the storied valley that the Spanish traversed on their way to Santa Fe, where the Puebloans dwell and the river shapes the land. Clouds were moving in and the air was bitterly cold. Snow was forecast for later in the evening.

Unlike most cities, which on Christmas Eve pause for a few hours of deep breathing and introspection, Santa Fe slips into a state of heightened activity. Strollers bundled in furs and ski jackets crowd the sidewalks. Carolers gather at street corners. Cars creep bumper to bumper around the plaza, and a driver occasionally lowers a window to shout greetings to a passerby. In the nearby neighborhoods, residents kneel in their front yards to kindle luminarias—small fires of piñon logs, symbols of the fires of the shepherds of Bethlehem. More light, and it is riveting: At each luminaria a crowd of revelers gathers to gossip or to stare into the coals, perhaps to enjoy warm drinks provided by the fire builder.

We passed through the center of town and exited the historical zone to the north. As though we had crossed a border into a new land, we saw the character of the surroundings change at once. The homes grew smaller and less imposing. Chain-link fences separated some of the lots. Old American-made cars stood in the driveways. Here and there, graffiti-marred walls crowded the sidewalks. As we drove down a dark street toward our destination, a Labrador retriever, lost and wild-eyed, charged past us into the night. We turned at the Praise Tabernacle and pulled into the parking lot at 804 Alarid Street—St. Elizabeth Shelter for the Homeless. It seemed a likely place to locate that shelter sketch I wanted for our tree.

St. Elizabeth's and its guests belie the myths of the homeless shelter. It's an attractive and dignified place, staffed by skilled professionals under the leadership of its imaginative and caring director, Hank Hughes. Volunteers and donations from concerned Santa Feans keep it afloat. The halls are clean and bright, lined with posters, photographs, and notices of job openings and support group meetings. One hallway leads to the dining room past an alcove containing a library and a television set. The other leads to separate men's and women's dormitories. (At another location, St. Elizabeth's maintains a complex of apartments for families.) Each evening, several dozen sane, sober, hardworking men and women come through the door seeking refuge from the night. It will be temporary refuge only; guests are expected to move on after a few days.

The sun had set by the time Carol, Jake, and I arrived, and the shelter was nearly full. We wandered through the building trying to seem festive and comfortable, without much success on either score. Some guests lay on their bunks reading, napping, or staring at the ceiling. Others drifted up and down the halls, stopping to study the bulletin board or to engage friends in conversation. Half a dozen people lounged on sofas in the alcove. In the kitchen a volunteer crew readied a special Christmas Eve supper. The food, like much of what is served year-round at St. Elizabeth's, had been donated by several Santa Fe restaurateurs.

Not long after arriving, I realized that something seemed to be missing: I had expected the atmosphere to be more frenetic. Perhaps I imagined rude, enraged, or deranged guests screaming or shoving each other in the hallways.

On the contrary, the shelter's most striking characteristic was its tranquility. No peals of laughter echoed up and down the halls, no shouts greeted new arrivals at the door. The guests were quiet and subdued—partly from exhaustion, partly from melancholy, I guessed, neither out of place under the circumstances.

Observing those around me and trying to imagine what had brought them there that night, I thought of Coronado and his mistaken belief that he would find the Seven Cities of Cibola, a place that did not even exist. Like him, the explorers of St. Elizabeth's had been tricked into believing that by proceeding diligently in a steadfast direction, they would reach their destinations—homes, jobs, financial success. The trick was that there were not enough of any of these to go around. Match up all the dwellings in America with people who have the means to rent or purchase them, and thousands of Americans will still be sleeping in the streets. Fill every available job from the ranks of the unemployed, and millions will still be jobless. Divide the wealth of the nation among all our citizens, and so long as some are millionaires, others will necessarily be paupers. It isn't that the guests at St. Elizabeth's were stupid or lazy or unworthy, though some of them may have been that; it's simply that even if all of them plus everyone else in the United States were bright, industrious, and eminently worthy, some would still be left out in the cold. In this relentless game of musical chairs, some of the players are practical, some are clever and quick, some are ruthless, some are wise. Some, like John Kluge, are lucky. And when the music stops, some, no matter what their attributes, will not find a place to sit down. I felt honored to be in the august company of a few of the latter, who persevered despite their circumstances.

My feeling of admiration grew during dinner as I spoke with some of the guests. Kathy McKesson is an articulate, animated woman with long brown curls and a brandy-smooth Louisiana drawl. A year before, after leaving a battered woman's shelter in Texas, she found herself in "a nowhere situation." With little money and no car, she worked her way at one job after another to Santa Fe—"riding buses, praying a lot." She hoped that in fabulous Santa Fe she would find friends, a good job, a new beginning.

So far she had found none of it. But like everyone I spoke with that evening, Kathy McKesson had a job: she worked at Taco Bell earning fast-food wages. At Taco Bell she would earn in a year what the CEOs of several American corporations earn in an hour, what pitcher Clayton Kershaw of the Los Angeles Dodgers earned for every pitch he threw in 2016. If she could save the several thousand dollars she would need to move into an apartment (which she could not), she would see 90 percent of her wages eaten up by rent and utilities. It seemed clear that Kathy McKesson would not be staying long in Santa Fe.

Nor would the others with whom I spoke. Martin Kelleher is a short, stocky man with a neat mustache and a sly smile. He is a writer of short stories, a fancier of the works of Gabriel García Márquez. For the past month Kelleher had played Santa Claus at Santa Fe's Villa Linda Mall. In the morning, his employment finished, he would climb into his truck and head for Seattle, where he had friends and, he thought, the prospect of a job. Martin Kelleher was not angry over the irony of a homeless Santa Claus but bemused by it. He had profited from the experience, he said, for it had given him the idea for a new story. In Kelleher's story, God will play Santa Claus and humans will sit on His knee asking for chocolates and eternal life.

Nor would the dark, intense young man who calls himself Christian Joe, a bell-ringer for the Salvation Army, be staying. Nor would Patrick Cleland, a Vietnam veteran, nor Anna Spence, a frightened, bewildered woman of sixty who arrived just as my family and I were about to depart, and who, in a hollow voice, told the receptionist that she needed a safe place to sleep. Surely they would not be long in Santa Fe, a city like every city in America, with a look and a feel—a style—that seem to define it and drive it and invest it with meaning and purpose, but which under scrutiny reveals a shattered core flying apart like fragments of an exploding star. On this night, at least, there was unity among the most distant and fastest-flying of the particles, a brief coming together into incandescence. And on dark Alarid Street, a light as bright as a million *farolitos*—a light of courage, resilience, and hope—shone at Number 804.

∿

THE POWER OF the mountains, cold and juniper-spiced, drifted down from the Sangre de Cristos and settled over the streets and houses of Santa Fe. In the magic of the evening, Carol, Jake, and I slipped and slid our way along Washington Street. Dangling at his mother's hand, my son took on his first icy sidewalk like a new ride at the playground.

St. Elizabeth's was behind us, its guests safe for another night. We were out to enjoy the evening and, just as important, to put distance between ourselves and the shelter as rapidly as possible, the faster to assure ourselves that we had stepped back to our side of the line.

As we rounded a corner and entered the old plaza, a dream of perfect Christmas opened before our eyes. Kids skated in the street. Blithe walkers, frosty breath at their lips, strolled arm-in-arm under the porticos. Shop windows glowed with displays of toys, canned hams, and crisp new clothes. Remembering my friend's homage to Santa Fe, I kissed a beautiful woman in the snow. Jake looked on jealously, then asked to be picked up and carried. We slipped in among the strollers, joined them as though we were all one family. I found myself smiling and wishing well to strangers who caught my eye. The chill night, the antiquity of the surroundings, the passersby bundled so fastidiously—it was the wrong time and place, but I couldn't help thinking of Dickens. I half expected to see Bob Cratchit hurrying by with a turkey under his arm.

In the park at the center of the plaza, an unearthly radiance rose up, the aurora of a thousand *farolitos*. We crossed the street and entered the brightness, gathering its warmth and its strength.

It was quiet there, and beautiful. We walked slowly among the candles, taking in the light. It seemed eternal, yet somehow fragile enough to be extinguished with a single breath.

And soon it was too much and we were in our car, driving higher and higher out of the city and the light, up winding streets where old men walked in the shadows, over dark arroyos harboring the sleeping millions, past battered Fords and Chevies where children slept and parents kept watch in the night.

Amid the majestic hills that adorn Santa Fe like a crown we stopped and in a small clearing beside the road stood rapt in the deep silence of Christmas Eve—even Jake, bundled to the teeth against the bitter cold. To the east, Sun Mountain glimmered in snowlight. Above, the sky roiled with the harbingers of an approaching storm.

But to the south over the benighted valley of the Rio Grande the sky was yet clear. It was spangled in stars. They were brighter, sharper, and more immediate than I had ever seen them before. That fortune in crown jewels was fashioned in true Santa Fe Style! How clear it was to me then that the shelter I had been seeking to understand was much more than a simple clearing by the road, or a homeless refuge on the wrong side of town, or an old city in the Sangre de Cristo Mountains. Those are but tiny rooms in the only shelter we will ever know, this grand spinning planet we inhabit, one and all, our lifelong refuge from the storm. Here in our hallowed sanctuary we join in the pageant of life and death, cast ourselves as heroes or tyrants, and share in a common fate. Here like Londoners in the Underground we take on the monumental task of being human, and in our most solemn decision choose whether to hope or to despair.

The wind freshened, the mountain air coiled tighter around us. In the final moment before I escaped into the warmth of the car I thought of the ones we call the faceless, those stalwart souls who like the lights over Santa Fe burn with an unquenchable inner fire. I looked up and picked out a star, a silvery, blazing Christmas star, and I vowed that it would become the face of them all. From that moment till the end of time, the star will shine on, unmistakable in its meaning. Whoever gazes up will see it and recognize its countenance. And the stalwart will never be faceless again.

I gave a name to the star. I called it Thomas of Prairie Dog Town.

THE CONDOR'S LAST FLIGHT

"The Condor's Last Flight" appeared in The Progressive *in 1981. At the time, the entire population of California condors had dwindled to fewer than two dozen birds. With the strong backing of the National Audubon Society and a profusion of other conservation organizations, the U.S. Fish and Wildlife Service announced plans to implement a captive breeding program to save the species from extinction. In the article, I set forth my reasons for opposing the program, a position that generated considerable criticism and, in some conservation circles, disbelief. In a postscript, I'll report on the results of the recovery effort thirty-five years later.*

In the finest T-shirt tradition, the message emblazoned on the front summarizes a complex issue in a few simple words: "Nothing is quite so final as total extinction."

The artwork features the image of a condor, that high-rider of the warm California updraft, soaring in blissful majesty above the words "total extinction." The symbolism is hard to mistake. Whoever purchases this T-shirt, one reads in the design, has done his or her part to help the beleaguered California condor to overcome the grim fate that now threatens to wipe it off the face of the earth.

The National Audubon Society is hawking this T-shirt to raise money for its California Condor Fund. But before laying down your

$6.95 to help save the condor, be apprised that the solution to the condor's problems that the society has in mind may not be nearly as uplifting as a warm California updraft. On the contrary, the condor recovery plan that the society and a whole flock of conservationist organizations and government agencies hope to implement may fail to rise above even the minimal standards of charity set during the several centuries of mistreatment that the condor has suffered at human hands. Nothing is quite so final as extinction, it's true; and no means for averting that end may be quite so insensitive to the condor's needs as captive breeding.

The models for the T-shirt design—only about twenty of the birds remain—inhabit the rugged mountains of California's Los Padres National Forest. There, the long and lately disheartening saga of the California condor shows unmistakable signs of drawing to a close. For reasons that are not fully understood, the huge bird that has plied the skies of the western United States for possibly ten thousand years may be on an irreversible course toward extinction.

Now, in an effort to save the species, the U.S. Fish and Wildlife Service—the agency charged with the care of all officially endangered species—proposes to initiate a captive breeding program for condors. In the first stage of the program, condors will be trapped, rigged with tiny radio transmitters, and then released. During the ensuing months, wildlife biologists will study the birds' habits and movements from afar through analysis of radio telemetry signals.

Then, a year later, nine of the birds will be recaptured and transported to breeding facilities in San Diego or Santa Cruz, where wildlife biologists will try to persuade them to proliferate in cages, although the birds have lately shown little ability to do so in the wild. The goal of the program, one that may take decades to achieve, will be to assemble a large population of cage-reared condors; these will be given a suitable course in survival training and then released. Fish and Wildlife Service biologists are cautiously optimistic that captive propagation may be the key to the eventual establishment of a healthy, self-sustaining population of condors in the wild.

Joining the Audubon Society in endorsing the proposed program are some of the most august conservation and research organizations in the United States. The World Wildlife Fund, the International Council for Bird Preservation, the Cooper Ornithological Society, the New York Zoological Society, the American Museum of Natural History, and the Smithsonian Institution have all thrown their support behind the program. So have the U.S. Forest Service and the Bureau of Land Management. Indeed, the technique of captive breeding has been used so widely in recent years, and has met with such notable success, that until now almost no one has questioned its legitimacy as an ethical approach to the problem of endangered animals.

That is changing. A small but growing number of people are taking a hard look at the proposal to capture condors for breeding—and turning their thumbs down at what they see. David Brower, founder of Friends of the Earth and a strong opponent of captive breeding, points out that until the causes for the condor's decline are fully understood, it makes no sense to raise the birds in captivity; upon release, cage-reared condors may well fall prey to the same hazards that led to the species' decline in the first place. Stanford biologist Paul Ehrlich bluntly characterizes the trapping of condors as "harassment," and former Berkeley zoologist Carl B. Koford, whose three-year field study of the condor resulted in the most exhaustive report on the species yet published, was an outspoken critic of the proposed breeding program before his death in 1980. Koford was convinced that the condor could make a comeback without direct interference in the birds' affairs by scientists. What was needed, he claimed, was not cages but comprehensive studies of the condor's life cycle, increased protection and enlargement of its habitat, and a thorough cleanup of its environment. Koford argued that captive breeding would expose condors to a whole new set of uncertainties: Birds could be injured or traumatized during capture; they might not, in fact, reproduce in captivity, leaving potential breeders in cages rather than in the wild where they might be doing more good; and even if they did reproduce, cage-bred condors might never adapt to the wild. In Koford's view, captive breeding was a classic example of a cure that is worse than the disease.

His fears were realized in June 1980, when a two-month-old wild condor chick died after being removed from its nest for weighing and measuring by a member of the Condor Research Center, a team of scientists supported jointly by the National Audubon Society and the U.S. Fish and Wildlife Service. The chick was one of only two nestlings known to have hatched during the previous year. Following its death, the California Fish and Game Department withdrew all permits for the handling or capturing of wild condors. The ban will remain in effect until a final decision is made on whether or not to go ahead with the captive breeding program.

Whatever the merits of the proposed program, there exist some disturbing, unanswered questions about the practice of capturing wild animals for breeding in cages. They strike at the very heart of the issue of captive breeding itself and cast doubts on its legitimacy as a means for preserving not only condors, but any other wild animals as well.

"With a cage-bred animal, you may be able to preserve genes and cells and organs," Koford told me in an interview a few months before his death. "But a wild animal is much more than these. Can you preserve its wildness? Can you preserve the complex cultural heritage that animals in their natural habitat pass along from one generation to the next?"

For Koford, there was a serious fallacy in the argument that endangered species should be preserved in captivity, even if future generations of those species were to be released into the wild. What is the point of saving genes, he wondered, if in its *behavior* the animal you engender is different from the one you began with?

Beyond logic, there is an ethical component in the captive breeding issue as well, as Mark Palmer, the Sierra Club's regional vice president for Northern California and Nevada, points out.

"The crux of the matter has as much to do with the ethics of artificial maintenance of a species as it does with the feasibility of captive breeding," says Palmer. "However well-intentioned it may be, isn't captive breeding yet another manifestation of our presumed right to manipulate all life on this planet for our own interests?"

The human interests in preventing the extinction of the condor are clear indeed. Surely one of the most important derives from the simple fact that animals give us pleasure, and the specter of extinction threatens that pleasure. Preventing the extinction of a species might further serve human interests by seeming to demonstrate the triumph of compassion, and possibly technology, over the grim forces of evolution. And it could furnish self-satisfying, though no doubt self-deluding, evidence that the human excesses which may have driven the species to the brink of extinction in the first place were not really so excessive after all.

In the present case, breeding condors in captivity would yield several additional benefits to humans. Wildlife biologists would be afforded a fine opportunity to add to their knowledge of avian reproduction. And for the U.S. Fish and Wildlife and the U.S. Forest Service, both stung by charges that their own past neglect and mismanagement of the condor have contributed directly to the species' decline, captive breeding offers a chance to pull off a spectacular public relations coup and clutch victory—in the form of condor eggs—from defeat.

Such a victory would be one for birders as well, who would have California condors to check off on their Life Lists. (The consequence of extinction that most distressed several birders with whom I spoke is that they would lose the opportunity to *see* condors.) Indeed, it would be a victory for all of us who are saddened at the condor's plight. Saving the species might mitigate some of the guilt we feel over the sordid treatment that condors have been receiving since November 18, 1805, when, as William Clark noted in his journal of the Lewis and Clark Expedition, "Rubin Fields Killed a Buzzard of the large Kind."

Since Rubin Fields happened onto the scene, the war on condors has continued almost unabated. Hunters have blasted countless numbers of them out of the sky. Because the California condor is the largest bird found in North America—its wingspan can reach nine feet and its weight twenty pounds—some have been shot simply to see how big they were. Others have died in the name of higher learning: Today more than two hundred skins or skeletons of California condors enhance museum collections around the world.

Following World War II, a new and insidious menace began to threaten the condor. The proximity of the species' habitat to prime agricultural land exposed condors to a battery of herbicides and pesticides. Widespread use of DDT over condor range is now known to have caused a thinning of the birds' eggshells, resulting in easy breakage and the consequent deaths of the undeveloped chicks inside.

DDT has now been banned, but other potentially harmful chemicals, including an agricultural poison called Compound 1080, have not. The effects of 1080 are disputed, but many authorities on the condor believe that the poison may be as hazardous to the species as DDT was. Lacking irrefutable evidence linking 1080 to the condor's decline, ranchers continue to spread the poison over condor range in massive amounts.

The egg collectors have disappeared, but disturbance of condor nesting activities continues. Sonic booms and low-flying aircraft, hikers and off-road vehicles, oil wells and mineral exploration, developers clearing land: All are common near California condor habitat, and all have a potentially adverse effect on the skittish bird's ability to reproduce in the wild. Koford observed condors for some five hundred days while carrying out his primary field research and concluded that a single flushing of a nesting condor could result in nest desertion. Unfortunately, the protection from illegal disturbance that the officially protected condor has received from agencies charged with its care has not always been of the first order. During the 1960s, to cite two extraordinary examples, both the U.S. Forest Service and the California Department of Fish and Game appointed condor wardens who could not identify condors when they saw them.

As the assaults on the species mounted, one upon another, the dimensions of condor territory—which once extended from Baja California to British Columbia, and may have spanned the southern United States—drew inexorably inward, like the perimeter of a slowly fading spotlight. Today only a glimmer of the species' former range remains, a wild and rugged mountainous area that overlaps several counties north of Los Angeles.

If today's condors had nothing to lose in being pressed into our service and that of their descendants, there might be no need to question the propriety of captive breeding. But they stand to lose on at least two counts, as a consideration of two aspects of condor behavior will show.

The first is that a California condor spends a considerable portion of its time flying. Because of its huge wings, a condor can soar with an endurance and efficiency that is almost unknown among other birds. Taking off on a feeding mission, a condor will beat its wings a few times, then glide along smoothly until it senses the subtle rush of a warm updraft. Now gathering the rising air beneath its outstretched wings and banking its body to adjust for local thermal conditions, the condor will begin to climb skyward, slowly carving a great ascending spiral around the warm column of air. That the bird is a living creature and not, say, a runaway kite, may not again be manifest until it levels out at twelve thousand feet and flaps its wings for the first time in half an hour. When the condor at last sets down to feed, it may be forty miles from its takeoff point.

Opportunities for such excursions in a captive breeding program would be nonexistent. Captured condors would be consigned to cages about the size of a trailer home, where they would remain for the rest of their lives.

A second aspect of condor behavior is of equal importance in assessing the impact that captivity may have on the birds: Condors prefer to be left alone. They are not tame or inquisitive birds that perch dilatorily beside highways or search for food in suburban backyards. Condors nest and carry out their other affairs in remote locations, as far from civilized activity as possible. They do this voluntarily, clearly demonstrating their aversion to disturbance. When humans intrude—as they did, for example, with a second home development on California's Mount Pinos—the birds will quickly move elsewhere.

The National Audubon Society has been the prime mover in efforts to initiate a condor breeding program. I wondered how the society could justify a solution to the condor's problems that would force the birds into close contact with people—something condors themselves have shown no taste for and which furthermore would permanently deprive them of flight. So I put the question to John Borneman, who since 1965 has held the position of Condor Naturalist with the Audubon Society.

"The evidence indicates that condors are very adaptable birds,"

Borneman answered. Topa Topa, a condor that has lived in the Los Angeles Zoo since 1967, "adapted to captivity very quickly. Several California condors have lived in cages for more than thirty years. There is probably some trauma initially, but I'm sure that there are no permanent effects."

Borneman then invoked a greatly misunderstood term that has become a prime source of confusion in efforts to determine how animals ought to be treated.

"People sometimes look at Topa Topa and imagine that since they would not like to be in a cage, Topa Topa must be saying, 'Gee, I wonder if I'll ever get out of here so that I can fly again.' That is anthropomorphism. It can lead one to draw conclusions that are simply not justified."

Anthropomorphism—the ascription of human characteristics to things not human—has clearly fallen on hard times. Today the term is almost always used negatively and derisively, to describe nearly any opinion about animals with which the speaker disagrees. This may be a result of such embarrassing and ill-begotten phenomena as beauty parlors for pets, hydrant-shaped dog snacks, and the talking, singing, and chow-chow-chowing cats featured in television commercials. Whatever the reason, it is a mistake to deny the possibility that we may share *some* of our attributes with animals simply because we patently do not share all of them. No sensible person would claim to know that condors *enjoy* flying, or that a condor that appears to be sulking in a cage is a bored and unhappy bird. But one must not dismiss the possibility that condors *might* enjoy flying, or that they might despise captivity.

It is specious to argue that because condors might adapt to captivity—that is, might make the best of what may be a bad situation—they may therefore justifiably be captured. The burden of proof should lie with the prospective captors, to demonstrate that removing condors from their natural habitat and forcing them into confinement and close contact with humans will not prove harmful or traumatic to the birds. Given the preponderance of evidence to the contrary, it seems unlikely that any such demonstrations could be made.

Paradoxically, one of the strongest arguments that today's condors ought to be permitted to remain in the wild is provided by proponents of captive breeding themselves. The goal of the proposed breeding program is precisely to establish a self-sustaining population of condors in the wild. Condor freedom is taken by the program's supporters as self-evidently desirable. Having acknowledged the validity of that principle, it is a mystery how they can justify applying it arbitrarily, granting its benefits to the condors of the future while denying them to those alive today.

If captive breeding is to be forgone, what then can be done for today's condors? Part of the answer has already been given by the U.S. Fish and Wildlife Service. Its recovery plan for the condor proposes numerous remedial measures in addition to captive breeding—and those that do not involve capture should be implemented as soon as possible. Among the measures recommended are studies of the effects of pesticides and other poisons on condors, studies of the species' nesting cycle, and surveys to identify and secure additional suitable condor habitat. This last is particularly important and promising. Several hundred thousand acres of roadless lands in Los Padres National Forest could be set aside as officially protected wilderness by Congress. Future developments of these lands would thereafter be forbidden, and an area large enough to encompass most of the condor's wide-ranging activities could become the species' permanent home.

In addition, all local, state, and federal agencies charged with protecting condors should strive to immediately halt disturbance of the birds by human beings, and to eliminate contamination of the species' habitat by harmful chemicals, once studies to identify those chemicals have been completed. Only then can the condor make the best of its now meager chance to survive in the wild. One advantage of forgoing captive breeding would be that several million dollars now targeted for that phase of the recovery program could be redirected to effect an even more comprehensive environmental revitalization than is now feasible.

Not long ago, a doctor who was able to prevent a patient's death—in other words, to conserve a human—recognized a moral obligation to do so, no matter what the circumstances. Today, following the emergence of the concept of "death with dignity," the issue is not so clear-cut. If death is prevented only for the benefit or comfort of despairing relatives, if life is preserved only in a narrow legal sense through the aid of a complex array of life-support systems, if a patient is somehow denied a dignified death—then preventing that death may be wrong.

A consideration of these contingencies may shed some light on the nature of our obligation to endangered species. If the prevention of a species' extinction is sought only for the benefit of us, the grieving bystanders, or at the cost of an animal's dignified— that is, natural—life, and perhaps death, in its normal habitat, then it may be wrong to seek that goal. It is possible that there are endangered animals whose lives in the wild can reasonably be duplicated in captivity, and for them, captive breeding may be a justifiable solution to their problems. Condors, however, are not among them.

But let there be no mistake: If condors are not bred in captivity, it may come to pass at some time in the foreseeable future that the last wild condor will die. This potential consequence of our choosing not to capture condors should be stated unequivocally and understood fully.

If that happens, it will be—for us—a tragedy of huge proportions. But it won't be a tragedy for condors. Condors will have lost nothing that they ever coveted. It is we who will come up short, for we will have lost two things that we covet very much: confidence in our ability to manage the affairs of the world, and condors. Troubling as those losses may be to contemplate, we should recognize that we are to blame for bringing them dangerously close to realization. For us to now involve condors in what is nothing more than a face-saving scheme will only increase our culpability.

～

Epilogue

The California Condor Recovery Program was inaugurated by the U.S. Fish & Wildlife Service in 1979. The goal of the program was to establish two geographically distinct, self-sustaining condor populations, each with a wild population of one hundred and fifty birds, including at least fifteen breeding pairs, with a third population retained in captivity.

When "The Condor's Last Flight" was published in 1981, a single California condor, a bird named Topa Topa (mentioned in the article) was being held in captivity. Topa Topa had been rescued in 1967 in a canyon near Ojai, California, where he was found near death, hanging upside down from an injured wing. He was taken to the Los Angeles Zoo and has remained there ever since.

Between 1982 and 1987, the entire remaining wild condor population of eleven birds (comprising adults, fledglings, and nestlings) was captured, along with eggs taken from wild condor nests. All were transferred to breeding facilities at the Los Angeles Zoo and the San Diego Wild Animal Park. Fifteen of the eggs hatched, bringing to twenty-seven the total number of condors held in captivity.

The growth of the condor population since the recovery effort began has been dramatic. In 1992, two captive-bred condors were released into the wild in Ventura County, California. By 2008, the number of free-flying condors exceeded the number of condors in captivity. By 2015, the total condor population exceeded four hundred, with some two hundred and twenty in the wild, the rest in captivity.

Of the twenty-seven condors that composed the original captive breeding population, four had been released into the wild by the end of 2016. Three had died in captivity. The other twenty remained in captive breeding facilities, where they had resided for at least thirty years; Topa Topa marked his forty-ninth year in captivity in 2016.

The fourth of the original twenty-seven birds to return to the wild was a condor named AC-4. Captured in 1985, AC-4 was released into the Bitter Creek National Wildlife Refuge in 2015, after having spent thirty years in the San Diego Zoo. Let it be noted that upon release, AC-4 did not go for a short flight and then, given the choice between freedom and captivity, return meekly to the truck that had brought him and hop back into his cage. In fact, AC-4 took off into the sky. The same was true for the three thirty-year members of the breeding program that were freed before AC-4, effectively putting to rest any claims for the "adaptability" of condors to captivity. For anyone who still has doubts, it has been firmly established that the birds prefer freedom to cages.

Yet some two hundred condors remain in captivity. The primary rationale for their incarceration is to ensure that humans will forevermore have the opportunity to see condors, whether caged or in flight. That was insufficient justification in 1979 when the captive-breeding program was hatched, and it remains so today.

LING-LING HAS KILLED ANOTHER BABY

The cub had appeared healthy earlier Friday, but its squeals suddenly stopped at 11:41 P.M. Fifteen minutes later Ling-Ling put the cub down and went into an adjoining room, Mr. Hoage said. The cub did not squeal as she did previously when she was briefly separated from her mother. At 12:05 A.M. Ling-Ling returned, picked up the cub, licked and cradled her, but again there was no sound and the cub appeared motionless.
—THE NEW YORK TIMES, JUNE 28, 1987

In response to certain stories you may have heard
Ling-Ling wants to say:
People of America, I greet you!
Thank you for your friendliness!
You are very well-intentioned!
Many of you come to see me, the famous
     panda at the zoo.
You wave to me and shout, "Ling-Ling, we love you!"
I am sure you mean no harm.
You say, "There is the goodwill ambassador from China!"
Well, I have been an ambassador for 15 years.
Believe me, it's not such a great honor.

Now I think I have done enough good will.

Please, I would like to go home.

I wish to return to Yunnan forest, where I can be alone.

There, no one will yell "Ling-Ling!" at me.

Ling-Ling is not even my name.

You say, If Ling-Ling returns to Yunnan forest she will die.

The poachers will find her and present her with a bullet.

Believe me, that's not so bad!

I will die wherever I go, even the zoo.

In Yunnan forest, at least I will recognize my surroundings
    when I close my eyes.

Another thing: that guy Hsing-Hsing.

Everybody wonders why we fight.

Everybody wonders why we do not snuggle and have babies
    who wave back at you.

The answer: Hsing-Hsing is a monster.

Look at him.

Please do not allow him to come near me anymore.

In Yunnan forest we no longer have arranged marriages.

Which brings me to what I want most to say:

Why are you so crazy for me to have babies?

If you love me so much, why do you do that terrible thing to me?

Sure, there are not many of us left.

That's not my fault.

I am sorry if it is yours.

But listen, when you squirt me full of

Hsing-Hsing's seeds,

you are no better than poachers.

You kill me, too.

You say, Ling-Ling, it is for the good of your species.

You say, If we do not put you in the zoo and squirt you full of seeds,
your species will die.
I say, Fine, that is your problem, not mine.
Adjust to it.
In the meantime, I do not care to be squirted with Hsing-Hsing's seeds
    just to solve your problem, thank you.
People of America: Already you have caused enough problems.
Please do not cause more.
I do not worry about species.
I worry about Ling-Ling.
You want species, you get in the cage.

Finally, about all those babies who died.
I know you think I am a careless mother.
I know you think I killed my babies accidentally.
But, really—three times?
I am a panda, but I am not stupid.
Let me go home to Yunnan forest, and there I will have
    a thousand babies.
Here, no.
I do not wish to have babies who will grow up in a zoo.
I do not wish to have babies who will grow up to be
    squirted with monster seeds.

Now I think I have said enough, so I will stop.
I am sorry if I have offended you.
Believe me, that was not my intention.
I hope you will accept my apologies.
Now I will go and sit at the spot where you like to watch me.
"Hello, people!" I will shout.
"I am the one you call Ling-Ling!"

⁀A POEM, ᶏGATHERING IN ᶆY ᶆIND

The following essay appeared in the catalogue accompanying From
Exploration to Conservation: Picturing the Sierra Nevada, *a
1998–1999 exhibition organized by the Nevada Museum of Art and
the Wilderness Society.*

Trying, yet again, to wring light out of stone.
—DOUG ROBINSON, BRINGING LIGHT OUT OF STONE

ike the painters and photographers whose works distinguish
the exhibition *Picturing the Sierra Nevada,* writers who hope to
reveal the essential matter of their subjects must have the patience,
the facility, and, not least of all, the good luck to discover the
proper light. I was reminded of this fundamental law of artistic
creation recently when I found myself in one of those grand settings that is so typical of the Sierra Nevada, and that has challenged the eyes of artists and writers for more than a century and a
half. With my son Jake, I had traveled to Calaveras Big Trees State
Park near Arnold, California, where in 1852 a hunter named A.T.
Dowd "discovered" sequoia trees, the enormity of which quickly
gained them fame throughout the world. Jake was only seven and
had never seen sequoias before. I was interested to see what his
reaction would be.

We parked near one of the principal groves. While a friend and I strolled down the path, chatting idly, Jake raced on ahead. Before I had walked fifty yards, he had taken a gander at one of the trees, read the sign posted beside it, and raced back. The information that the sign conveyed must have electrified him, for his eyes appeared ready to explode from their sockets.

"Dad! Dad! Dad! You've gotta see something!" He grabbed my hand and began pulling me down the path. "You won't believe this! There's a tree down there that's as big as a blue whale!"

A few moments later I stood gaping at the immense tree. Just as my son had predicted, I didn't believe what I saw. I had viewed sequoias many times before, yet there I was, once again, thunderstruck as always, as I'm thunderstruck each time I see Half Dome, Cathedral Peak, the Sawtooth Ridge, Lake Tahoe, Evolution Valley, the East Face of Mount Whitney, or, at the more subtle end of the spectrum of Sierra grandeur, huddled whitebarks at the tree line or shooting stars on a windswept ridge. From the widest panorama to the smallest detail, each thread in the Sierra's miraculous tapestry renders the observer momentarily speechless. It's no wonder writers have been drawn to this extraordinary scenery from the moment it first became known, and why they have failed so often to deliver. The task of discovering the essential light of something that seems beyond comprehension, and then rendering it so as to *transform the way the reader sees the world*—the central challenge facing the writer—is brutally difficult and achieved by few.

We should not be surprised to discover that among the first generation of writers who came to the range, none was up to the challenge. Before 1860 the Sierra was a mysterious and dangerous place. The goal of visitors was to save their skins, not to produce great literature. Documents from the period are plain and practical as juniper tea. There's mountain man Jedediah Smith's stark description of tough slogging on the Upper Stanislaus in 1827; fur trapper Zenas Leonard's record of an arduous traverse of the range in 1833; Army Lieutenant John Charles Fremont's report of his wanderings in the vicinity of Carson Pass in 1844; seventeen-year-old emigrant Moses Schallenberger's tale of his winter alone at Donner Lake, also in 1844; Donner party member Patrick Breen's wrenching diary of his ordeal in 1846.

The Sierra that we learn about in these documents is an unknown and fearful place, one to be done with as quickly as possible. Even when gold was discovered in the western foothills in 1848 and a rush of miners at last found a reason to put down stakes, they stayed only long enough to jot down their languid comments about the food, the weather, and the fellow from Cincinnati who'd just lost his arm in a mine accident. As historical documents, such observations make for fascinating reading; as works capable of transforming our view of the Sierra, none is up to the task.

By 1860 the range's Native Americans had been pacified, its major passes cut, its premier attraction, Yosemite Valley, discovered and widely publicized. A hundred two-bit mining towns dotted the range from one end to the other. Plans for a railroad through Donner Pass were underway. Physically and psychologically, the Sierra had been tamed, a development of enormous significance. No longer was the range something to be done with as quickly as possible; suddenly it was a place to which one could travel for enjoyment, reflection, and, most of all, to be moved by the same senses of wonder and astonishment that my son and I experienced at Calaveras.

"He dashed ahead, shouting and gesticulating and tossing his arms in the air like a madman," John Muir writes of the artist William Keith at the moment Keith first laid eyes on Yosemite's Mount Lyell. Muir himself suffered practically daily from such epiphanies. "Exhilarated with the mountain air, I feel like shouting this morning with excess of wild animal joy." In the new and gentler Sierra, visitors rediscovered their lost innocence, their childlike senses of awe and curiosity. To the writer searching for inspiration, those were huge benefits.

Inspiration alone, however, was not enough to produce memorable writing. A glance at the lengthy shelf of syrupy, clichéd prose and poetry "inspired" by the grandeur of Yosemite Valley during the first years of the tourist trade confirms this only too quickly. El Capitan is inevitably "sublime"; in the late-afternoon it tends to brood. Half Dome—"butments sounding back the thunder of the winds," as one amateur poet put it—is a proud monarch towering grandly and inaccessibly over its insignificant worshippers below. The authors of these encomia obviously had strong feelings about the miraculous valley. Rarely, however, were they able to translate their emotions into first-rate poetry or prose.

Perhaps the first writer with something new to say about the Sierra arrived in Nevada Territory on the Overland Stage from Missouri on August 14, 1861. Two weeks later, twenty-five-year-old Samuel Clemens, soon to be known as Mark Twain, hiked from his boarding house in Carson City to desolate Lake Tahoe. There, in the rather forlorn hope of becoming a wealthy man, he claimed three hundred acres of timber. In *Roughing It*, his memoir of five years in Nevada and California published in 1872, he recalled the moment when he saw the lake for the first time.

> *Thus refreshed, we presently resumed the march with renewed vigor and determination. We plodded on, two or three hours longer, and at last the lake burst upon us—a noble sheet of blue water lifted six thousand three hundred feet above the level of the sea, and walled in by a rim of snow-clad mountain peaks that towered aloft full three thousand feet higher still! It was a vast oval and one would have to use up eighty or a hundred good miles in traveling around it. As it lay there with the*

shadows of the mountains brilliantly photographed upon its
still surface I thought it must surely be the fairest picture the
whole earth affords.

In the spirit of the times, Twain succumbs to one "noble" sheet
of blue water. Then, his homages paid, his inspiration spent, he
is off and running to fresh new ground. In the pages that follow
we find no aching paeans to Tahoe, no godlike mountain peaks.
Eschewing received wisdom and style, Twain treats us to a simple,
from-the-heart, good-natured account of a swell time—floating on
the lake in a skiff, fishing, swimming, pipe-smoking, joking, camp-
ing at lakeside. Measured beside other contemporary accounts, his
is positively revolutionary.

In due time we spread our blankets in the warm sand between
two large boulders and soon fell asleep, careless of the proces-
sion of ants that passed in through rents in our clothing and
explored our persons . . . We never moved a muscle all night,
but waked at early dawn in the original positions, and got up
at once, thoroughly refreshed, free from soreness, and brim full
of friskiness. There is no end of wholesome medicine in such
an experience. That morning we could have whipped ten such
people as we were the day before—sick ones at any rate.

Twain was still finding his way as a writer, but the irony, the
gentle leg-pulling, the self-deprecation of his mature style are to
be found on every page. "Three months of camp life on Lake Tahoe
would restore an Egyptian mummy to his pristine vigor, and give
him an appetite like an alligator. I do not mean the oldest and
driest mummies, of course, but the fresher ones." To Twain, the
Sierra was a beautiful, congenial place where a fellow could relax,
play euchre by the campfire with a deck of greasy cards, and have

a fine old time. No one had said that before. The explorer's fears and the conventional vacationer's flowery prose are absent from Twain's account; instead we have a fond tale that but for an occasional reference to snowy peaks and forested mountainsides might be mistaken for two weeks on the Mississippi.

Only a few months before Twain's arrival in Carson City, the California legislature authorized a wide-ranging exploration of their state under the direction of the geologist Josiah Dwight Whitney. For the next five years, dauntless members of the California State Geological Survey hiked their mules over every Godforsaken corner of California, drawing maps, assessing geological and biological resources—in general, seeing what they could see. They saw a lot, especially during the summers of 1863 and 1864, when five members of the team struck deep into the wild Sierra. They were the first whites to view many of the range's grand sights. From their experiences came two classics of Sierra literature.

The first was by William Brewer, Whitney's chief assistant on the survey. A scientist of considerable accomplishment, Brewer was also a tough-as-nails adventurer capable of leading the survey team over rivers and up mountains the mere thought of which, even today, induces sweaty palms in seasoned backcountry travelers. His notes of his explorations have been collected in the volume *Up and Down California in 1860–1864*. It's a wonderful book, easy and hopeful, brimming in the kinds of details one expects from an experienced observer like Brewer, yet without the numbing objectifications of science or the self-importance of conventional nature writing. Brewer strikes one as a first-rate hiking companion: He's smart, he's tough, he's uncomplaining, and he enjoys a good time. Like Twain, Brewer is charmed by the Sierra. Like Twain, too, he shows us something in the Sierra that we haven't seen before.

This granite is of a uniform light ash-gray color, inclining to pearly, and by the lights of sunset showed the most beautiful rosy tints. Scraggy pines grew in the crevices up to eleven thousand feet, gnarled and twisted by the winter storms of these desolate regions. One new species I found here, not known to botanists. By day the sky is generally of a deep blue-black; the stars shine with a mild silvery luster almost without twinkling.

Brewer was curious about rocks and trees, but he loved sunsets and star-shine, too. If he could enthuse over the composition of granites and schists, he was equally fervent about billowing clouds and the scent of pine needles. Like few who have written about the Sierra, he understood both the art and the science of mountains. Though he was not writing for publication, he produced some of the most lyrical and engaging prose on the entire shelf of Sierra literature. Here he is on the Great Western Divide on July 4, 1864:

We were back before sundown; a hearty dinner and pleasant camp fire closed the day. We sang "Old John Brown" around the camp fire that night—we three, alone in these solitudes. Thus was spent Independence Day. The last was with Hoffmann alone, in the Sierra farther north. We heard not a gun. Would that we might know the war news—we are over a month behind.

The next morning we lay in our blankets very late, after the fatigue of the previous day—in fact were in bed eleven hours. We stayed in camp and took latitude observations. It was a most lovely day.

The second notable work to come out of the survey was written by Brewer's assistant Clarence King. Brash, courageous, and burning with ambition, King accomplished a great deal of derring-do while with the survey, including an extraordinary assault on Mount Whitney, the highest peak in the continental United States. Though he failed in his bid, he and his companion Dick Cotter managed to traverse the Kings-Kern Divide, an accomplishment of such severity that Sierra historian Francis Farquhar has credited the two men with inaugurating, on their epic journey, a new era in American mountaineering.

King achieved considerable fame later in life as a writer and the first director of the U.S. Geological Survey. His book *Mountaineering in the Sierra Nevada*, published in 1872, is a collection of articles recounting his exploits in California. Within its pages King offers some fine descriptions of scenery and perceptive if not always sympathetic commentary on the human inhabitants of the range. The book's fame, however, rests on its author's seat-of-the-pants accounts of climbing in the High Sierra. King's tales abound in swagger and fabrication, partly because they were intended to entertain an audience of armchair adventurers in the east, and partly because King was something of a swaggering fabricator. Never a man to choose an easy route when a harder one lay nearby, he took on his mountains as St. George took on dragons. Here he is tackling Mount Clark in Yosemite:

About seven feet across the open head of a cul-de-sac (a mere recess in the west face) was a vertical crack riven into the granite not more than three feet wide, but as much as eight feet deep; in it were wedged a few loose boulders; below, it opened out into space. At the head of this crack a rough crevice led up to the summit.

Summoning nerve, I knew I could make the leap, but the life and death question was whether the debris would give way under my weight, and leave me struggling in the smooth recess, sure to fall and be dashed to atoms . . .

There was no discussion, but, planting my foot on the
brink, I sprang, my side brushing the rough projecting crag.
While in the air I looked down, and a picture stamped itself
on my brain never to be forgotten. The debris crumbled and
moved. I clutched both sides of the cleft, relieving all possible
weight from my feet. The rocks wedged themselves again, and
I was safe.

King has taken a good deal of heat from critics—some of it undoubtedly deserved—for his Perils-of-Pauline style and his shameless embellishments. Yet there is something in his writing that is truer and more accurate than any "objective" report of his experiences could ever be—if such were even possible. A journey into the Sierra, even today, is a journey into ambiguity and mystery. Climbing a difficult rock face, gazing across a gulf into misty morning, cupping a tiny wildflower in one's hand, one is never entirely certain of what one sees or feels, conceits of science and journalism to the contrary. Such uncertainty, indeed, is one of the reasons we are drawn to nature: we *cannot* put our fingers on it, no matter how hard we try, and that inability enchants us. Any account of a wilderness journey that omits the ambiguity, or that does not include a generous helping of the writer's fancies or fantasies, is bound to be false. If King's tale of climbing Mount Clark fails as journalism, it succeeds in conveying something of the *inexplicability* of the mountain, and of his experience of it. As the Yokut Indians tell of a hawk and a crow that created the Sierra, King tells of fantastic adventure on the slopes of a beguiling mountain in Yosemite. Both stories are necessary. Both reintroduce us to the Sierra as myth. It's a view of the range we cannot do without.

Three years after the members of the Whitney survey laid down their barometers and measuring rods, the single most important event in the human history of the Sierra took place: John

Muir showed up. Determined to reinvent himself by throwing off the shackles of society, Muir had set out from Indiana in search of the "divine beauty" and "harmony" of wild nature. His journey took him a thousand miles to the Gulf of Mexico, on foot, then by steamer to San Francisco. In March 1868 Muir stepped off the ship and asked directions from the first person he saw.

"But where do you want to go?" asked the passerby.

"To any place that is wild," Muir replied.

A few days later he set out on foot for Yosemite. At Pacheco Pass, southeast of San Jose, Muir had what we can only call a religious experience. Like St. Paul's vision on the road to Damascus, it set the young Scotsman on a path from which he would never stray.

> *At my feet lay the Great Central Valley of California, level and flowery, like a lake of pure sunshine . . . And from the eastern boundary of this vast golden flower-bed rose the mighty Sierra, miles in height, and so gloriously colored and so radiant, it seemed not clothed with light, but wholly composed of it, like the wall of some celestial city . . . Then it seemed to me that the Sierra should be called, not the Nevada or Snowy Range, but the Range of Light.*

Can there be any doubt what the writer is telling us? At Pacheco Pass, John Muir saw Paradise.

We should not be surprised by his choice of words, for Muir was a disciple of the Transcendentalists Ralph Waldo Emerson and Henry David Thoreau, who preached that nature is the dwelling place of good, not evil, as Judeo-Christian tradition would have it. Wilderness, they affirmed, is an earthly heaven where God's word is revealed. In years to come, on long journeys of discovery from one end of the Sierra to the other, in his primitive quarters in Yosemite Valley or huddled beneath a rock in a driving storm, praising God through the raindrops, John Muir, the essential madman of the Sierra, would live what the Transcendentalists only preached. At Walden Pond, after all, Thoreau was only a short distance from his mother's house, to which he sometimes repaired after dinner for berry pie. When he ventured into the wilds of Maine, he was ambivalent about what he found. The wellspring of wisdom and strength, wilderness was also "savage and dreary," wrote Thoreau; he couldn't wait to get home.

About wilderness, John Muir was never ambivalent. Unlike Emerson and Thoreau, he insisted on physical connection to wild places as a precondition for psychic connection—for understanding. The lesson he teaches is that to understand the Sierra, we must get out of our cars and dig our hands into the soft earth. "Climb the mountains and get their good tidings. Nature's peace will flow into you . . . while cares will drop off like autumn leaves." Accustomed to our hermetic urban lives, to nature as Disney and adventure as LeBron James slam-dunking a basketball for us, we struggle to make sense of the real-life majesty and drama of a Yosemite or a Kings Canyon. Says Muir: You wouldn't attempt to learn French without speaking the language, would you, or baseball without picking up a bat? Be like me: Ride an avalanche! Ford a river! *Climb a tree!*

After cautiously casting about, I made choice of the tallest of a group of Douglas spruces that were growing close together like a tuft of grass, no one of which seemed likely to fall unless all the rest fell with it. Though comparatively young, they were about one hundred feet high, and their lithe, brushy tops were rocking and swirling in wild ecstasy. Being accustomed to climb trees in making botanical studies, I experienced no difficulty in reaching the top of this one, and never before did I enjoy so noble an exhilaration of motion. The slender tops fairly flapped and swished

in the passionate torrent, bending and swirling backward and
forward, round and round, tracing indescribable combinations
of vertical and horizontal curves, while I clung with muscles
firm braced, like a bobolink on a reed.

In his journals and major writings—*My First Summer in the*
Sierra, The Mountains of California, The Yosemite—Muir preaches
that the embodiment of our hopes and dreams are to be found
etched in granite walls. In the petals of a flower, in gossamer crystals of falling snow, we glimpse our very images, and that of the
Divine. For, as he says, it is all one. "When we try to pick out
anything by itself, we find it hitched to everything else in the universe." Muir's belief in the unity of nature explains his rage in the
face of efforts to destroy it: It is the rage of a man whose leg is
about to be chopped off. "Dam Hetch Hetchy!" he thundered at the
proposal to turn Yosemite's magnificent Hetch Hetchy Valley into
a reservoir. "As well dam for water-tanks the people's cathedrals
and churches, for no holier temple has ever been consecrated by
the heart of man." It is a testament to Muir's achievement that he
stands as a monument who will long outlive the O'Shaughnessy
Dam at Hetch Hetchy—a man as inextricably linked with the
Sierra as Jefferson with Monticello, as Thoreau with Walden
Pond. Muir wrote the bible on the range, casting it in a light that,
perhaps more than any other, has come to seem essential to any
understanding of the Sierra.

Muir's equal has yet to appear, but during the twentieth century a few writers came along to fill the gaps he left. Mary Austin
was one. Like Clarence King, Austin spent a few unremarked years
in the Sierra before departing for widespread acclaim (in her case,
as a writer and social activist), leaving behind a single work to
deepen our understanding of the range. For a few years at the turn
of the century she resided in the threadbare landscape between

Death Valley and the High Sierra, an area she called "the land of little rain." In her book of the same name, published in 1903, she turns her gaze upon the borderlands between desert and mountain, a region about which John Muir had little to say.

> *Cattle once down may be days in dying. They stretch out their necks along the ground, and roll up their slow eyes at longer intervals. The buzzards have all the time, and no beak is dropped or talon struck until the breath is wholly passed. It is doubtless the economy of nature to have the scavengers by to clean up the carrion, but a wolf at the throat would be a shorter agony than the long stalking and sometimes perchings of these loathsome watchers.*

Austin went on to become a novelist of considerable repute. Although *The Land of Little Rain* is not a work of fiction, it evinces a novelist's interest in the people of the Sierra, who are almost nowhere to be found in John Muir. Austin casts a discerning light on wagon drivers, Native American basket makers, and Latino prospectors. Like few Sierra writers before or after her, she draws our attention to the interplay between people and landscape, suggesting that neither is complete without the other.

> *Perhaps to get into the mood of the waterways one needs to have seen old Amos Judson asquat on the headgate with his gun, guarding his water-right toward the end of a dry summer. Amos owned the half of Tule Creek and the other half pertained to the neighboring Greenfields ranch. Years of a "short water crop," that is, when too little snow fell on the high pine ridges, or, falling, melted too early, Amos held that it took all the water that came down to make his half, and maintained it with a Winchester and a deadly aim.*

It's regrettable that Austin never used her borderlands as a setting for a novel, for the Sierra has not proven a fertile ground for fiction writers. For many decades the same was true of poets. Hamstrung by their strong feelings for the Sierra, they applied their talents and their breathless language to the unnecessary task of glorifying the range, with mostly unremarkable results.

During the 1930s, however, the acclaimed poet and longtime Sierra traveler Kenneth Rexroth began using the Sierra not as his predecessors had, as an end, but rather as the beginning of explorations that took him to distant corners of the earth—and the heart. Rexroth used mountains as both memory and metaphor. With deceptively simple language, he draws us in, then springs his trap, showing us that there is much more to the Sierra than meets the eye. "For a month now, wandering over the Sierras, / A poem had been gathering in my mind," he begins "Climbing Milestone Mountain, August 22, 1937." A few lines later he is ruminating on the tragedy of Sacco and Vanzetti:

> *And I told Marie all about Boston, how it looked*
> *That last terrible week, how hundreds stood weeping*
> *Impotent in the streets that last midnight.*

Familiar backcountry sights—"blue damsel flies," "the pollen of the lodgepole pines," "the melting snow and broken rock"—become conduits into history.

> *I kicked steps up the last snow bank and came*
> *To the indescribably blue and fragrant*
> *Polemonium and the dead sky and the sterile*
> *Crystalline granite and final monolith of the summit.*
> *These are the things that will last a long time, Vanzetti.*
> *I am glad that once on your day I have stood among them.*
> *Some day mountains will be named after you and Sacco.*

Like Rexroth, the poet Gary Snyder has used images of the Sierra to illuminate his major themes, particularly the theme of the journey of discovery that leads to an understanding of one's unity with all creation. Snyder found his voice as a poet during a 1955 sojourn with a trail crew in northern Yosemite. In a few days he completed the poems that became the foundations of his collections *The Back Country* and *Riprap and Cold Mountain Poems*, including the poem "Water":

> *Pressure of sun on the rockslide*
> *Whirled me in a dizzy hop-and-step descent,*
> *Pool of pebbles buzzed in a Juniper shadow . . .*

"Pounded by heat," the poet races downward, plunges into a creek—a mirror of water:

> *Stretched full on cobble—ears roaring*
> *Eyes open aching from the cold and faced a trout.*

More economical than Rexroth's rambling excursions, Snyder's Sierra poems are hard-breathing, step-like—brief lives lived within a framework of bare-earth imagery, culminating in enlightenment and release.

No discussion of Gary Snyder or of Sierra literature would be complete without mention of Snyder's association with Jack Kerouac and the spirited adventure the two enjoyed, with the poet John Montgomery, on Matterhorn Peak in Yosemite National Park. The tale is told in Kerouac's 1958 roman á clef, *The Dharma Bums*, a hymn to both Snyder and Zen Buddhism. No mountain climber, Kerouac nonetheless manages in a few pages to fashion one of the most exhilarating and insightful climbing stories in the literature. Terrified as the ascent begins, Kerouac ("Ray Smith" in

the book) overcomes his fears by watching Snyder ("Japhy Ryder")
and by absorbing Snyder's wisdom. At climb's end, though Smith
fails to reach the summit, he suddenly sees the light:

> *It happened in one insane second or so: I looked up and saw
> Japhy running down the mountain in huge twenty-foot leaps,
> running, leaping, landing with a great drive of his booted
> heels, bouncing five feet or so, running, then taking another
> long crazy yelling yodelaying sail down the sides of the world
> and in that flash I realized it's impossible to fall off mountains
> you fool and with a yodel of my own I suddenly got up and
> began running down the mountain after him doing exactly the
> same huge leaps, the same fantastic runs and jumps . . .*

Kerouac's Matterhorn saga ushered in the modern era of
Sierra writing, an era that, coincidentally, has belonged almost
exclusively to the climbers. By some cosmic accident, Yosemite
Valley turned out to be Valhalla for rock climbers and the High
Sierra a mecca for mountaineers. Over the past half century,
mountaineering journals have brimmed with accounts of aston-
ishing ascents on smooth, vertical rock in the Valley and in the
Sierra high country.

The great majority of these reports are humorless, jargon-
choked exercises in self-congratulation. A few, however, tran-
scend even their airy settings to provide breathtaking and
illuminating glimpses into life at the edge. Several writers stand
out, among them Galen Rowell, Royal Robbins, Yvon Chouinard,
Steve Roper, and Doug Robinson. By their words and deeds, the
authors of these accounts attest that climbing is more than sport;
that, at its finest, it is an opportunity to bask in life at its lofti-
est, then to return to earth richer for the experience. "The view
below our hammocks was terrific—2,500 feet between us and

the ground," Chouinard writes of the beginning of Day 7 of his historic first ascent, with T.M. Herbert, of El Capitan's three-thousand-foot Muir Wall in 1965.

> *We now felt at home. Bivouacking in hammocks was completely natural. Nothing felt strange about our vertical world. With the more receptive senses we now appreciated everything around us. Each individual crystal in the granite stood out in bold relief. The varied shapes of the clouds never ceased to attract our attention. For the first time we noticed tiny bugs that were all over the walls, so tiny they were barely noticeable. While belaying, I stared at one for 15 minutes, watching him move and admiring his brilliant red color.*
>
> *How could one ever be bored with so many good things to see and feel! This unity with our joyous surroundings, this ultra-penetrating perception gave us a feeling of contentment that we had not had for years. It reminded TM of his childhood days when the family all came together on the porch of his home to sit and watch the setting sun.*

Later, returned safely to terra firma, Chouinard gazes up at the wall he has climbed. El Capitan, he tells us, no longer seems as fearful as it once did. Strangely, however, it appears "even more aloof and mysterious than before. It is far too deep-rooted to be affected by the mere presence of man. But we had been changed. We had absorbed some of its strength and serenity."

In that crystalline moment, Chouinard recognizes both the central paradox of the human relationship with the Sierra and a means for understanding it. The continually shifting character of the range that writers have described over the past hundred and fifty years springs not from plate tectonics, or biology, or meteorology—for, indeed, as Chouinard reminds us, the mountains are immutable; rather, it arises in spirit, in the human need to reinvent the world continually in our own image. Each fresh imagining alters our relationship with the mountains, putting us on a new path in search of a primal link with nature and the reassurance that we matter..

INTRUDERS ON A LIFELESS RIDGE

Now that our once-mysterious planet has been leveled, fenced, plowed, and planted in luxuriant enterprises like Quiznos and Jiffy Lube, it's easy to imagine that the term "terra incognita" is obsolete, a quaint reminder of a time when maps had blank spots, explorers used sextants to figure out where they were, and *National Geographic* had not yet published photos of every last pile of rocks and trickle of water on the face of the earth. No Air Canada passenger who gazes down on the 12 degrees of latitude that separate Vancouver, British Columbia, from Whitehorse, Yukon, can suffer from such a delusion. For nearly three hours, an inscrutable landscape unfurls below. Peaks and glaciers, glaciers and peaks heap and churn in all directions, lawlessly, like a rampaging sea. When the aircraft reaches one horizon, the thoroughly flummoxed passenger observes the arrival of yet another riot of mountains just like the last. In the first hour the spectacle is thrilling; sometime during the second it begins to wear; during the third, one prays for deliverance. "The increasing prospect tires our wandering eyes, / Hills peep o'er hills, and Alps on Alps arise!" Did Alexander Pope take this flight? Yes, every inch of the globe has been seen, mapped, photographed, and measured. But is it *known*? I don't think so. To draw a circle and calculate its diameter is not to know the circle.

I was on my way to the Yukon in the hope of tracking down members of the Porcupine caribou herd on their winter range.[1] My keenest desire during the flight to Whitehorse was to catch a glimpse of Mount Logan, Canada's tallest peak and the second-tallest in North America. Logan resides in Yukon's southwest corner, at the nucleus of the third-largest concentration of glaciers on Earth. (Bigger ones carpet portions of Antarctica and Greenland.) Remarkably for a peak with a high point nearly ten thousand feet lower than that of Mount Everest, Logan may be the biggest mountain on Earth. It owes its great bulk to its extraordinary length—more than twenty miles; a huge vertical relief—the mountain rises some fourteen thousand feet above the surrounding field of glaciers, several thousand feet more than Everest extends above her own; and to an architecture that more resembles a hotel than a pyramid: In its upper reaches, instead of angling to a sharp summit in the customary fashion, Logan widens into a plateau some ten square miles in area. Nine locations along the plateau exceed eighteen thousand feet in altitude; the peak's actual high point is reckoned at around 19,550 feet, just seven hundred fifty feet below that of Denali (Mount McKinley). Three thousand feet below the summit, at the altitude of the summit of Mont Blanc, Western Europe's tallest mountain, Logan's cross-section measures some thirty-square-miles in extent.

By my calculations, the product of all these heights and widths is a mountain with a volume of some four hundred cubic miles. Photographs of the peak taken from fifty miles away show the earth buckling beneath the feet of what appears to be a very large elephant draped in a white blanket. Surrounding king pachyderm is a court of countless smaller but only marginally less imposing

---

1. Part of the story of that adventure is told in "The Porcupine in Winter" elsewhere in this volume.

subjects. The poor climber who sets out for Logan's summit from the ice fields below has a long and very trying ascent ahead.

The mountain's climbing history is stirring. Because of Logan's remote location, simply getting to it presented a major hurdle for the first ascent team. Eight climbers departed McCarthy, Alaska, in early May 1925 and walked one hundred and fifty miles, eighty of them on glaciers, just to reach the mountain. Even then they found themselves barely a mile above sea level and twelve thousand feet below the summit. Atrocious weather and temperatures as low as −33 degrees Fahrenheit dogged the team over the three weeks that followed (the mercury topped zero exactly once during that period). At an altitude of around seventeen thousand feet, climber R.M. Morgan, whose feet were badly frostbitten, turned back; Henry Hall, a strong and healthy member of the party, unselfishly volunteered to accompany Morgan down the mountain. Two days later, the six others topped a thirty-foot platform of ice and stepped onto Canada's highest point.

That might have been the end of the climbers' troubles, but in fact they had only begun. The men arrived on the summit at 8 P.M., dangerously late to find themselves on the top of a big mountain. They stayed half an hour. Moments after beginning their descent, they were enveloped by clouds, then hit by a ferocious windstorm. For five hours they wandered aimlessly in a white-out, a frightening and harrowing meteorological condition where shadows disappear and earth and sky seem to merge; within, the bewildered victim is hard-pressed to tell up from down, forward from back. At 1:30 A.M., thoroughly lost somewhere on Logan's huge summit plateau, the six found the willpower to carve holes in the snow, then to burrow in for the most miserable bivouac of their lives.

A blizzard raged as, late the next morning, the team resumed its descent. Andy Taylor fell over a cliff, landing thirty feet below.

Somehow he was unhurt. Minutes later, Albert MacCarthy duplicated the feat. All six men would surely have perished but for a
stroke of luck: Peering through thick cloud cover, team member
Norman Read spotted a thin willow wand stuck in the snow. It was
one of many that the climbers had planted during their ascent to
mark the route. Read, Taylor, and Fred Lambart followed the lifeline of wands through the storm to the camp they called Plateau
Camp, two small tents perched on a shelf at 17,800 feet.

As those three were finding their way to shelter, the others—
MacCarthy, Allen Carpé, and Billy Foster—stopped to adjust one
of their packs. Within a moment they had lost touch with their
companions. When they resumed their march, they did so in the
wrong direction. An hour later, MacCarthy noticed that the mountain was sloping upward to his right instead of to his left, as it
should have done. In their confused states of mind, he, Carpé, and
Foster had reversed course and were now heading back toward
the mountain's summit. Unnerved, dangerously demoralized, and
still beset by storm, the three turned around and trudged on for
another hour in the proper direction. But it was late and the men
were exhausted. Realizing they would never reach the tents in
time, they prepared to spend a second night out.

It was a night of terror and wretched cold. All three men suffered hallucinations. "High cliffs of ice would seem to rise up before
us," MacCarthy later recalled, "and yet we never encountered them.
Barns and shelters would suddenly appear that we knew could
not exist, for otherwise one's companions would surely suggest
taking refuge in them." At some point, understanding that they
would not survive the night if they remained where they were,
they hoisted their packs and moved off down the slope. Now and
then they paused to sink down into the snow and fall asleep for a
few moments; then one would awaken and alert the others, and the
three would resume their descent.

They plodded on through the night. At 5 A.M., thirty-three hours after leaving Logan's summit, they stumbled into Plateau Camp. Andy Taylor prepared boned chicken, potatoes au gratin, and mugs of Ovaltine for the missing trio. The entire team spent the day and night in the tents, sleeping, eating, and readying themselves as best they could for the dreadful ordeal they knew lay ahead.

Late the next morning, feeling like anything but conquering heroes, the men abandoned most of their equipment, including tents, extra clothing, and most of their food, and beat an all-out retreat. Shortly after leaving camp, they were hit by a storm that all later agreed was the worst thing they had experienced on the mountain. The temperature plunged; hurricane-force winds whipped over the ground surface, hurling needles of ice into the men's faces. On one especially slippery stretch, they were forced to stop to remove their snowshoes and don crampons, an agony of bare fingers in boreal winds. All six now suffered from frost-bite and exhaustion; mid-storm, several began to exhibit symptoms of snow-blindness.

Had a cup of hot tea and a warm bath awaited the beleaguered group at the base of the mountain, the tale of their ill-starred retreat might have contained a hint of justice. But they had no such luck. Still a hundred miles from safety, in the nearest town of McCarthy, the team located the first of their previously stashed food caches. Alas, there was nothing to eat: Bears had found the site first and destroyed it. Two days later they found a second cache; it too had been trashed. Lambart, Carpé, and Read walked as far as they could on frostbitten feet. With eighty miles to go, they could go no farther.

The men set up camp for several days beside the Chitina River, which was in full flood. During the layover they cut a dozen logs and used them to construct two sixteen-foot rafts. Each craft the carpenters graced with a small platform, which they hoped would keep their few remaining possessions above water. On July 11, they resigned themselves to the Chitina and its caprices. Taylor, Read, and Lambart made fifty miles. After several days off his feet, Lambart was strong enough to walk the remaining thirty miles to McCarthy with almost no assistance from his two mates.

The other raft dumped its passengers into the freezing river after eighteen miles. MacCarthy, Carpé, and Foster managed to save their skins, barely, but lost everything else, save for a few scraps of food. Over the next four days the trio hiked seventy miles, Carpé on black, frostbitten toes. On July 15, sixty-four days after departing McCarthy, the last three members of the success-ful ascent team walked into town. As they were doing so, they ran into their pal Andy Taylor, who had organized a search party and was just then setting out to comb the sandbars of the Chitina for their bodies.

~

THE STORY OF the first ascent of Mount Logan has taken its place in the annals of mountaineering as an astonishment of the first order. The willow wands, the night of terror, the tiny rafts in the big Chitina, the marathon miles on frostbitten feet—those are signature episodes in climbing history. "For endurance and courage," mountaineering historian Sir Arnold Lunn has writ-ten, summing up the ordeal of the six, "their achievement has rarely been surpassed."

By the mid-sixties, four decades after this audacious enter-prise, most of the world's great peaks had been ascended for the first time, usually by the easiest route. Denied opportunities to be first on top, ambitious climbers now sought out new lines on the big peaks—lines notable for the directness of their approaches to the summit, or for their aesthetic qualities, or simply for their difficulty. Mount Logan had by then been ascended nine times, always by the 1925 route or by the East Ridge, a more technical route climbed for the first time in 1957. Then, over thirty-one days in July and August of 1965, the peak was the site of one of the luminous achievements in mountaineering history. If the 1925 ascent was noteworthy for the sheer grit of its participants, this one distinguished itself as a work of art.

Six visionary alpinists—Richard Long, John Evans, Allen Steck, Jim Wilson, Frank Coale, and Paul Bacon—set their sights on Logan's six-mile-long south ridge, a wild zigzagging feather-edge of raven-black rock and teetering cornices, much of it little wider than a bootprint. The six flew to their base camp on the Seward Glacier on July 7. They set up their tents twenty-eight hundred feet below the crest of the ridge they hoped to climb, near the run-out from a steep and very nasty couloir—a gully—that flowed almost constantly in avalanches and rockfall. In an article in the 1966 edition of the *American Alpine Journal*, Steck, a celebrated climber renowned equally for the boldness of his routes and his serene appreciation for the absurdities of his craft, recalled that base camp was near enough to the couloir that the avalanches could be viewed "in the most personal way, reminiscent of the surf where, with your toes digging in the sand, you watch the foaming mass come in to expend itself virtually at your feet, all the time wondering about that ninth wave supposedly so much larger than all the others."

To attain the ridge, the team had to ascend a buttress on the right side of the couloir. With time out for storms and for dodging rocks and cascades of snow, those twenty-eight hundred feet of precious altitude consumed ten of the thirty-five days the men had allotted for the entire climb. They called the couloir Osod, a word that seemed to convey, in Steck's words, "the full-flavored, all-pervasive feeling of fear" they felt in its grips. There was nothing kind about Osod. Its ice-coated ledges—tiny skating rinks—sloped downward. Looking for something to grip so that you didn't zip off all the way down to base camp, you found holds that inevitably faced in the opposite direction from where your fingers would like them. Perilously loose rock ribboned the final yards to the ridge itself. In one grueling twenty-two-hour effort, Evans and Long opened the route to within two hundred feet of the ridge, negotiating one section that in rock-climber's parlance they rated 5.7— challenging on warm rock at sea level, many times so here. Alas, with the ridge in sight, the two were forced to descend all the way to base. "Not even a place to sit down comfortably," Long reported. "A campsite is out of the question."

New storms pinned the men in base camp. Finally, on July 17, they mastered the final two hundred feet to the ridge. Up came personal gear, a month's worth of food and fuel, and forty-two hundred feet of rope. Ten days into the climb and they were at ninety-six hundred feet, with two vertical miles to go.

In Osod the fear was being hit by a projectile. On the ridge, the fear was becoming one. A cornice is an overhanging roof of snow, a great white comma, a curl at the front edge of a wave. A cornice is formed when prevailing winds sweep over a ridge, building and rounding the snow-cover farther and farther away from the solid mountain beneath. The result is exquisite, a creation that for pure elegance is unsurpassed in the teeming museum of mountaineering delights—"a creation of absolute beauty" noted Steck, adding quickly, "to be observed from as great a distance as possible." Which is to say, you are welcome to stand atop a cornice to admire the view, or even pitch your tent on it; but do understand that the thing could collapse beneath you at any moment with a distressing *"WHUMMMP!!!"* as though some joker had blown it to bits with a stick of dynamite. Your next stop, or that of your tent and everything in it, will be the glacier, located some distance below. ("How far is it down to the glacier?" goes the rookie's question in an old climbing joke. Veteran climber responds: "About nine seconds.") The south ridge of Mount Logan is a six-mile-long alleyway of magnificent, ready-to-crumble cornices, with occasional interruptions of hairy, splintery rock. To climb the ridge, you surf the white wave and tiptoe the black one.

Or you burrow beneath the wave. Perched under a big one, protecting Bacon, who was inching up the curl at the other end of the rope, Evans shouted: "If that cornice falls, don't tell me about it. I want to be surprised!" Two hours later, the cornice fell. Steck: "All of us had been on the buttress and had watched the ice crystals shoot into the sky as that ghastly thing raced into the catchment basin, cleansing and scouring the . . . couloir as it went, with a roar that remains in our ears to this day."

Once on the ridge, the team was unable to find a spot spacious enough for the tents. They set to work carving a narrow ledge in the ice—an effort that took twelve hours. Once Camp 1 was established (eventually there would be ten camps), snow began to fall. It continued for six days.

The men climbed when they could. A routine developed. Two in front would push the route higher, fixing rope to snow or rock as best they could, scooting past towers of ice, tunneling through cornices, ascending crumbly rock pillars. The others would clip onto the rope using a device called a jumar and follow behind, hauling loads. At day's end, all would follow the ropes back to camp. The next day, weather permitting, more of the same and another step higher. When a spot big enough for a new camp was located—an apparently stable mushroom of snow, a tiny ledge that could be carved into something homey—they brought up the tents, pulled up the fixed ropes for the next stage, thereby cutting off their retreat line, and started over.

In some ways, the two in front had it easier: Despite the dangers, they at least had the pleasure of solving problems, of getting up and getting past and being first. Coming along behind, the load-bearers had little to do but mutter and fret and offer earnest incantations to the mountain gods. To follow the leaders' shallow boot holes in the snow, especially in fog or high winds, they needed courage and skill, of course, but also no small amount of simple faith. If the weather was clear, the porters were in constant sight of the terrible drop-off just a foot or two to their right or left, a sight none of them ever got used to. Standing in some forlorn spot, waiting for the two up ahead to anchor the rope with an ice picket or a rock piton, Steck sometimes played his harmonica; but even sweet music drifting down the Arctic airwaves couldn't quell the surges of fear. Falls on the fixed line were routine. "Of the many mishaps on that little jaunt, one was memorable," Long recalled, of a stretch where a rare jab of sunlight had softened the snow, making treacherous the footsteps he was following. "This time I pitched off headfirst with my heavy pack and thus enjoyed an exhilarating snap when my jumar finally picked me up on the fixed line."

Camp 2 was a thousand shovel-blows in the side of a cornice. The six climbers were trapped there for seven days by on-and-off storms. The main topic of conversation that week was, "When will it go?" The men got moving again on the morning of July 29. The cornice collapsed a few hours later. Bacon surmised that perhaps it had been held together by their tent lines.

What possessed those six characters, taunting death by the minute, pressing on in the face of what all of them now regarded as certain defeat? Madness? The desire to die wretchedly but in a beautiful spot? They were, of course, volunteers in their endeavor, at a time well before the age of corporate sponsorship, endorsements, book deals, and the Travel Channel, any one of which might have provided them with at least a moment of notoriety and a few bucks for their wallets. Few people even knew they were there. In the event of trouble, there wasn't an iota of hope they would be rescued.

It's commonly asserted that climbers do what they do because they have a deep-seated wish to die. Having known many climbers, and having myself climbed for many years, I can attest that mountaineers haven't a scintilla of interest in dying; all of them want quite voraciously to live. These men and women have learned that life is most easily understood for the sublime gift that it is when it is viewed in close proximity to its alternative. This seeming contradiction is regarded as perverse when stated by climbers but moving and insightful when asserted by someone who has had an unprovoked near-death experience—with cancer, say, or in a car accident. Having stared into the jaws of death and survived, many such people suddenly realize what they had not before: that life is precious. Their lives are changed. Thereafter, they cherish each day in a way they never did before.

People who fall in love with climbing achieve this same understanding but without having near-death experiences thrust upon them. Instead, they thrust them upon themselves. Moreover, they do so cheerfully and as frequently as possible. Like people who survive illness and accidents, climbers know that life is beautiful; their sport, if that's what it is, is an expression of their love for life, their realization that it is short and irreplaceable, and their ever-growing appreciation for the crazy mystery of existence. It's my belief that climbers are, at heart, humorists who are deeply in touch with the essential facts of life, the most essential of which is death; they don't want to die but they get a good laugh out of trying.

> *But Steck, we cannot be saved if we get in a jam!*
> *Wonderful—isn't that why we came here?*
> *Yikes, that cornice may go at any moment!*

But how beautiful it is!
Yes, but my fingers are freezing!
But most of the time back home, you don't even remember that
you have fingers!
What if I fall?
Don't!

Team members were often exhausted, uncertain, cold, scared, and they still had miles to go. There was no sensible conclusion to their pursuit. The top of a mountain! What to do? Well, go on, of course! The great French alpinist Lionel Terray put it this way: We are, he said, "conquistadors of the useless." There are touches of Don Quixote in the six perched on their ridiculous cornice, but equally of Leif Ericson and Neil Armstrong.

"I am terrorized by each blow of the shovel," Steck admitted. "Our panic threshold has soared." Observed John Evans, of pushing the route higher, with Paul Bacon, in a 50-knot wind: "The wind was blowing up from the nearly invisible camp, and we could occasionally hear the singing and the strains of Steck's harmonica. The boost this incongruous bit of elegance gave our morale was remarkable; a great part of the charm of the mountains surely lies in the climber's awareness of this strange combination of beauty and discomfort."

Of the many unforgettable episodes that distinguish the south ridge climb, one stands above the rest. On the final day before exiting Osod onto the ridge itself, Steck was last in line, waiting his turn to clip into the fixed line and to follow his companions onto the crest. He was, to put his location in perspective, one hundred miles from the nearest flower, in a steep, icy, awful slide, on a perch the size of a dinner plate, on the world's biggest mountain: alone in ghastly Osod. Exactly the spot for an epiphany.

Suddenly I am aware of a whirring sound . . . a falling rock!
Instinctively I press myself close to the cliff, but the sound per-
sists and as I turn to investigate I notice a tiny hummingbird
hovering over my bright red pack, darting in and then retreat-
ing, with that delightful grace peculiar to its kind. Is he merely
curious or does he wish to stop and rest awhile on something
other than rock and ice? In a moment he has flown away,
consuming his fuel supply at a rate perhaps 30 times my own.
My little friend, you and I are both intruders on this lifeless
ridge; you have been blown off course by chance, while I, owing
to forces I do not fully comprehend, have come voluntarily—
like a moth to a flame—attracted by the elemental dynamism
of the mountains. We are now both engaged in a struggle with
our environment, though mine appears the more absurd . . . I
wonder which of us is the better prepared to meet the trials to
come? Somehow, I think you may even reach the world of green
things by nightfall . . . In any case I shall be thinking of you.

To those who accomplish the first ascent of a new route goes the privilege of giving it a name. On big mountains, geography often wins the day. On Everest, most climbers follow Tenzing and Hillary up the South Col route. On Denali, the West Buttress is the standard way to the top. Sometimes the team leader is honored, as on Denali's Cassin Ridge.

But irony is permitted in these baptismal rites, as are whimsy and even tenderness. In dreadful Osod, then, a small miracle. Steck passed the news of his encounter along to the others. They agreed unanimously to replace "south ridge" with the name that this beguiling, terrifying feather of snow and rock has answered to ever since: the Hummingbird Ridge.

～

AMAZINGLY, MIDWAY UP the Hummingbird there's a level stretch. It's five-eighths of a mile long. Needless to say, it's corniced all the way. Photos show what appears to be the long, level top of a white cathedral. On either side, a roof pitches downward at an 80-degree angle. The ascent team stopped climbing upward and for two days moved forward, each step in hard snow on a walkway the width of a dictionary, the first man probing, whacking the lip off a cornice, kicking a bucket, attaching the rope to an ice screw, his roped companion dug in behind—one step, one step, one step.

Steck recalled:

> *I drew the last lead, took the shovel, and bade farewell to John. The air was still, the sun incredible. The cornices and ice towers were balanced on a slender spine of rock, the culmination of this giant ridge that formed a 7000-foot barrier between two glacial cirques. A soft mist rose to the east of the crest. I turned for a moment and was completely lost in silent appraisal of the beautifully sensuous simplicity of windblown snow.*

Reverie quickly gave way to reality: there were still seven thousand feet of up to go. Retreat was inevitable. And yet unthinkable—to retrace those steps! As a safeguard, the men had left ropes strung back to the third campsite, the better to assist them in their retreat when the weather turned, as they knew it would.

Miraculously, the next day dawned clear. Abandoning their earlier plan, the team pulled up the ropes and committed themselves to the summit. Evans called it a forward retreat. The packs were lighter now. The sky was clear. Spirits soared. Duly naturalized citizens of the mountain, the team moved rapidly. Standing on a cornice, Wilson felt it start to break off; with scarcely a thought, he simply leaned the other way, shifting his weight. The snow broke, fell to kingdom come, Wilson admired the sheered-off edge and moved on.

At 16,300 feet they encountered the only section of the ridge where they could safely progress two hundred feet unroped. Camp 7 at 16,500, Camp 8 at 18,200. Then, on August 6, thirty-one days after landing on the glacier, Richard Long, John Evans, Allen Steck, Jim Wilson, Frank Coale, and Paul Bacon lunched in sunlight at the top of the ridge. For the first time in a month, they could fall unroped without dying.

"Weaker than we realized," Steck recalled, "we staggered like drunks, and often stumbled waist-deep into crevasses." Determined to finish the job—they were at the top of the ridge but not the mountain—they descended a demoralizing five hundred feet, then struck out for the highest of Logan's many high points. Minutes from the top, perhaps overcome by a condition called "summit euphoria," they decided that the true summit was not enough, that they needed the mountain's second- and third-highest points as well. Duly emboldened, they dropped their packs and traversed down and over to Logan's east summit. There they enjoyed a view of their magnificent ridge. Dropping down again, they ascended to the main summit, picking up their packs on the way.

The temperature was 12 degrees. Gazing west, they could see the Pacific a hundred miles away. They camped and the following day took in Logan's third-highest point. Descending to the west by the 1925 route, they found the food cache that Coale had air-dropped thirty-two days before. They pitched their tents, and then a storm moved in.

Few ascents before or since have demanded greater levels of imagination, commitment, audacity, fortune, or technical skill. No newspapers reported the achievement. The six went home and slipped quietly back into their lives—Steck as a designer of climbing and backpacking equipment, Long as a physician, Coale as an electrical engineer, Bacon as a ski racer, Wilson as a physicist, Evans as a geologist. Five decades have passed, and though many mountaineers have dreamed of the Hummingbird and a few have attempted it, no one has ever repeated that giddy tightrope walk in the sky. The Hummingbird belongs to a rare club, the "fewer ascents than deaths" club. As of 2015, the tally stood at one ascent, two deaths.

~

SEATED AT MY portside window on Air Canada Flight 6344, I studied the view to the northwest. The horizon in that direction had been clear since takeoff. Now, as the end of my flight neared, the sky grew dark. Lightning flashed. The entire St. Elias Range, of which Mount Logan is master, slipped beneath a tumble of clouds. Whether Logan could be seen from that distance on a sunny day, I didn't know; in any case, she would not be seen today.

Naturally, I was disappointed. And yet, it would have seemed unsporting to glimpse that hallowed temple of snow and rock on my first try! There's an old mountaineering adage, designed to assuage the climber who, for some reason—bad weather, bad equipment, a bad feeling in the pit of his or her stomach—decides to turn back from an ascent: The mountain will always be there. So will its stories. Not to be defeated, I closed my eyes, burrowed beneath the clouds, and summoned up the myth of the Hummingbird Ridge, where long ago, six stouthearted warriors engaged the goddess of Logan in hand-to-hand combat, and won.

~

Epilogue

In the fall of 2014, as the fiftieth anniversary of the Hummingbird approached, I found myself wondering about the fates of the six men who had accomplished that historic ascent. Jim Wilson, Frank Coale, and Paul Bacon, I learned, were deceased. John Evans was retired from an eclectic career that included stints with Outward Bound and the U.S. space program, and that centered on supporting field research in Antarctica. As a mountaineer he participated in expeditions to the Pamirs, to Mount Everest, and to Antarctica, where he made the first ascent of Mount Vinson, the continent's tallest peak, and the much more difficult second-tallest peak, Mount Tyree.

I found Allen Steck in the hills above Berkeley, in the house where he has lived for more than fifty years. Two years after returning from Mount Logan, Steck and Steve Roper founded ASCENT, one of the world's classiest mountaineering publications. Two years later, Steck created, with Leo Le Bon, Mountain Travel, the first adventure travel firm.

In his late eighties when I caught up with him, Steck lamented that his climbing days were behind him, though until two years earlier he had been doing mid-level routes at the local climbing gym. One wall of his den featured a huge photograph of the south façade of Mount Logan, with a thin and daunting Hummingbird Ridge climbing steeply from lower right to upper left. Allen walked me up the ridge, educating me on certain features of the ascent that I hadn't heard about. The name of the dreaded Osod couloir, I learned, was chosen not to call to mind some evil ancient god, but rather for its utility as an acronym: O Shit! O Dear! And he speculated on why, after fifty years, the ridge hadn't seen a second ascent. Fortune, or lack of it, was partly responsible. An attempt on the Hummingbird in 1987 by world-class alpinists Catherine Freer and David Cheesmond ended when a cornice broke and the two were swept to their deaths.

But failure to appreciate the magnitude and nature of the undertaking has played a role, too. One team ran out of food far down on the ridge; another foundered due to dissension among its members, who were not sufficiently prepared to handle the weeks of continual stress and fear that the ridge is sure to dole out.

I struck out at first in my attempts to locate Richard Long. One evening at an event at the local high school in Carson City, where I live, I struck up a conversation with the father of one of my son's friends. When

I learned that the man was a climber, I mentioned the Hummingbird Ridge and my interest in finding Long.

He laughed. "Richard Long? I'm guessing you can find him. He lives a couple of miles from here. He's been an orthopedic surgeon in Carson City for decades." Shortly thereafter I hooked up with Long and spent an enlightening couple of hours with him, talking mountains and enjoying bountiful portions of a very fine cabernet. Long was eighty. Altogether fitting for a surgeon who has replaced a thousand hips, he possessed a plastic one of his own. He still swam and hiked in the nearby hills.

We talked about departures from the normal routine of climbing a big mountain that the Hummingbird demanded—the elevation of the lowly snow shovel to a position superior to that of the iconic ice axe as a practical tool for moving upward, the constant fear of plunging through a cornice, the use of 600-foot ropes rather than traditional 150-footers, allowing the man in the lead to move four times farther than normal before securing himself, sort of, to the mountain.

I asked Long what he thought when, staring up at the Hummingbird for the first time, he contemplated the ordeal before him.

He answered without hesitation: "I knew there was nothing there we couldn't climb."

SIX EXCERPTS FROM ARCTIC CIRCLE

I. To Feel the Earth Turn

When you set out on your journey to Ithaca,
pray that the road is long.
—CONSTANTINE P. CAVAFY

Lead me from the unreal to the real!
Lead me from darkness to light!
—BRIHADARANYAKA UPANISHAD

In the vast literature of polar exploration, certain moments blaze with almost celestial splendor. One of the brightest, arguably saintly in its proportions, is British Army Captain Lawrence Oates's transcendent sacrifice on the Antarctic plateau, a stunning, nearly inaudible whisper near the end of explorer Robert Scott's journal, when the gravely ill Oates eases himself painfully from his sleeping bag and exits Scott's tent into a blizzard, knowing that he must die if the other members of the party are to live. "I am just going outside," Oates says almost offhandedly to Scott, "and may be some time."

On an altogether different scale—big, brawling, arduous to a degree that defies comprehension—is Ernest Shackleton's miraculous eight-hundred-mile journey over the tempestuous South Atlantic in his ridiculous rowboat, then foot by frostbitten foot across the brutal mountains of South Georgia. His mission: the salvation of the men of his expedition, stranded an ocean away on a flyspeck of rock called Elephant Island. Can anyone read these passages and ever again question the capacity of the human animal for greatness, or the heights to which it is capable of rising?

Yet for each such moment, there are a thousand others that reveal not the nobility of our species nor the triumph of the human spirit, but the rather more down-to-earth and often quite nasty details of daily life in the harshest environment on the planet. Certainly there is a kind of heroism to be found running between even the most pedestrian of lines in these riveting journals and memoirs. But let's face it: That's not why we read them. We read them for *the good parts*. We read them for the bone-snapping temperatures and the ten-day blows, the polar bear attacks, scurvy epidemics, and exploding camp stoves. Ungodly darkness, not celestial brightness, draws us to these tales, and in all the literature there is scarcely a sentence that fails to satisfy.

The shadow falls for the first time in A.D. 997. The Norseman Thorgisl Orrabeinfostri wrecks his ship on the northwest coast of Baffin Bay, laying the groundwork for a two-year ordeal of starvation and madness. A millennium later, the means have changed but the gloom persists. April 1998: The Russian diver Andrei Rozhkov cuts a hole in the ice precisely at the North Pole, observes a beautiful and haunting light beckoning deep in the water far below him, and dives fifty meters to investigate. His equipment fails in the demanding conditions of 90 degrees north, and he dies. (Rozhkov's demise is, ipso facto, the most northerly ever recorded.) Between the two events, the official record is pretty much one of hell on earth. And however sympathetic we may feel toward the condemned in their plights, something in these fiendish, callous, ambulance-chasing souls of ours makes us want to pull up a chair, pop open a beer, and watch.

"Great God! This is an awful place," Scott mourns upon his arrival at the South Pole, and we can scarcely wait to find out why. Crime novels disturb us, and Stephen King scares the bejeezus out of us. But the annals of cannibalism and blackened limbs . . . for sheer day-to-day horror, nothing can match 'em!

"When I awoke my long beard was a mass of ice, frozen fast to the buffalo-skin: Godfrey had to cut me out with his jack-knife." So writes the physician and polar explorer Elisha Kent Kane of his somewhat melancholy emergence from a snooze on the sea-ice west of Greenland in March 1854. The dismal scene is one of many that enliven *Arctic Explorations*, Kane's bestselling account of his attempt to become the first person to reach the North Pole. Alas, things are not going well. The doctor and fifteen of his seventeen-man crew are purple with scurvy; the expedition's precious supply of hardtack and rotten potatoes is running low; the ship, in which the party has been icebound for six months, has been taken over by rats.

We have been terribly annoyed by rats. Some time ago we made a brave attempt to smoke them out with the vilest imaginable compound of vapours: brimstone, burnt leather, and arsenic, and spent a cold night in a deck-bivouac to give the experiment fair play. But they survived the fumigation. We now determined to dose them with carbonic acid gas.

Before long, half the crew will mutiny. First, however, there is the matter of the lost patrol. Five crewmen have been missing for more than a week. They are assumed to be in a desperate state. Kane and nine of his men are afoot on the ice, searching for the beleaguered five. Where are they? "Somewhere within a radius of forty miles." The temperature is −46 degrees Fahrenheit.

"It required brisk exercise to keep us from freezing," Kane explains helpfully. He faints twice. McGary and Bonsall are seized with trembling fits and shortness of breath. Ohlsen, who had been with the missing five and who somehow made it back to the ship to report their predicament, now returns with the rescuers, strapped to a sled. "Mr. Ohlsen, who had been without rest for fifty hours, fell asleep as soon as we began to move, and woke now with unequivocal signs of mental disturbance."

The party marches twenty-one hours without pause. Then, miraculously, they see footprints; a moment later they spot an American flag fluttering atop an ice hummock.

So: Farther from help and from the good graces of God than anyone else on Earth, we find fifteen cold, sick, hungry, exhausted men, plus one tent with space for eight. Lots are drawn. The eight winners pile into the shelter and fall into a sleep of desperation; the others pace outside continually to keep from freezing.

Two hours pass. The groups switch places. The thermometer reads −56 when the party begins the long march back to the ship. On the way, Bonsall and Morton beg permission to sleep. Hans is found nearly stiff under a drift. John Blake throws himself into the snow and refuses to rise. The men camp again, without food or water. Kane's beard freezes to his sleeping bag.

We could not abstain any longer from eating snow; our mouths swelled and some of us became speechless. Our halts multiplied and we fell half-sleeping in the snow. I could not prevent it. I ventured upon the experiment myself, making Riley wake me at the end of three minutes; and I felt so much benefited by it that I timed the men in the same way. They sat on the runners of the sledge, fell asleep instantly, and were forced to wakefulness when their three minutes were out.

Three days after leaving the ship, the men are back. The missing five have been saved, if that is the word. Dr. Hayes administers morphine freely. Mr. Ohlsen suffers from snow blindness.

"The week that followed has left me nothing but anxieties and sorrow," Kane laments.

Nearly all our party, as well the rescuers as the rescued, were tossing in their sick-bunks, some frozen, some undergoing amputations, several with dreadful premonitions of tetanus. I was myself among the first to be about; the necessities of the others claimed it of me.

Early in the morning of the 7ᵗʰ I was awakened by a sound from Baker's throat, one of the most frightful and ominous that ever startled a physician's ear. The lockjaw had seized him; that dark visitant whose foreshadowings were on so many of us. His symptoms marched rapidly to their result; he died on the 8ᵗʰ of April.

～

THE NORTH! I fell in love with these amazing stories, real and true and honest as a chomp on the thigh by a rabid wolverine, when I was in my early twenties. Whatever had gotten into me? Was it rebellion? A cry for help? No doubt the seed was sewn early, perhaps by Jack London's *Call of the Wild*, which I read in junior high school, or Vilhjalmur Stefansson's *Unsolved Mysteries of the Arctic*, which I received as a Christmas present at around the same time. Stefansson's book fairly sang with the mystery and enchantment of the North—even more, with the peril. Those associations became my primary links with the region. A few years later I began reading the hair-raising words of the explorers themselves: Elisha Kane's *Arctic Explorations*, Isaac Hayes's *The Open Polar Sea*, Fridtjof Nansen's *Farthest North*, Frederick Cook's *My*

Attainment of the Pole. Any doubts I may have had about the true
nature of the North were quickly erased. The men who took on the
Arctic were cool and tough as icebergs, and they had to be. They
wrote about the region as though it were some distant and sinister
planet to which they had been dispatched, usually by themselves, to
wage war against an enemy, and the more spears and cannonballs
it rained down upon them, the happier they were. They seemed
almost disappointed if there was enough food to eat or if the sun
came out.

The idea of the North that I drew from my reading was only
incidentally rooted in the physical character of the region. Partly
that was because the authors rarely had much to say about geology, flora, or fauna, or even about the Inuit, who so often saved
their skins. (Thoroughly at home in the North, the native people
are usually consigned to a spot on the frozen edges of these high
misadventures, like so many icicles; the reader can sense them
shaking their heads at their strange visitors, so out of place in
those harsh surroundings, and muttering, "Who *are* these guys?")
Written as they were on the fly with frozen fingers, in the dark,
the hastily scribbled notes and diaries of the Arctic explorers are
understandably deficient in scientific observation and sociological commentary.

What they brim with, however, and what formed the basis of
my understanding of the place, is the notion of the Arctic as a
big, empty, dangerous place where life is lived in extremis, and
where one goes to put oneself in contact with the elements, even
perhaps to risk death (or at least amputation) in order to achieve
some grand reward. It was the same notion that a few years earlier
had attracted me to the idea of climbing mountains. That infat-
uation, too, began with books. At the age of sixteen, faced with
the grim task of preparing in one night a book report for a high
school English class, I quite arbitrarily pulled a volume called *The*

Conquest of Everest from a shelf in the public library in my home-town of Titusville, Pennsylvania. Written by Sir John Hunt, the leader of the 1953 British expedition to Mount Everest, the book told the story of the first ascent of the world's highest peak by expedition members Edmund Hillary and Tenzing Norgay.

I was a lowlander who had never before given a thought to the idea of climbing mountains. Yet something in the book's climactic chapter (the only one I read) struck a chord in me. In those sixteen spellbinding pages, the triumphant Hillary recounted in his own measured, precise, and thrilling words the story of the final assault on the summit. His tale provoked an epiphany in me. Suddenly I longed to be atop a towering peak, alone, enveloped in cold and mist and silence. I knew nothing of mountains, but I understood intuitively that they were more than mere topography, that they had a spiritual side, too, and that the determined seeker could go to them, as I believed Hillary had, to find happiness and peace.

I emerged from the book on fire. I decided that I wanted to become a mountain climber. During my final year in high school, I found and devoured other mountaineering titles in the library: *Annapurna*, Maurice Hertzog's stirring account of the first ascent of an eight-thousand-meter peak; *K2, The Savage Mountain*, Charles Houston and Robert Bates's monumental, heartbreaking tale of an attempt on the world's second-highest mountain by a star-crossed team of American climbers. When I went off to college I took up backpacking, then rock climbing, then the entire art of rock and snow and ice. I was never an especially skilled climber, and I set no records and gained no fame; but for a quarter century I was delirious with mountains, drunk with them. I climbed year-round throughout the Western United States and Canada: peaks, hills, boulders, crags—anything that went up. In the accepted fashion and usually with a few close friends, I put my life on the line rock after rock, mountain after mountain, and sometimes I achieved my summits. But even when I didn't, I understood myself to be a kind of pilgrim on a quest that transcended mere sport, one that inquired obsessively into eternal questions of life and death. I was not alone in this conceit: Of all the reasons that motivate climbers to pursue their dangerous sport, this one is perhaps foremost.

I climbed until I was in my early forties. Then a series of lamentable events, including a divorce, the deaths of my parents, and the death of a dear friend in a rock climbing accident, caused me to rethink my commitment to mountaineering. I was growing older. I was losing the physical and mental edges I needed to climb safely. Worst of all, I was becoming afraid. When, a year after my divorce, I fell in love and remarried, I realized how utterly stupid it would be for me, at that joyful moment of starting over, to perish in the mountains. Reluctantly, I hung up my rope and crampons and vowed to never use them again.

∼

MOUNTAINEERING AND ARCTIC exploration have much in common. Both are dangerous games conducted under difficult circumstances in extreme environments. Both beg of their players unanswerable questions about life and death, and about what in the world they are doing there, playing the game, *that* game, rather than, say, tennis. Both attract the type of person who, given the choice between flying four thousand miles in a private jet to sleep in silk pajamas at the Ritz and hiking twenty miles in the rain to sleep in wet underwear on a pile of rocks, would choose the latter. Having fallen for Arctic literature as helplessly as I had fallen for *The Conquest of Everest* and *Annapurna*, I might have been expected at some point in my young life to make a decision to go north, just as I had made a decision to go climbing.

But I did not. I made several feints in that direction but each time slunk away having barely tested the wind. While teaching high school in New York City, I attended evening classes in celestial navigation at the Hayden Planetarium. I was motivated by the romantic and requisitely crazy notion that I would one day command a dog team across some perilous northern landscape, finding my way by sun and stars. When I retired from teaching, my students presented me with a handsome sextant to use on my journey. Sadly, I never fulfilled their dream for me. For a few years I kept up my navigational skills, occasionally shooting the sun to learn that, yes, I was in Palo Alto or Albuquerque. But never Greenland or Melville Island or Repulse Bay.

At about the same time I was attending classes at the planetarium, I concocted a halfhearted plan to attempt a peak on Baffin Island—real North!—with a fellow climber. The expedition died, ostensibly for lack of funds but more accurately, for me, for lack of will. As I pored over maps with my friend and studied the difficulties and dangers of living for even a short while in that forbidding environment, I began to grasp in a way that I never had before the true and uncompromising hostility of the North. If climbing a mountain on Baffin Island were simply a matter of technique, of putting one foot in front of the other, I might have gone ahead with the plan. But there was a psychological component to the exercise—that pervasive Arctic darkness—that rendered such an effort beyond my mental reach.

The difference between climbing mountains and exploring the Arctic; the reason, I think, that I climbed for a quarter century but never set foot north of the fifty-fifth parallel, was that for all the trouble mountains are capable of meting out, they have a bright, beautiful, spiritually grand side that I knew well and that I reveled in. No climbing account is complete without its long and painstakingly composed passages extolling the beauty and wonder of the mountain landscape, and of the act of climbing. For most mountaineers, those pleasures are central to their enjoyment of the sport.

During my years as a climber, I knew many scary ledges, dangerous slopes, and cold, wet nights; despite them, light and pleasure
were the pre-eminent associations I always made with mountains.

By contrast, I continued to see the Arctic as unrelievedly
gloomy. Most of the explorers' accounts that formed my understanding of the region fell into the "Great God! This is an awful
place" category—riveting reading but poor advertisements for the
territory. Rarely did the authors of those works throw their arms
skyward and cry out in ecstasy at the grandeur of the North or at
their joy in being there. With only the teeth-gritting explorer's
model of the Arctic after which to pattern my understanding, I
looked northward with ambivalence. The idea of the place, I loved;
the thought of going there gave me the shivers.

~

A CHANCE ENCOUNTER in 1977 with a man named Fred Meader
turned my notion of the Arctic on its head. I was living in the San
Francisco Bay Area, climbing as often as I could in California's
High Sierra and on friendly neighborhood crags like Castle Rock
and Pinnacles National Monument, and attempting the rest of the
time to make a living as a freelance magazine writer. Recently I
had come across John McPhee's "Coming Into the Country," a
long article excerpted from his book of the same name, in the
New Yorker. McPhee's subject was Alaska. Naturally I devoured
the article in one sitting. Much of the story was given over to a
discussion of the Alaska Lands Bill, a grandiose piece of Carter
Administration legislation that proposed carving up huge portions of Alaska's wildlands into national parks, monuments, and
wildlife refuges, thereby providing them with permanent protection from development.

I had never heard of the bill, but it sounded like a good idea
to me. At the time I didn't know much about the way Washington

works, and I assumed the bill would pass with ease. After doing a little investigation, I learned that although the legislation was widely supported in the lower forty-eight, it was stalled, perhaps permanently, in Congress. The reason: loud and cranky opposition by many Alaskans, including the governor, the Congressional delegation, the publisher of the state's largest newspaper, and most of the regulars at Rosie's Bar on Nugget Street in Fairbanks, none of whom wanted Washington laying its grubby paws on their scenery.

The thought that the bill might not pass threw me into a panic. My theoretical model of the North was under attack! That fearsome and inviolable landscape where one hundred and thirty men of the Franklin expedition had perished from hunger, where Elisha Kent Kane had suffered a frozen beard on the sea-ice west of Greenland, was about to be overrun by hotels, gas stations, and fast-food joints!

I had never written about a political issue before, but I made up my mind to write about this one. After querying a few magazines, I managed to nail down an assignment to write an article about the Alaska Lands Bill.

Fred Meader, too, had been goaded into action, though for reasons far more urgent than mine. He and his family lived in a cabin by a lake in northern Alaska's Brooks Range. There they had fashioned for themselves lives of almost unimaginable simplicity and self-sufficiency. Meader rarely left his homestead, but so distressed had he become when he learned that the parklands legislation was in trouble that he had uprooted himself and hastened to teeming, barbarian San Francisco to speak out for passage of the bill. He had a huge stake in the outcome: His cabin lay within the boundaries of the proposed Gates of the Arctic National Park. As subsistence hunters, he and his family would be permitted to stay on if the bill passed; development over the huge portions of the Brooks Range that the new park would encompass, however, would be forbidden.

Development of the Brooks was no idle threat. Once the end of the earth, northern Alaska now crawled with petroleum engineers, geologists—even real estate agents. Anyone with a passable set of eyes and a vague sense of how the world works could see that civilization was coming to the Arctic wilderness.

One evening I got a call from a friend. He told me that some rough-and-tumble sourdough was in San Francisco, preaching the gospel of wilderness preservation to anyone who would listen. I was interested at once. The article I was writing was a hodgepodge of amazing facts and noble sentiments, but it hadn't an ounce of life. What it needed was a shot of Yukon Jack. So I decided to track the fellow down. At the least, he might be able to jumpstart my story with a few outrageous anecdotes about life on the Alaska frontier.

I met Meader a few days later at my friend's office on Bush Street. My first impression was encouraging. He was clearly a candidate for All-Arctic: a towering figure, lean, strapping, a bit intimidating, with a raggedy black beard, a nearly bald head, and piercing, heavily lidded eyes. He walked into the room silently and sized me up slowly, as though he hadn't decided whether to talk to me or to tear my head off. He was outfitted in standard backwoods issue: work boots, dungarees, a long-sleeved green-and-black checkered shirt. He didn't have a long-handled axe in his hand, but I was happy. He looked perfect for the job I'd hired him for: slugging a grizzly bear, say, or whooping it up with a bunch of the boys in the Malamute Saloon.

Then he shook my hand and introduced himself, and as quickly as I had sized him up, my impression of him as combination bearslayer and shitkicker vanished. It wasn't simply that I saw at once he was no threat to man or beast; he was, on the contrary, one of the gentlest, most self-effacing people I had ever met—an old potbellied stove of openness and warmth. He thanked me for seeking him out, for giving him a chance to jawjack a bit about life in the Brooks, about what had gone wrong for the wolves and the caribou, and about what he thought the world was coming to. Despite his great height and his craggy presence, he had a voice that was feather-soft and a manner of speaking that was dreamy and allusive; he seemed more a poet or a monk just down from a Himalayan mountaintop than a frontier hell-raiser.

In one respect, at least, Meader reminded me of stateside portraits of tough-as-nails Arctic explorers I'd seen—men like Robert Peary and Roald Amundsen and especially Charles Francis Hall, the Cincinnati printer who achieved "farthest north" in 1871 and who, more than any other person, showed how to accommodate oneself to the peculiarities of the North rather than fight against them. Like the gazes of those men, Meader's was distant and pensive; he seemed unable to focus on objects in the room—desk, chair, photos on the wall. He looked frequently toward the window, not because he was ill at ease or bored, but because something beyond the glass tugged at him. What it was was obvious: latitude. Fred Meader was homesick.

But no rough-and-tumble sourdough. About all he had in common with North Slope hellbenders was an address; in the Malamute Saloon, he would have been holding belligerents apart with his cedar-branch arms, encouraging them to behave.

With no prompting from me, Meader launched into a monologue on life apart from civilization in a two-bit cabin in the Alaskan wilds. He went on for an hour, scarcely pausing to take a breath. The tale he spun was enthralling, astonishing. He spoke not of hardship or struggle or pain but of enchantment, beauty, quiet marvels, sweet mysteries. He described a place that reminded me not of the terrible struggle for the Pole but of the peaceful landscape I had imagined on first encountering Edmund Hillary's story of his climb to the top of the world. Meader's Arctic was rich and grand and, most of all, *alive.* As I listened, I was aware of being drawn into his world, mesmerized by it and by him. I began to wonder if years of living close to the earth might have rekindled in him powers that humans once possessed but had lost in their ascent, if that was the word, to civilization. Meader was an atavist, a throwback to an earlier type—maybe even a caster of spells. In words charged with passion, he told me about an Arctic I had never imagined: a beautiful, bountiful, generous place—not a dark and dreadful wasteland, but an abode of light.

～

HE CAME OF age in the fifties, as a graduate student in philosophy at Boston University. His view of the world—part Rousseauian, part Jeffersonian, part Saint Jerome of the Desert—sprang from his experiences growing up on a dairy farm in upstate New York during the Depression. A background like that can lead a young man to decide early in life to get as far away from dirt and hard work as possible, as quickly as his feet can carry him. For Fred Meader it had the opposite effect: He came to believe that there was dignity to be found in physical labor and fulfillment in a simple life lived close to the earth. Unusually for the time and place, he saw nature not as servant or foe, but as partner, teacher—perhaps even as divinity.

On the streets of Boston, in the classroom, in interactions with neighbors, community, and friends, what Meader observed failed entirely to square with what he believed. An intolerable disconnect grew. Facing a career as a teacher, a home in the suburbs, a life of commuting, shopping, and mowing the lawn, he despaired. Today, hip social historians tell us that the famously bland fifties were not as bad as their reputation. To Fred Meader they were. Fancy new products, light entertainment, mindless conversation, upward mobility, luxury, power, security—those meant nothing to him.

In his wife Elaine he had found a woman who not only understood his despair, she shared in it. A nursing student at the college, Elaine Meader had, like her husband, acquired a world-view so distant from that of contemporary society, it might have seemed Plutonian. At its core lay her belief that the planet on which she lived and the universe through which it spun were more than physics, geology, and biology, and were anything but an accident. Rather, planet and universe constituted a single, eternal, and living organism through which life energy coursed like blood, and purpose like patterns of thought; whose tiniest parts were joined as molecule to molecule; whose nature was spiritual and whose central and defining properties were benevolence and love. The fully realized life was the life lived in awareness of, and gratitude for, one's small but essential role in this vast drama—one's vital *cellness.*

In the compulsively busy lives of the people she observed around her, in the arrogant, contentious chess game of neighbors and of nations, she saw little that resembled attention to this grand design. Modernity had brought comfort and wealth, but it drowned out the music of creation's heartbeat. Where others looked at a group portrait of America and saw a smiling, contented family, Elaine Meader saw fragmentation, alienation—desperate men and women out of touch with the cosmos. Civilization, she and her husband both believed, was a code word for life out of balance, even life without meaning; to participate was to risk losing one's soul. At a moment when the environmental movement was a mere gleam in the eyes of a few fantasists, these two defiant, prescient individuals understood the earth as a perfectly evolved organism whose integrity was threatened by progress. They craved simplicity, honesty, communion with the elements; moreover, they believed it was still possible to find those elusive qualities and to organize their lives around them.

Fred applied for a job at the Boston Museum of Science. He was perfect for the position, he was told, but he could not be hired unless he shaved off the small beard he had grown. The beard, it seemed, might prove disturbing to museum visitors.

Meader kept the beard. With Elaine, he dropped out of school. For a few years the couple wandered—Europe, Colorado, Arizona, Mexico. Vaguely an idea began to grow: to escape from the world. They scoured maps in search of places where they might put their ideas to work. For a time they homesteaded in British Columbia, perfecting the survival skills they would need to live apart from civilization. Then, in the fall of 1960, they gathered up their three-year-old son Dion and a few belongings and headed for Alaska. There they found the paradise they had been seeking: a lake in the heart of the Brooks Range, eighty miles north of the Arctic Circle, fifty miles from the nearest neighbor, two hundred miles from the nearest road.

Time was short. Winter lay just around the corner. The couple flew in provisions to see them through the long night to come. Then they set to work shoring up a dilapidated prospector's cabin they had found near the lake.

Each day they worked from dawn to dark, laboring in a kind of ecstasy. Both understood clearly the extraordinary opportunity they held in their hands. They were free and independent, as few have been. They even believed that they controlled their own destinies, though in that they would prove to be grievously mistaken.

When the first snow fell, they were ready. Tempering their anxieties over what lay ahead was a feeling of profound contentment. The sun slipped lower in the sky. The last geese disappeared over the southern horizon. Sometimes in the dimming light the couple stood with their son beside the lake and thought about friends in New England and California. Then they heard a chorus of wolves or felt an icy breeze skidding off the surface of the water, and they understood that there was no Boston or California on the distant planet where they had chosen to live, the planet that would be their home for the next seventeen years.

~

We found what we were looking for. During those first years it was magnificent, unbelievable. Elaine and I came from a culture where people lived their lives in bits and pieces. In Alaska we found connection and continuity. We could watch the rhythms and patterns of life as they unfolded. There was an organizing principle, a structure to our existence. The sun returned, the ice broke up, the caribou came north, the wild-flowers appeared. The seasons came and went, always bringing their expected treasures, but surprises, too, and those we learned to recognize and appreciate. I could close my eyes and feel the earth turn. I knew where the wild sheep were. The wolves accepted us as neighbors. Sometimes they left their pups with us while they were off hunting. Dion grew up in direct and intimate contact with nature in its purest form. He had innocence and joy. He wore an expression on his face that you don't often see on kids today.

To a degree that most people with a yearning for wild country could only dream of, Fred, Elaine, Dion, and later the Meaders' two daughters Heather and Dawn entered into the cycle of the seasons, the caribou, the willow, and the alder. Their goal, astonishing in its ambition and its symbolism, was to rid themselves of all vestiges of civilization—to leave the modern world behind and return to a pre-agricultural, hunter-gatherer way of life. For much of the year they subsisted on a diet of wild meat, fish, and berries. They rejected the use of sled dogs, which they believed would involve them in a master-slave relationship with the animals, a corruption of civilization. Fred continued to use a rifle to secure game. But he was learning to shoot a bow, which he had fashioned by hand, and he intended to begin using the weapon exclusively before long.

Before meeting Meader, I might have imagined such a life to be one of unrelenting drudgery, with few pleasures and little to look forward to. Those illusions vanished as he spoke.

"In spring when you first hear the water trickling and the birds singing . . . there's power in that that's greater than anything I know. It teaches you something. You know that you're not alone, that you're a valued part of something that's bigger than anything you could ever understand."

The place and the way of life that Meader described were utterly beyond my experience, yet somehow I recognized myself in his story. Odd as the details were, he invested them with a universality that anyone could relate to. I had gone to him wondering about 60-below-zero winters and caribou-skin clothing. I came away marveling at the beauty and mystery of the most common chunk of earth—even Arctic earth, which previously had seemed so forbidding to me, and of the connections that link each fragment of the natural world, one to the next. Meader's relationship to land was one of kinship; as one comes to know the patterns and habits of one's spouse and children, he knew the patterns of wind and snow, the habits of wolf and hare and Arctic moon. His conclusion was that the world is not a strange place, though it is quite enchanted. To grasp this, he seemed to be saying, it is only necessary to be still and watch.

Meader was one of the few people I have ever met who fully embodied the concept of "real assent." The term was coined by the nineteenth-century theologian John Henry Newman, who distinguished between what he called "notional" assent to a proposition such as "Humans must live in harmony with nature," and the far more difficult "real" assent. Notional assent is the classic liberal approach to thorny issues. It involves nodding one's head gravely, writing checks that don't hurt too much, signing politely worded petitions, scolding the riffraff for their foolishness and their profligate ways, and paying solemn lip service to the proposition, so long as doing so doesn't require one to change one's own ways in any significant manner.

Real assent is assent of the heart and soul. Real assent is stringent, uncompromising, complete. Real assent to the proposition "Humans must live in harmony with nature" might compel a person to separate himself from the rest of humanity for seventeen years, to suffer hordes of mosquitoes stoically, to bear up philosophically under weeks of drizzly rain and months of darkness, to forgo television, films, telephones, indoor plumbing, and internal combustion engines, to raise one's son without formal schooling or Little League.

Meader possessed that rarest of qualities: authenticity. He struck me as not so much the vanquisher of the mighty mountain he had conjured in Boston so many years before, but the mountain itself, an integral chunk of its geology. Like the title of the celebrated Aldo Leopold essay, Meader had become a man capable of "thinking like a mountain." This allowed him, like the subject of Leopold's piece, to listen objectively to wild country and to understand its meaning. That meaning was patent: Wilderness is essential to human survival.

"Man has boxed himself in. He's like a caged animal. He's created something he calls civilization, a schizophrenic way of life whose primary features are alienation and disillusionment. In wilderness it's possible to overcome civilization and to find the answers that we've lost. Wilderness is a template that allows us to measure where we're going and where we've been."

Meader had come at last to the rationale for his trip to San Francisco and for his decision to lobby for passage of a bill written in a modern, schizophrenic city by civilized, disillusioned legislators: The gauge on the template had skyrocketed into the danger zone. He knew where we'd been: Eden. He feared where we were going. He had seen what the first blush of civilization had brought to the Brooks Range. Since the discovery of oil in Prudhoe Bay and the beginning of construction on the Alaska Pipeline, natural patterns thousands of years in the making had changed. Wolves no longer called at Meader's front door. The Arctic caribou population had fallen to less than half its pre-pipeline size. Meader needed fifteen caribou a year to feed and clothe his family. New hunting laws now restricted him to six. Finding even that many was becoming harder and harder, for the Western Arctic herd, which once had migrated practically through the Meaders' backyard, now sometimes failed to show up at all.

Meanwhile, lakes throughout the Brooks Range had become field-dumping stations for oil and mining exploration crews. Fred and Elaine sometimes saw helicopters passing overhead; Fred, hunting for game, had come across spools of cable, pasteboard boxes, discarded fifty-five-gallon oil drums.

He regarded development of the Arctic as flagrantly shortsighted. "There's probably a few months' worth of oil to be found up there," he allowed. "There's probably enough minerals so that if you divide up the profits, everyone will get a few dollars. The cost, however, will be beyond measure. And there will be no way to go back."

In a final disaster, a Fairbanks realtor had purchased an old hundred-acre mining claim at the Meaders' lake. On the drawing boards were plans for a fifty-cabin development in sight of the mountains where Fred stalked moose with a homemade bow and arrows.

∼

LIKE MY ENCOUNTER with John Hunt's *Ascent of Everest*, my hour with Meader changed the way I viewed the world. With a few deft

brushstrokes, he had painted over the ferocious Arctic of Elisha
Kent Kane, transforming that harsh and unforgiving land into a
bright, vibrant, and—this was the hardest to believe—fragile place.
The transformation was enormous; it was as though I had walked
into the room Norwegian and walked out Japanese. I wrote earlier
that on first meeting Meader I had wondered if he might not be a
caster of spells. Now I knew that he was. A few dashes of poetry and
music, a dollop of philosophy, spritzes of truth, justice, and righ-
teousness—*Here, take this . . . you won't know what hit you . . .*

He wrapped up his story. In something of a daze, I shook his
hand and wished him well. As we were about to part, he turned to
me and, staring me straight in the eye, spoke two words that were to
him as momentous as any he had spoken during the previous hour.

"Loon Lake," he said. He paused. "Loon Lake. That's where
we live." He shook his head. "I've never told that to anyone before."

He waited for me to catch the significance of what he was saying. "I don't feel too good about it," he went on. "I thought that by
keeping the name a secret, we could prevent it from being discovered." Now, of course, he knew: The world is a small place. There
are no more secrets.

"So write it in your article. Tell people where we are. I want
them to know where this is happening, to give a human dimension
to the threat that we all face."

Meader's final words were an invitation for me to visit him at
his cabin. "Come and see where I live," he said. "Write about what
you find. That's all you can do. Time is short. You must come."

Little realizing the commitment I was making, I promised
him that I would.

~

OVER THE NEXT few days I began thinking about making my
way north. My old fear of the region had vanished. Meader had

introduced me to a landscape I suddenly longed to see: not as adventurer or explorer, not as dog-team driver (a notion I now saw as bizarre), not even as tourist, but as a kind of citizen of the country who belonged there, whose inalienable rights included vastness, emptiness, and silence, whose birth certificate read "Born wild and free!," who knows that he's a valued part of something bigger than anything he could ever understand.

And then, as suddenly as this revolutionary view had been thrust upon me, it was violently snatched away. At the home of friends with whom he was staying in Bolinas, California, Meader grew restless. He gave a few public talks, spoke to a few reporters. But phantoms stalked him—dissatisfaction, alienation, that old familiar fear of being buried alive. Gazing north he saw freeways and shopping malls—the architecture of oppression. Beyond, the earth curved sharply away, and no matter how keenly he trained his eye, he could not see past the crowded horizon to the shining country of mountains and rivers, to the trackless wild.

He returned to Alaska. For a number of years, using borrowed equipment, he and Elaine had been making a film about their lives at Loon Lake. On the surface an adventure story about a remarkable family's struggle to survive in the wild, the film was, on a deeper level, a work about the integrity of the natural world, and about threats posed to that world by modernity and progress. Fred and Elaine knew that hunter-gatherers typically did not employ movie-making equipment. But they also saw in an honest, well-made film a powerful tool for telling their story and, perhaps, for pointing viewers in new and life-changing directions. Producing a film was a compromise with their primitive lifestyle that they were willing to make.

By the time I met Fred, he had found a distributor for the film. Back at Loon Lake that fall of 1977, he shot the final scenes. Then he made arrangements to fly to New York City to complete production of the movie and to arrange for its distribution. On the first leg of the journey south, he took a bush plane to the village of Bettles, Alaska, landing on the Koyukuk River.

Of Meader's many such landings, most had been on lakes, where the routine was familiar: The plane lands and approaches the dock, the pilot shuts down the propeller, someone on shore wades out to grab the line, which is attached to the front of the plane. On this occasion, repeated radio calls failed to rouse anyone on land, so the pilot decided to dock himself. He instructed Meader to climb out onto the plane's float and to grab the tie-up rope. To prevent the plane from drifting away from the dock in the river current, the pilot kept the propeller turning.

Meader stepped onto the float and closed the door behind him. Elaine later theorized that her husband may not have understood that the rope now lay at his feet, having been carried there by the current. All he had to do was reach down, grab it, and jump to the dock.

Instead, recalling lake landings, Fred began inching his way forward on the float toward the spot where the rope attached to the front of the plane. There was a moderate swell on the Koyukuk that day, and the plane was rocking noticeably. Meader may have missed a step, or he may simply have misjudged the reach of the propeller blades, the tips of which are practically invisible when the apparatus is spinning. Whatever the reason, he failed to give himself sufficient clearance from the propeller. He was struck by the blades and killed instantly.

I heard about the accident two days later. I had called the phone number Fred had given me, to ask him a few questions about the Alaska Lands Bill and how it would affect his homestead. A grief-stricken voice at the other end of the line told me what had happened. I muttered a few inadequate words of condolence and hung up.

The news from Bettles had a curious effect on me. Naturally, I was distraught. But I was angered, too, not only at the terrible manner of Meader's death but at my own naïveté, in having abandoned so swiftly that long-held idea that I now knew to be true: The North was indeed a brutal place.

I knew, of course, that accidents could happen anywhere. But this one seemed pinned to geography. This one seemed pointedly Alaskan. Before long, the painful memory of what had happened to Fred joined in my mind with the invigorating spell that he had cast over me, producing an ambivalence about the North that was to last for many years. I came to believe in two places: the benevolent Arctic of Fred's life, and the fearful one of his death. Logically, this realization allowed me to see that good and bad, light and dark, cannot be attributes of place at all. Such words describe the acts and experiences of human beings at precisely defined points of land, not inherent qualities of land itself. When I dreamed of Loon Lake, as I sometimes did during the years to come, it was the boundless faith of that mad couple standing beside the lake with their three-year-old son, watching a small plane receding into a great sky, that informed my dream. Loon Lake was only a place; faith was the glow that lit it, the rapture that pervaded it, the color that imbued it with a sense that anything is possible.

Whenever I felt my compass needle tugging northward, I quickly brushed aside any thoughts of the promise I had made to Fred. In their place I substituted the illusion that, thanks to him, I had experienced the Arctic with an intensity that the real place could never match. Before meeting Meader, I boasted that I had visited forty-eight of the fifty states, with only South Carolina and Alaska yet to be checked off my list. Afterward, I sometimes told people that only South Carolina remained. If they asked me about Alaska, I said, "Yes, I was there once, for about an hour."

~

ONE AUTUMN, A quarter-century after Fred's death, I began making plans to celebrate an upcoming milestone birthday: my sixtieth. Thirty, forty, and fifty I had released to the wind without a blink, but sixty seemed worth blinking over. Recently a small, rather high-toned voice had begun to pester me—not often, maybe once a week, at the oddest of times. (Now that I've passed the milestone without serious incident, I hear the voice practically every day. I think that at about my age, the onboard solid-waste detector finally gets fed up with all the crap and begins to demand of its host a measure of seriousness and honesty about things like goals, purposes, the meaning of one's life—little things!—that in earlier years it was willing to overlook.) What the voice said went something like this: Good morning! I've been thinking about something and I believe I should mention it. Remember how you've always said that one day you were going to make up with your cousin Phil? So here's my question: *When exactly are you going to do that?* Oh, and another thing: Remember how you've always said that one day you were going to dump all that baggage about the math professor who humiliated you in front of the entire calculus class? Here's my question: *When exactly are you going to do that?*

Most of the prompts I managed to fend off. One, however, cropped up so persistently that I began to pay attention to it. It went something like this: Remember the last words that Fred Meader spoke to you? *Come and see where I live. Write about what you find. That's all you can do. Time is short. You must come.* And remember the promise you made to him that you would go? So here's my question: *When exactly are you going to do that?*

Of all the vows I had made over the years, this was the most confounding. During the short time I had spent with Meader, he had transformed my long-held fantasies about a brutal and unforgiving

North into belief in a place that was bright and beautiful and benevolent, and so fragile it was in danger of being destroyed. His death a few weeks later left me unsure of what to believe. Now, at last, my uncertainty had vanished. I knew with complete confidence that the time had come for me to make good on my vow.

I had no conceits about what I might accomplish on the long-imagined journey. Balls-out, death-defying, *Outside* magazine–approved Arctic adventure, which in my younger, more foolhardy mountaineering days had figured prominently in my plans, no longer interested me. If I had once imagined that I might be willing to sacrifice a few toes to the achievement of a worthy goal on an Arctic mountain or on the polar ice, I was now firmly committed to preserving every cell I had left in my body. My greatest desire now was simply to taste, if only for a short while, the vastness and wildness of the North.

By doing so, I believed, I might find a serenity I had not known for a very long time. For nearly fifteen years, my wife Carol had suffered from the flagrantly misnamed disease: chronic fatigue syndrome. (Calling the illness "chronic fatigue syndrome," one wag has observed, is like calling diabetes "excessive peeing disorder." It's true that on the Centers for Disease Control's list of primary indicators for the disease, one is "incapacitating" fatigue. There are fourteen others.) Years of searching for the cause of Carol's condition and procuring effective treatment for it, at stupefying prices, had drained our financial resources nearly to zero. Doing triple-duty as breadwinner, house husband, and soccer dad for our son Jake had further worn me down. We three had been adrift in windswept boreal seas, through a polar night that seemed endless.

Now, suddenly and miraculously, the end of that long night seemed to be at hand. With the help of a brilliant and caring physician, Dr. Daniel Peterson, and an experimental drug called Ampligen, Carol had turned a corner on her illness. Her symptoms had begun to recede. A significant portion of her old energy had returned. Wrenching pain—a constant companion since the first day of her illness—no longer hounded her. She still had bad days, but no more bad weeks or months. For the first time in years she was leading something like a normal life—even contemplating a return to her career as a counselor.

At such a time, I ought to have been a supremely happy man. But years of emotional ups and downs associated with Carol's illness, of alternating joy and grief and hope and despair, had taken their toll. Deprived of an object for my dread, I now lay awake at 3 A.M. dreading unnamed future woes. Anticipating a phone call from a creditor, I literally shook from fear. One winter morning, my car stopped dead on the highway. As I watched that faithless piece of junk being towed away, I guessed correctly that it was going to need a new engine. That afternoon, as I sat dazedly by the phone waiting for the mechanic to call, my entire body began to quake. I was unaware of what was happening until suddenly I was awakened from my stupor by a rapid clattering sound: the sound of my chair jackhammering against the edge of the desk.

In his poem "The Peace of Wild Things," Wendell Berry offers as an antidote to the dissonance of daily life the "still water" of the natural world:

> *When despair for the world grows in me*
> *and I wake in the night at the least sound*
> *in fear of what my life and my children's lives may be,*
> *I go and lie down where the wood drake*
> *rests in his beauty on the water, and the great heron feeds.*
> *I come into the peace of wild things . . .*

Nature has the capacity to heal the frazzled soul, Berry reminds us, bringing with it freedom and "the grace of the world."

I had known that poem for years. Decades of climbing mountains and wandering the wilderness of the American West had led me to much the same conclusion Berry had reached. But during the years of my wife's illness, I came down from the mountains of rock and snow to take on mountains that were psychological and emotional in character. I retreated from the physical wilderness into the realm of the beleaguered spirit. For reasons not hard to understand, I lost touch with the world's grace. Now, as I prepared to enter my seventh decade, I wanted to find that grace again. And something told me I could do so in the vastness and wildness of the North.

I had no idea where I would go on my journey. One evening I paid a visit to the public library. Finding my way to the section on Arctic travel, I pulled a book from a shelf and opened it at random. My eyes fell on a photograph of a knot of caribou swimming across a river. The caption said that the animals belonged to the Porcupine caribou herd, and that once a year they undertook a long and hazardous migration from their winter quarters in the mountains of northern Yukon to their calving grounds on Alaska's north coast, a section of the Arctic National Wildlife Refuge that the Inuit call *ivvavik*: "a place for giving birth to and raising young."

I knew I had found my destination. My excitement mounted as I read on about the amazing journey of the caribou. In a vague but unmistakable way, their story reminded me of my own. The animals faced enormous obstacles, met them with alternating courage and faintheartedness, bumbled toward their goal with a hit-or-miss pace that I knew well. Yet they pushed on, with something that seemed a little bit like faith, toward a place that seemed very much like still water. I wanted to do that. Ten thousand times the herd had returned to the calving grounds, to be born and reborn and reborn. In that unbreakable cycle of renewal, I found hope for Carol's rebirth, and for my own.

Six months later, seven days after my sixtieth birthday, I kissed my wife and son goodbye, boarded an Alaskan Airlines jet at Reno-Tahoe International Airport, and headed north. Caribou were descending on *ivvavik*, and I wanted to be there to see them.

~⁓

II. Honeymoon Blues

[Late May, a campsite in the Arctic National Wildlife Refuge, thirty miles south of the Arctic Ocean. The site is bounded on one side by the Kongakut River, now rampaging in spring runoff, and on the others by several smaller streams. My friend Shaun Griffin and I call our habitat "the island."]

ABOVE THE KONGAKUT, gulls endlessly patrolled the air space, cool and cocky as top guns. Never were more than two or three of the birds to be seen, but rarely was there a time when, glancing toward the bare hillside on the far side of the river, I didn't have my view momentarily tweaked by the sight of one of them slipping diagonally across my field of vision.

Gulls I knew, but most of the other birds that inhabited the island were new to me. Northern Alaska is the Grand Central Station of the bird world. Millions of birds representing some seventy species visit each summer from around the globe—semipalmated sandpipers from Brazil, bluethroats from India, smews from Russia, northern wheatears from Egypt, wandering tattlers from New Zealand, loons and pipits from the American Midwest. Birds like Alaska.

Because the island is a spell north of the tree line, the birds that summer there must build their nests on the ground. Tramping about, I had to watch my step for fear of accidentally crushing a clutch of eggs beneath my boots. Several times I unintentionally

walked too close to a nest. Suddenly I would be aware of a screeching sound, then a pesky dive-bomber of a thing strafing my head
and making repeated runs at my nose and ears. Not ten yards from
the campsite, a semipalmated plover contrived for herself a nest of
pebbles and dead grasses. In it she deposited four lovely brown-
speckled eggs. So successfully were she and her digs camouflaged
that several days passed before I stumbled onto the nest.

It was a valiant life she led. Rain, snow, foxes, photographers—they meant nothing to her. Because her headquarters
were so close to our camp, it was inevitable that several times a
day one of us would pass nearby. Each time, she put up a terrible
fuss and rose fiercely to defend her nest. Pulling herself up as
tall as she could (not very tall, as it happened; maybe six inches),
rocking back and forth from one foot to the other, she dared the
intruder to take another step. Such courage! A human being must
look like a battleship to a plover. But she held her ground successfully, and the last time I saw her she was still at her post, her
eggs and her resolve unbroken.

Except for a few year-round residents—ptarmigan, ravens,
snowy owls—the birds on the island had traveled great distances
to get there, none more so than the Arctic terns. Shaun and I
found a pair of them nesting not five minutes from our campsite. The two had appropriated a snarl of sticks and twigs that
looked as though it had probably begun life as part of a very dis-
orderly shrub upriver and then got swept away, finally running
aground on a spit of sand and gravel at the island's edge. The nest
reminded me of Le Corbusier's famous Chapelle Notre Dame du
Haut in France; it had the same curvy boat shape sweeping up to
a peak at one end, the same sense of the calm and the primitive
teetering on the edge of chaos.

In such a place, the terns settled down to a short but event-
filled residency. She was a beautiful thing, and both of them knew

it. The male worked his tail feathers off for her. Not yet having laid her eggs, she spent most of her time perched very still and regally on the steeple of the church, pretending not to know her mate. Terns are of the same lineage as gulls but generally smaller— perhaps a foot in length. The Arctic model wears a trendy black beret down to its eyes; below, the head is white. The bill is a nasty-looking red dagger as long as the bird's head. The breast, back, and wings are mostly gray. The tail is long and narrow; in flight it opens into a two-pronged fork.

What a fuss the female's partner made, and what he wouldn't do for her! Hour after hour he took to the air in search of insects, small fish—snacks and desserts of every description. North and south he prowled, east and west, long angel wings carving marvelous love letters in the sky. Spotting a delicious minnow in the river below, he would hover for a few seconds, reading his instruments, furiously beating off gravity with his wings. Then he would fold them and drop like a flaming arrow to the water.

He rarely came up empty. Obviously pleased with himself, trophy dangling from his bill like a hipster's cigarette, he rose into the air. He always took the long way home—three or four extended swings across the river, swooping down at the right moment on each pass so that his mate would see him cutting his fancy route. She, of course, feigned indifference—but was anyone fooled? Hardly! On his arrival home, she shivered like a bumblebee. But the drama was not yet over. Now he would hover above his darling, his back arched, his wings pumping, and she would look straight up and crank open her bill, and he would look straight down and take aim, and then—*bingo!*—he would poke his catch into her mouth, as though it were his tongue and they had just discovered French kissing.

Sometimes the lady's beauty and the male's excitement and their pleasure in each other overcame them, and he would mount her and flutter above her, and she would flutter below, both of them quite flushed with passion. As far as I could tell, this orgy of spooning and feeding and fluttering and carrying on continued twenty-four hours a day. They were quite a pair. They knew how to enjoy life.

What they had done to reach their cozy love nest by the river defies reason, common sense, and quite possibly the Second Law of Thermodynamics. The annual migration of the Arctic tern is one of nature's great stupefactions. The birds summer in the Arctic. They winter a world away, in the pack ice off Antarctica. Twice a year they fly from one end of the earth to the other, some eleven thousand miles in each direction; with added mileage for normal deviations from a straight line, each bird logs close to twenty-five thousand miles annually. That is a distance equal to the circumference of the earth. Arctic terns have been found wearing leg bands placed twenty-five years before. A twenty-five-year-old tern must have seen some two-thirds of a million miles pass beneath its wings—to the moon and back and then some. All this by a creature weighing no more than a bran muffin.

How to understand such a journey? It seems to me that the migration of the Arctic tern is most usefully viewed not as a record-setting flight, or an oddity of nature, or one stage in the life cycle of an interesting bird, but rather as a work of epic poetry—*The Odyssey* of migrations. Understanding the journey—no, not understanding it: *glimpsing* it, tentatively, distantly, imperfectly—requires not a map or an odometer but an imagination, the more fanciful the better. After all, beyond mileages and flight times—beyond what one might learn in *Guinness World Records 2017*—we know nothing. We have no photographs of Arctic terns in clouds. We do not know if they sing while they fly, or if they chant ternish chants. We do not know if they fly in a "V" or in a straight line, or in long swoops left and right, or in roller-coaster curves up and down. We do not know if they travel with other birds who happen to be going their way—sandpipers, say, or cranes—and we do not know how far they fly each day, and we do not know how they apportion their time. Do they fly for a few hours, then stop somewhere to feed for a while, like most birds? Or do they fly for days before taking a breather? We do not know.

Imagine them over the coast of British Columbia. Do they fly in tens or twenties or hundreds, or do they fly alone, each bird miles from its neighbors? How high do they fly? Small birds sometimes fly as low as two hundred feet on their migration paths; we could see them if we looked up, which we don't. Big birds fly higher, a mile or two or three.

A mountain climber in Nepal did look up once and was amazed to see a goose flying over Mount Everest. That's up there. Arctic terns are medium-size birds, so you would expect them to fly one or two miles up. But they fly so much farther than other birds—maybe they fly higher too! Maybe they fly in the stratosphere, at the altitude of test pilots and ozone holes. I know, there's not enough oxygen up there to keep a bird alive. But this isn't just a bird, it's an Arctic tern! Maybe they store oxygen in the hollow quills of their tail feathers and sip it when they get thirsty. There are big advantages to flying in the stratosphere. It's less crowded up there than it is down below with the riffraff. Plus, you can see Antarctica sooner. Imagine them over Peru. Peru! A storm front is ahead. Do they see it? Do they care? Perhaps they'll fly above it. Perhaps they'll fly through it. What's it like in a storm cloud? Is it cold? Is it eerily silent? Is it dark and scary? Do Arctic terns worry about falling behind schedule when they're flying through storm clouds? No one knows.

Imagine them over Patagonia. What do they do to pass the hours? Film director Stanley Kubrick once speculated that dolphins spend their free time solving complex mathematical theorems. Do

Arctic terns play games or write poetry or find new solutions to the longitude problem? They would be good at that. In any case, no one knows.

Bulletin! We know this: Arctic terns love the sun. Arctic terns know the sun better than any creature on Earth. The birds summer in the Arctic, where the sun is above the horizon twenty-four hours a day. They winter in the Antarctic, where the sun is above the horizon twenty-four hours a day. Late in the summer, as the long days begin to move south from the Arctic, Arctic terns move with them, following the light. Late in the winter, as the long days begin to move north from the Antarctic, Arctic terns move with them, following the light. As bats and worms spend their lives in darkness, Arctic terns spend their lives in light. They go where the light goes. Does this explain their inexplicable journey—that they love the light? No one knows.

Years ago, when I first imagined that I might someday like to write a book, I came up with a vegetable stew of an idea for a novel that involved Arctic terns, the legendary blues singer and guitarist Robert Johnson, and the notion that Earth is a spaceship forever crisscrossing the cosmos, calling at various interesting destinations as it goes. As I saw it, Arctic terns would symbolize the indomitable spirit, Robert Johnson would symbolize art, and Starship Earth would symbolize the hope for eternal life. It all made sense until you tried to write a novel about it. Mine, if I had ever written it, which I didn't, would have been all symbols. It represented everything: struggle, hope, art, life, death (what else is there?)—and so it represented pretty much nothing.

What I had was more a novel idea than an idea for a novel. It happened that, at the time, I was interested in Arctic terns, I was interested in Robert Johnson, and I was interested in space travel; so I tossed the three willy-nilly into my stew and figured that that was how you outlined a book. But when I tried to turn my outline into pages and chapters, I had no idea what to do. I had no characters and no plot. I couldn't find a single connection among my themes. My novel collapsed under its own weightlessness.

I hadn't thought about the book for years. Then one day, as I watched my beautiful, giddy terns whooping it up beside the Kongakut, I suddenly recalled my masterpiece in all its weirdness. It occurred to me that the reason the project had foundered wasn't the lack of a plot or characters or connections among its themes; it was that I had chosen the wrong form for my material. What I'd dreamed up wasn't a novel at all. It was a song. What's more, someone else had dreamed it up before me. His name was Robert Johnson, and the song was "Honeymoon Blues." It was about spirit, art, and the hope for eternal life. Johnson wrote it during the 1930s and recorded it in 1937, six years before I was born.

Robert Johnson spent the bulk of his brief and mostly unlucky life (he died at the age of twenty-seven, probably a murder victim) in the Deep South, a long way from the island. Nevertheless, on the evidence of "Honeymoon Blues," it's clear that he would have recognized the place at once if he had suddenly been transported there. He would have seen that the Kongakut is just a big old guitar strumming heartfelt blues down the rocks and gravel bars of the valley, and that sometimes the song is fast and wild, and sometimes it's slow and peaceful. He would have known that the island is the words of the song, that some of them are joyful and some of them are sad. He would have understood that the theme of the song—and the theme of the novel I never wrote—is simple human yearning, for a good and happy and useful life that will never end.

I could probably have figured out most of that if I had been in some other wild and musical place. But I needed to be on the island, situated among its multitudinous vagaries and curiosities, to discover something I had never known before. And that was that no one is willing to go farther or search harder for a good and happy and useful life than the little birds with the black berets and the forked tails. Robert Johnson was no ornithologist, but he came to that same conclusion, decades before I did. Even more amazing, he knew the name of one of the birds. She was the one who spent her days perched on the steeple of the cathedral at the edge of the river, pretending to be bored. Her name was Betty Mae, and he wrote his song for her.

"Honeymoon Blues" by Robert Johnson

Betty Mae, Betty Mae, you shall be my wife someday.
Betty Mae, Betty Mae, you shall be my wife someday.
I wants a little sweet girl, that will do anything that I say.
Betty Mae, you is my heartstring, you is my destiny.
Betty Mae, you is my heartstring, you is my destiny.
And you rolls across my mind, baby, each and every day.
Li'l girl, li'l girl, my life seem so misery.
Hmm hmm, little girl, my life seem so misery.
Baby, I guess it must be love, now, hoo mm, Lord, that's takin'
   effect on me.
Some day I will return, with the marriage license in my hand.
Some day I will return, hoohoo, with a marriage license in
   my hand.
I'm gon' take you for a honeymoon—
                    in some long, long distant land . . .

This was the island. It was a peaceful, earnest place where life unfolded effortlessly and seamlessly, where you could drop in at an arbitrary moment and get swept up in the flow and the feel of the place, as though you were part of the plan, even if you didn't understand a word of it, even if you didn't know that there *was* a plan.

Where you felt a kind of deliverance from everything that had come before your arrival, and where, mysteriously, you could find the patience to await whatever was to come next. Each moment was the same as the last; both had a familiar shape and sound and taste. But each was different, too, for it always brought something new—a breeze, a crocus wakening on a logjam, the plaintive cry of a curlew, blue clouds crowding over bare brown hills. Lichen and wolf, plover and ground squirrel—each was inventing a life, each was going about a business I couldn't fathom but which I understood to be quite important. The island was a diligent, deadly serious place, but one without airs.

If there was a purpose here, it was new life—new buds, new eggs, new creatures large and small; and, to my mind at least, new beginnings. One particularly exuberant morning, watching the grand preparations for the next generation of every kind, I realized that I was witnessing nothing less than the first day of creation. The Sioux believe that all animals came from the same valley. Now I knew that they were right, and the valley was here. The world was being born before my eyes.

And such a nursery the parents had contrived! Icy mountains to grace the walls, lullabies of wings and waters, spinning mobiles of gulls and dragonflies, cuddly blankets of phlox petals and willow buds. Twenty-five years earlier Fred Meader had told me this was going to happen: "In spring, when you first hear the water trickling and the birds singing . . . there's power in that that's greater than anything I know. It teaches you something. You know that you're not alone, that you're a valued part of something that's bigger than anything you could ever understand."

And, millennia before that, that old backcountry traveler Isaiah: "Let the wilderness and the dry land be glad, let the wasteland rejoice and bloom . . . let it rejoice and sing for joy . . . "

~~~

III. Very Close to Everywhere

*[Shaun and I reached "the island" thanks to a lift from bush pilot Walt
Audi, who flew us in from Kaktovik, a town on Barter Island, just
off the northern Alaska coast. Audi operates a small hotel in Kaktovik
called the Waldo Arms, where Shaun and I spent several days prior
to our flight. Once on the island, we became good friends with the
renowned Japanese photographer Toru Sonohara, whom Audi had
dropped off at the same spot several weeks earlier. No caribou were to be
seen, but we remained hopeful.]*

I AM NOT a fisherman but Shaun is, and during our stay at the
Waldo Arms he had been disheartened to learn from several leading
authorities that he was not likely to have any luck with a hook and
a line on the island. The season was too early, one guest told him.
The fish were still comatose beneath the ice; even those that were
stirring would be too stupid to recognize a decent worm if they saw
one. Another explained that the issue was not stupidity, it was visibility. Because of melting snows in the Romanzof Mountains and
the furious rains of the preceding few days, the Kongakut River
would be so choked with mud and debris that even smart, happy,
hungry fish would be unable to see anything my friend might dan-
gle in front of their noses, no matter how tempting.

Discouraging words, those. And yet, such words mean nothing
to members of the brotherhood of bullheaded anglers, of whom my
friend is a regional vice president. During Shaun's final moments
at the Waldo, after he had climbed into the back of Audi's truck for
the hop to the airstrip, and many minutes after he and I had made
our final and irrevocable decisions about what we would take to
the island, a look of profound fear came over his face. It was the

look of a man who has seen the future, and it is bad. He leapt from the truck and raced into the Waldo. Moments later he was back, pole and tackle box tucked safely under his arm, a sigh of relief murmuring devoutly from his lips.

Not long after we took up residence on the island, Shaun mentioned to Toru his disappointment that, because of the poor conditions, there were no fish to be angled. Toru's forehead wrinkled.

"I saw fish," he said. He pointed at a pool of meltwater that had calved off from the river. "Over there. Big ones. You can catch them."

The words were scarcely out of the man's mouth before Shaun was feverishly ransacking his backpack for tackle and pole, as though a phone was ringing in there. Minutes later the two men were poised at the edge of the pool, peering down into blue-green water for signs of life.

What followed was one of the great chapters in the annals of fishing. Shaun tied a rooster tail onto his line and aimed it at a spot by the edge of an ice shelf on the far side of the pool. The plash of feather and hook on water was enough to wake the fish, of which many were indeed present. He tried again, this time securing their attention.

On the third cast the lure had barely touched down when it was assaulted by an Arctic char of great length and volume. Toru let out a hoot. Shaun dug in his heels. Man and fish battled briefly. Fish lost. In a minute, the creature was flopping in the gravel at Shaun's feet.

He cast again. This time he reeled in a cousin of the first catch, slightly less handsome but bigger. I was on the other side of the island during this developing story and learned the details only later.

"I was feverish," Shaun told me. "I was crazy. I was casting like a madman. I'd reel one in, take it off the hook, cast again, reel in another one." The look in his eye as he talked was new to me—and unsettling. "I've never had so much fun in my life." At some point he passed the rod to Toru, whose results were the same.

The pair's final tally was eight Arctic char in ten casts in twenty minutes. None of the fish taped in at under twenty inches. With visions of a grand banquet in the wilderness forming in his mind, Shaun kept three of his catch and threw the rest back.

As I said, I am not a fisherman. But I know a thing of beauty when I see it, and these babies were centerfold material. Arctic char belong to the salmon family. Some exhibit red or green coloration; the three that Shaun had selected for dinner were electric silver in hue and dotted with tiny pink spots. In their essential qualities they presented reasonable facsimiles of Jennifer Lopez's legs in silk stockings: long, slender, supple, muscular, curvy—delicious looking!

Toru offered to clean the three chosen specimens. Shaun graciously accepted. On their way back to camp, the two men cut willow branches, one for each fish.

I had returned to the campsite by this time and was privileged to witness the homecoming. My two friends strolled into camp like Peter returning with the wolf. For the first time I understood the expression "drunk with victory." One welcome result of the warriors' giddiness was their conviction that they alone were worthy of preparing dinner. I was put in charge of snacks and drinks, but otherwise ordered not to interfere.

I found a rock and flopped down in the dirt beside it to watch. Above, long trains of ashen clouds chugged across the sky. They were harbingers; soon a light rain began to fall. I slipped on my rain parka and flipped the hood over my head. Blue mist crept through the gate of bare hills to the north, dropped to ground level, skulked across the rocks and into the banquet hall. Rain fell intermittently but never with any conviction; before long it gave up. Left in its wake were a slow, loping wind and a deep chill.

My hosts collected driftwood and fashioned a tidy fire pit. Toru whittled points on the willow branches. Earlier, cleaning the char, he had slit each open to the neck; now he mounted a fish on each branch, poking the stick clear through from tail to mouth. When the fire was blazing, he and Shaun angled the branches over the flames, securing them with rocks. A patient grilling began. The two men planted themselves beside the fire to await the outcome.

I sprang into action. I located crackers. I located some lovely Japanese cookies in Toru's pack. I located a hefty bottle of Canadian Mist in my pack. I showed the bottle to Toru, and he expressed interest.

"Yes," he said, his eyes narrowing. "I believe I would like to try that."

I rounded up coffee cups. We made a toast, to international peace and to the gallant fish that had donated so generously to our meal.

As the fish smoked, as we delved deeper into the bottle, crystalline silence drifted into the campsite. Just beyond my extended arm, a creamy moon joined the party, hunching down musefully on a hilltop behind gusty clouds. A pair of gulls grabbed a small breeze and rode it down the valley. Moon glow, bird flight, firelight: How quiet the evening was!

We were very far from anywhere. Gazing into the fire I tried to process that fact, without success; it seemed so clear that we were very close to everywhere. Now the flames crackled, shattering the silence. The steel-stringed river broke into song. We spoke of the animals that had lived here. How many? A million? Ten thousand grizzlies? Imagine! All seemed to be present, going about their business in the shadows, pausing at intervals to take in our words. With the animals were Inuit and Arctic Indians of a thousand years ago, following the river north or south to whatever it was that animated their dreams. The world seemed like firelight, something you gazed at with a far-away look in your eyes.

Shaun moved one of the willow branches closer to the flames. Toru added a stick to the fire and spoke lovingly of his family in Japan. His words, all our words, were simple and fervent and true; they seemed more important than usual; they had a sparkle and a glow, like the driftwood coals that glimmered beneath the flames.

Long after we flopped down in the dirt, the char began to droop from their supports. The flesh was deep orange by now, flaking from the bones. The two chefs laid it on hot rocks at fire-side to allow the flames to do their final subtle work. Toru collected his giant bottle of soy sauce.

I ate slowly and in amazement, with my fingers, with the knowledge that like the creeks and the ptarmigan and the women and men of a thousand years ago, I was now part of the history of this place, etched onto its rocks like a petroglyph, celebrated in song like the little birds that lived by the river: an intrepid explorer in some long, long distant land.

∽

AT SOME POINT it was over. Toru had returned to his tent; or, intrepid photographer that he was, perhaps he went out searching for wolverines. Shaun and I lay in our sleeping bags with the side flap of the tent pulled open. We chatted quietly. The north half of the earth lay before us: damp, bright, cold, misty, full of promise. The sky over the ocean was yellow and gray. I started to move away from the door when I heard my friend say something. His voice was quiet and calm.

"Caribou at twelve o'clock."

It took a moment for the words to sink in. I looked north, toward the hill that fell to the river's west side. There atop the ridge, silhouetted against the sky, stood seven caribou. They were perhaps a quarter mile from us, one with a modest set of antlers. Several were feeding; the others stood motionless but alert, as though they knew they had been spotted.

We watched, rapt, for a few seconds. Then one of the seven moved, and then they were gone, over the ridge, slipping silently toward *ivvavik*. Shaun and I said a few words, expressing a well of gratitude for what was surely one of the grandest days we had ever known. Then I scrunched down in my bag and fell into a deep and dreamless sleep.

~~~~~

IV. Travels with Lucky

THE PORCUPINE CARIBOU herd is one of more than a dozen barren-ground herds that endlessly crisscross the bleak, treeless latitudes of northern Alaska and Canada. With a population estimated at around 169,000 in 2010, the Porcupine is a considerable collection of animals, but by no means the largest of the barren-ground herds. Several others, including the Western Arctic (235,000 in 2013) and the Qamanirjuaq (349,000 in 2008) are larger. In all, as many as 2 million barren-ground caribou may inhabit the North American Arctic.

Given the huge numbers of animals, and the fact that at certain times of the year major portions of a given herd move together toward the same destinations, it's little wonder that Arctic travelers sometimes return home with stories of throngs of caribou streaming across the tundra, grunting and bleating, hooves clicking *en masse*, like Alaska-size orchestras of castanets. (Caribou hoof clicks are produced by ligaments slipping over bones in the feet.) In *Midnight Wilderness*, an engrossing account of her travels in the Arctic National Wildlife Refuge, Debbie S. Miller recalls a warm July afternoon on the Egaksrak River when what she at first thinks is a mirage shimmering in the distance turns out to be "a living, breathing, pulsating mass of animals." Later she learns that the multitude, which eventually surrounds her, contains some ten to twenty thousand caribou. Visitors to caribou calving grounds may see practically entire herds gathered in one place. Writer and photographer Kennan Ward camped at *ivvavik* with most of the Porcupine herd, a number that, in Ward's passionate work *The Last Wilderness*, he estimated at some one hundred thousand caribou.

Before heading north, I had read so many of these accounts that I had come to think of the sights they described as commonplace. I began to imagine that when I first saw caribou I would see a ton of them—perhaps hundreds swimming an ice-choked river, or thundering thousands such as Debbie Miller saw, a sight some writers have compared to the great herds of buffalo that once romped over the American West.

Like my back-home-in-Nevada fantasy of the Kongakut valley as a glacier-strewn wasteland, my idea of what I would see when I at last laid eyes on *Rangifer tarandus* turned out to be somewhat overblown. Instead of hundreds of caribou furiously dog-paddling across a river, or thousands steamrolling over the tundra, I saw, well, seven, and they weren't doing much of anything. Grazing is what they were doing, like cows, atop an unremarkable ridge beside the Kongakut River.

But such a seven! I didn't need thousands of caribou, or even hundreds, to count my trip a success. One would do. Even a small one. Even a sick one. Even a homely one whose hooves didn't click. By the time I crawled from my sleeping bag many hours after last call at the Grand Fiesta of the Humongous Char, the seven had grown in my estimation to a newly discovered herd, the noblest and bravest caribou of them all: the Canadian Mist herd! If I had observed its members for mere seconds, I nonetheless held a vivid picture of each: two handsome ones on the left, one grazing expertly, one with her head cocked in my direction, perhaps in a gesture of welcome; next, the antlered one, a bit arrogant, pushy, one of those tiresome individuals who never admit they're wrong; then two grazers; then a sentinel; then the last, somewhat apart from the rest, the rebel of the bunch, headstrong, rascally, impulsive. Certainly as fine a team as has ever been assembled on an unremarkable ridge beside the Kongakut River! I felt that I knew those stalwart beasts. I felt that we had communicated with one another, using the same trippy, mysterious, Esperanto-like dialect that my golden retriever and I employ to talk to each other, even though I wasn't sure what the message from the other side had been. I even believed that one of the seven might have been Lucky.

Lucky was one of ten female caribou that were captured in late 1997, outfitted with satellite collars, and then released. The operation was carried out near Old Crow, Yukon, by two Old Crow residents, Robert Kay and William Josie, and a team of wildlife biologists representing a consortium of Canadian and U.S. agencies. Schoolchildren in Alaska and Yukon competed in contests to christen the ten. The winning names were Dasher, Gus-Gus, Homer, Blixen, Lynetta, Cupid, Dormer, Vixen, Springy, and Lucky.

With their collars sending out steady streams of data, the test subjects could be followed on their meandering journeys across the North with great precision. This was true not only for the scientists who were studying the animals, but for anyone with a connection to the internet. Maps pinpointing the caribou's positions were posted and updated regularly on the project website. As a security measure, the animals' locations were kept at least two weeks behind, to prevent anyone with a hankering for a certain dim kind of notoriety from going out and plugging one of the famous caribou. When you checked a map you didn't see where the animals were at that moment, only where they had been a few weeks before.

With the aid of the maps, a visitor to the website could play a humbling and thoroughly exasperating game of Where Will the Caribou Be Next? This exercise was based on Aldo Leopold's exhortation to "think like a mountain," but with a new twist that asked players to think like a caribou. The idea was to attempt to get into the head of, say, Blixen, following her progress over several weeks, making sense of it, sort of, and then predicting where she would be when the next map came out.

~

OF COURSE, BLIXEN was never where you thought she would be when the next map came out. To anyone with an ounce of sense, it was obvious that she should have headed straight for Timber Creek, to avoid the Terrible Mountains. Instead, she turned left and ran straight for the Terribles. Two weeks after that she had reversed course completely and was heading back in the direction from which she came. *Hey girl! Where you going?* There was surely logic behind the movements of the animals, but it was caribou logic, which marched to the beat of a different drummer. The ten collared females demonstrated that caribou navigation was one part horse sense, one part goofiness, and one part riddle wrapped in an enigma wrapped in a great big clump of pickled reindeer moss.

Back in Nevada, where betting on caribou positions had not yet been discovered by the bookmakers, I happened onto the website early in 2003. Tables of historical data brought me up to date on the adventures of the fab ten since they had gone online more than five years before. The hard life of a caribou was manifest at once. Springy, collared in October 1997, died in August 1998. Vixen, collared in October 1997, died in June 1998. Dasher, collared in November 1997, died in August 1998. By May 2000, five of the original ten were dead. By that time, several new herd members had been captured and collared to augment the team. (The process of replenishing the group as old members fall by the wayside continues to this day, as does the satellite project itself. In 2007, biweekly updates of herd locations on the internet were switched to four updates a year in the face of mounting evidence that the two-week delay did not provide sufficient protection for the herd from hunters.)

Several months before my departure for Alaska, I decided to follow one of the caribou on her passage to *ivvavik*. In homage to my home state, I chose the animal named Lucky. She had originally been collared in October 1997, as she swam the Porcupine River some forty miles upriver from Old Crow. River captures do not allow for the collection of physical data, so at the time nothing much was learned about the animal herself; the entire process of roping a caribou, maneuvering it into position beside the capture vessel, attaching a collar, and releasing the animal takes only two or three minutes.

In March 1999, Lucky was recaptured—as each of the caribou must be, every couple of years—to replace her batteries. This time she was apprehended on land, with the aid of a gun-activated net fired over her from a helicopter hovering above. Blood samples and other measurements determined her to be a healthy animal, about five to six years old—middle-aged in caribou years. Her weight was two hundred pounds, her total body length just over 6 feet 1 inch, her height at the shoulders 3 feet 10 inches.

Thanks to the website's huge database of position coordinates, I was able to review in great detail Lucky's travels since her initial capture. Far from an immutable route followed year after year, this caribou's peregrinations more closely resembled the path of a shnockered soccer fan trying to find his car in the stadium parking lot after a game. Each annual cycle took Lucky to territory different from any she had set foot on before. Except at the northern and southern termini of these circuits, where there were occasional return visits, she appears never to have set foot on the same spot of ground twice. The idea of a "migration route" followed by members of the herd was clearly erroneous.

A look at Lucky's positions at the same time each year shows how widely she wandered. In October 1998, a year after her capture, she was 160 miles south of her capture spot, in Yukon's Ogilvie Mountains. A year after that she was 250 miles to the northwest, in the Davidson Mountains in the Arctic National Wildlife Refuge. The next year she was back very near where she had been two years earlier, in the Ogilvies. October 2001 found her 140 miles to the northwest, at a spot near the U.S.–Yukon border, southwest of Old Crow. Twelve months later she was 80 miles farther northeast, not far from her original capture spot. In October 2003 she was thirty miles east of her 2001 location. Each of those positions was a single point on an erratic, circuitous path several thousand miles in length, which changed utterly from one year to the next.

Equally characteristic of her species' fanciful nature is the fact that Lucky's October locations were often far from where her collared mates were at the same times. In October 2003, when Lucky was near Old Crow, Donner was one hundred miles south, in Yukon's Mahoni Range. Helen, meanwhile, was one hundred fifty miles northwest, in Alaska's Davidson Mountains. The entire herd was dispersed over an area in excess of twenty thousand square miles.

~

SPRING IS THE one time of the year when a pregnant female caribou might be expected to behave in a somewhat predictable fashion. And, indeed, in the spring of 2003, Lucky did just that. Through March, the traditional final month of an expectant female's winter gestation, she headquartered in the vicinity of the Eagle River, some forty miles north of Eagle Plains, Yukon. She hardly moved. During the week of March 22–29, she wandered south a few miles, where she remained until around April 5. Over the next seven days she moved slowly north again, about a mile a day.

Around April 12, she caught the fever. The following week she put sixty miles beneath her hooves, due north. The week after that she did sixty more, altering her course to the northwest. The migration was now in full swing. By the time I left Nevada for Kaktovik, at the end of May, it had long been clear from the website maps that Lucky had one thing in mind, and that was the calving grounds on the shore of the Arctic Ocean. By my reckoning, she should have dropped anchor in *ivvavik* a week or two before Shaun and I pitched our tent in the Kongakut valley. Even if she had visited the island along the way, she would likely have done so many days before we arrived.

Was Lucky one of the seven I saw poised atop the ridge? Probably not. Still, this was one happy-go-lucky caribou. Maybe instead of heading for Timber Creek, she had turned left and steered straight for the Terribles. Maybe she decided to lay over beside the Kongakut for a few days—you know, put her hooves up and listen to the grass grow. Maybe she was the appointed emissary from the other side. If so, she would have been expected to hang around until I arrived, so that she could deliver her message. *Welcome to caribou land, my friend. Geez, I thought you would never get here! Anyway, look fast, I have to am-scray. And, oh, by the way, you owe me one.*

And if she was not one of the seven, it didn't matter. Lucky or Unlucky, seven caribou or seven thousand, I emerged from my tent that day with a sense of a job completed, a goal fulfilled. It's okay, Shaun. I'm fixed. We can go home now.

~

V. The Porcupine in Winter

[As our stay on the island continued, Shaun and I were visited by many members of the Porcupine caribou herd. In late winter of the following year, we went north again, joined by my friend David Hertz. Our

destination: Yukon's Ogilvie Mountains, where we hoped to locate
caribou on their winter range. Because the only portions of the herd
we might hope to find were deep in the mountains, we determined that
we would need to go in by snowmobile. To guide us, we engaged two
members of the Tr'ondëk Hwëch'in First Nation, Peter Nagano and his
brother Richard. The first day we had great luck, finding several large
groups of caribou. Peter had an idea for a spot where an even larger
portion of the herd might be found, and we determined to check it out
the following day.]

THAT NIGHT THE temperature fell to 40 below. The next morning
was blustery. A storm seemed imminent. But amazing things happened that day, a day in which we clocked another fifty miles in the
wondrous Ogilvies. We headed out at midmorning. Somewhere,
Peter zigged where he had zagged the day before, and we entered
a new kingdom of snows.

The miles that followed were as thrilling and beautiful as it
would be possible to imagine. In the early afternoon the sun peeped
through the clouds, just as we drove onto an immense tableland, a
placid ocean of blinding white that stretched as far as the eye could
see. It was possible to move across this ocean at tarpon speed and
we did, heedless of the traffic laws. At last we came to the base of
a tall bluff. I understood that we were going to go to the top of the
thing, but I couldn't imagine how. The route looked foolhardy, like
something a teenager might try.

Peter called a halt to inspire the troops. He explained the plan.
He and Richard would go first. They would lay a bombproof path
up the slope, the wildest we had attempted. Richard had two sug-
gestions for the cheechakos: (1) be bold; (2) drive like hell.

All I remember of the next few minutes is a staccato of four-
letter words pouring from my mouth and a sure sense that the
five hundred pounds of steel on which I was riding would, at any

moment, be riding on me. But the path was sure and the leadership sound. In short order the entire team stood safely atop the bluff, gazing out at magnificent views to the horizon in all directions. In the near distance the great tableland flowed outward in waves, a high sea to anywhere you please. Beyond rose mountains upon mountains, blazing in pure light.

A few yards from where we stood lay signs of a different sort of drama: Strewn about in a vaguely defined circle were the scant remains of a caribou—a few bone fragments, part of a hoof, some clumps of fur. At several spots along the circumference, a clue to the perpetrator's identity: wolf scat.

The south side of the bluff consisted of a series of steep-sided snow bowls. It took me a few moments to realize where Peter had brought us. Call it Caribou Bluff, if you will, for in each bowl there were multitudes of caribou. Multitudes more ranged below, on the sloping run-out to the tableland. The entire formation on which we stood was something like a very large vanilla ice cream cake festooned with sprinkles, except instead of sprinkles it had caribou.

Peter said that he ascended the bluff perhaps once a year and that he rarely brought others with him. It was evident from his manner that the place had a hold on his heart. We each had a bite to eat and then we fired up our engines. For the next hour, our quintet wound slowly down and across the face of the bluff, from one bowl to the next, in and out, around and among the animals. We darted in close enough to arouse their interest, but almost never so close as to unnerve them. At each turn we came upon a crowd of onlookers. Once, scooting along a straight stretch beneath an escarpment, I looked up and saw a dozen heads peering over the edge at me. We came around a bend, and there were a hundred caribou; we zipped up a slope, and there were a hundred more. It was exciting to approach a blind spot, not knowing what we would find on the far side. Sometimes a dozen caribou would be waiting for us and they would scarcely look up. Other times a few would spook, then quickly give in to a famous family tendency toward curiosity. They would stop and turn around and then trot back in our direction, their heads cocked. Several times we stopped to take photos or simply gaze at the panorama of wildlife, to wonder if the animals knew they would be leaving this place in a few days to begin the long trek to *ivvavik*. And if they did not know, how would they find out, and how would they know the way?

Those were the last caribou I would see on my travels. I think about them often, especially when I read about yet another proposal to open the Arctic National Wildlife Range to oil and gas development, on the very spot to which the herd had returned to each spring for the past ten thousand years, the very spot where many of the animals I saw that day would bear their young, two months and many miles later. The common denominator of all such schemes, it seems to me, is their vulgarity. Oil development on Alaska's coastal plain is roughly analogous to public defecation at Ground Zero. It is crude, it is profane, and it is profoundly ignorant of history. That should be bad enough, but no. Undeterred, many advocates of development cheerfully take on the added habit of duplicity, dismissing as worthless and expendable lands in which they themselves have no personal interest, at the same time extolling as heaven on earth lands in which they do. Ronald Reagan was the first president to recommend oil and gas leasing for the Arctic National Wildlife Refuge. Now hear Mister Reagan, a few months before taking office, on why he intended to maintain the land on his 688-acre California ranch in its untamed, natural state: "Everybody has his own Shangri-La, his own way of getting away, and this is ours." No one would have blamed Mister Reagan for opposing oil exploration on his beloved ranch. And no one would blame former Vice President Dick Cheney—a prime mover behind efforts to open the refuge to drilling—for opposing oil and gas development on the Snake River, one of his beloved Wyoming fishing holes. Cheney grew up in Wyoming and has fished its streams avidly since he was a kid. "I love the setting where you get to do it," he told *Outdoorsbest* online magazine.

> *Fishing takes you to some of the most beautiful places in the world in terms of setting. But I have just as much fun with a day on the Snake an hour from the house, and I take just as much satisfaction from it. I've always firmly believed in the old saying that a day spent fishing is a day that doesn't count against your total time in life.*

Ten thousand trips to *ivvavik*, my friend—and you say enough? And who exactly are you? Someone who understands the world? I see! Tell me this: Why, then, are you blind to its majesty?

Years ago, my father, who was an Episcopal priest, told a story in one of his sermons that I'm reminded of when I picture roads, drilling pads, and airstrips on the calving grounds of the Porcupine caribou herd. I was probably eight or ten at the time and not in the habit of listening closely to my father's sermons, yet so powerful was the message of his story that I heard it clearly on that long-ago Sunday morning, and I've never forgotten it. It seems that an old monk was showing a group of American tourists around a great European cathedral. At the end of the tour the group came to a side chapel where a candle was burning. The monk explained that it had long been one of the duties of his order to tend the flame.

"How long has it been burning?" someone asked. The monk smiled. "A thousand years," he said.

There was a gasp from the assembled, and then silence. Then, while the others watched, one of the tourists walked over to the candle and cupped the flame in his hand.

"A thousand years," he said. "That's long enough." With that he blew out the flame.

Will that be the headline when the calving grounds are opened to drilling? *Officials say: That's long enough!*

But perhaps the story of the thousand-year flame was apocryphal. Never mind. Other flames far longer-lived than that one are routinely extinguished; of that there can be no doubt. Mayan ruins are looted, cave paintings defaced, antiquities destroyed. During the early days of the Iraq War, Baghdad's National Museum was pillaged, resulting in the destruction or disappearance of priceless artifacts four thousand years of age and older. A decade later, jihadist militants destroyed countless numbers of ancient shrines, statues, and other historical artifacts in Syria and Iraq. And such atrocities are not confined to foreign lands. In 1964 a geology student studying ice-age glaciation on Nevada's Wheeler Peak set about collecting tree-ring data from some of the bristlecone pine trees on the mountain. Bristlecones are known to be very old, and the student theorized that knowledge of their ages might assist him in dating contemporaneous glacial phenomena. He chose a tree known as WPN-114, which grew at an altitude of 10,750 feet in a glacial cirque on the northeast face of the mountain. The student drilled several holes in the tree with a twenty-eight-inch increment borer, an instrument that would have allowed him to take a sample of the core without harming the tree.

Unfortunately, he was unable to get a clear reading with the borer. His only other option was to examine a cross-section of the trunk under a microscope. With that in mind, he asked for permission from the U.S. Forest Service to cut down the tree.

Permission was granted. With the help of Forest Service personnel, the student chain-sawed the bristlecone. Subsequent counting of its rings established that the tree was about forty-nine hundred years old. That made it, to the best of anyone's knowledge, the oldest living thing on Earth.

It's true: WPN-114 was very old, and its downing was a tragedy. But it was not the oldest living thing on Earth. Not by a long shot. Terns have been migrating between the Arctic and the Antarctic since long before WPN-114 took root on the bleak northeast slope of Wheeler Peak. Fin whales have cycled between Antarctica and the coast of South Africa, monarch butterflies have plied the airways between California and northwest Mexico for just as long. The Porcupine caribou herd has staged an endless journey over mountain and river, from Yukon's Ogilvie Mountains to Alaska's north coast and back, for at least ten thousand years; there is evidence that the true timespan may be many times that number. The Porcupine's grand journey began in the unfathomable mists of prehistory, in a nursery of ice. It grew and prospered during fat times and waned during lean, engendering a unique narrative as surely as does a people or a nation. The chronicle of the Porcupine lives and breathes today where it has always lived and breathed: in a vital, enchanting corner of the world. Who now claims the authority to snuff it out?

Two weeks after I returned home from the Yukon, about the time that the Porcupine's 2004 run to Alaska shifted into full gear, Lucky's battery went dead. After broadcasting her day-to-day locations for almost seven years, her transmitter fell silent. Her last known position was 64.947°N, 139.030°W, which put her just a few miles from the spot I called Caribou Bluff. That left only Donner and Blixen, of the original ten caribou captured in 1997, still transmitting their latitude and longitude coordinates. In the meantime a new generation of test subjects had joined the satellite collar project—Aurora, Helen, Tundra, Iola, Arnaq, Cocoa, Catherine, Rocky, Isabella, and Pingo. A year later seven more were added, and the list continues to grow.

By my calculations, at the time of her disappearance, Lucky

had put some twenty-five thousand miles beneath her hooves—a circumnavigation of the globe, more or less. She probably put on a few more after the satellite lost track of her, though perhaps not many. She was, after all, getting up there in caribou years. As I write these words, twenty months later, she may well have seen *ivvavik* for the last time.

If so, she had a pretty good run, and she saw a lot of the world. I like to think that I spotted her that last day, up there in one of those sublime bowls of snow, not far from the top of the world. I like to imagine that even now she's okay, just being Lucky, racing for the next bright horizon, and the one beyond.

~

VI. A Vow Fulfilled

ON A CHILLY, early-summer afternoon, a de Havilland Beaver crested a circle of spruce-mantled mountains in northern Alaska and descended into the interior, toward the blue-black waters of Loon Lake. At the north end of the lake, where the plane touched down, the surface of the water rocked in a thin layer of ice. Steering northwest, the pilot navigated a path around the obstruction. In shallow waters he cut the engine and allowed the Beaver to drift to shore.

From a jumble of paraphernalia scrunched into the rear of the plane, I extricated my backpack and stepped out onto one of the plane's pontoons. One step ahead of me, my friend Bob Salerno tossed his pack into a thicket of vegetation at lake's edge and hopped to the ground. A moment later I did the same. With that, I made good on my promise to Fred Meader to visit him at Loon Lake. Fred was no longer resident physically at the lake, having for a quarter century lain under a pile of rocks a few hundred yards from where I now stood. But under the circumstances, it was the best I could do, and I was happy.

A month or so earlier, I had located Elaine Meader in California. One evening we spoke by phone. I told her of my plan to visit the lake with my friend. She at once offered us the use of the cabin that she and Fred had called home during their early years in the Brooks Range. Now as I stepped ashore and sensed the immensity of the mountains, the waters, the stillness—most of all, the *mosquito* that had just landed on my neck—I posted a silent and heartfelt thank-you note to Elaine for her generosity.

For the next week, Bob and I canoed the placid waters of the lake, climbed and explored the nearby mountains, solved the world's problems during happy hours that sometimes lasted somewhat more than an hour, slept sound as dormice in the tidy log cabin at water's edge that Fred and Elaine had cobbled together from the remains of an old prospector's cabin that long-ago autumn of 1960. Bob was the ideal partner to join me in tackling these difficult challenges. Like the giant porcupine that spent his days wandering the forest and his nights curled up cozily in the canoe beside the cabin, Bob has one foot planted firmly in the wild world, the other in the world of the civilized and the urbane. He reveres Henry David Thoreau and Gustav Mahler equally. Given the choice among a hike in the Adirondacks, a lecture on particle physics, and a concert by the Kronos Quartet at Carnegie Hall, Bob would fall to quivering pieces, unable to decide. A former marathoner, he's logged thousands of miles in wild country across the land, always with five pounds of literature crammed into his backpack.

At the time, when he wasn't wearing out a pair of hiking boots, he was selling them; or at least he would have been if Gucci made hiking boots. Bob was a lifer in retail at the very highest levels. When I met him he was senior vice president of Bergdorf Goodman, the super-high-end designer emporium at 57th and Fifth in New York City, where the ladies lunch, heads bow at the mention of the names Armani and Donna Karan, and thousand-dollar handbags

fly off the shelves faster than Fritos at 7-Eleven. Bob was responsible for all operational, financial, and administrative functions at
the store. He claims that his colleagues at BG were mystified by
his occasional withdrawal to places like the High Sierra and the
Brooks Range, rather than sensible spots like, say, Sedona or Costa
del Sol. The photos he brought back documenting what he had
seen and done during his bizarre sallies into forests primeval confounded many. What, no golf? Not even an herbal bath? Bob, who
does not play golf, has a white, neatly trimmed beard, thinning
auburn hair, and a wit as dry and salty as cocktail cashews. He
complains way too much on the trail but, because for some reason
he attracts every mosquito and gnat in the neighborhood, I regard
him as the ideal hiking companion.

Despite the long passage of time since the Meaders made their
home in that magnificent spot, it became clear to me during those
blissful days walking in their footsteps that, like the forests that
bound the mountainside behind the cabin and the wild creeks
that thundered into the lake, Fred and Elaine were still part of
that haunting landscape. Their images were sewn into the very
fabric of the place. The Dalai Lama has expressed his belief that
locations can become holy, intrinsically, in their very atoms, when
they are witness to transformative events. It seems to me that
Loon Lake is such a place. Here, two bullheaded, stoic, visionary individuals reminded the rest of us of something that humans
once knew but that has been pretty much forgotten the world over:
People and Planet Earth can live together in peace.

One morning, Bob and I threw daypacks over our shoulders
and set out up the flanks of the mountain that rose steeply to the
west of the cabin. For the first half hour, we beat our way through
a massive landslide of rocks, dirt, mud, and upended trees that
overhung the cabin like a giant nose on the mountainside. Within,
the thing was a mess, a primal coming undone of creation; neither

of us was sure that we weren't about to sense a subtle shift beneath our boots and then begin a slow, unhappy ride to the lake, perhaps picking up the cabin on the way.

Above, the mountain grew amicable. We moved upward on soft, damp earth, leaping friendly brooks, traipsing through gardens of blue anemones and sphagnum moss.

The forest thinned. After two hours, we emerged above the tree line. The sky was steely blue, the way obvious. We entered a zone of slabby rocks interwoven with brilliantly blooming wildflowers. As I stepped onto the peak's south shoulder I was greeted by a stunning view down into the watershed of a river that, as far as I knew, had not labored sufficiently in the cause of progress to have acquired a name. Even from several miles away, the roar was audible—a thunderstorm on the horizon. South and west through canyons unknown the waters flew, white streamers pluming behind like tail feathers.

The former marathoner plowed on ahead. Trailing by fifty yards, I needed someone to converse with. A moment later I came upon a bed of purple forget-me-nots. They appeared to be enjoying themselves. Why deny them a voice? We talked. They explained their purpose in life (I would reveal it here but I was sworn to secrecy). When I began to describe my own reasons for being there, they wagged their heads. *Don't bother*, they said. *Enjoy the view. Anyway, we already know.*

From the mountain's rocky summit, Bob and I enjoyed a grand panorama of the central Brooks Range. Barely visible on the northern horizon was seventy-five-hundred-foot Mount Doonerak, an unnerving (for a former climber) spike of ice that's named for an Inuit spirit. Doonerak has a name, but in all directions rose mountains that did not. Few have felt the bootsteps of climbers. In time-honored fashion, Bob and I used the view as a kind of travel brochure to spur plans for future adventures and misadventures.

Let's go there and then there, and then let's float a raft from there to there! Bob is one of those people who sees places like the Brooks Range and the Colorado Rockies and his beloved Adirondacks no matter where he stands. Sometimes he'll phone me from his office in New York, and we'll make small talk for a minute or two. Then suddenly he'll mention Alaska or Nevada's Black Rock Desert, and I'll know he's had a sighting.

Just a few miles north of where we stood was the boundary of Gates of the Arctic National Park. Fred and Elaine worked hard for the creation of the park, driven by their belief that, without protection in the National Wilderness Preservation System, Loon Lake and vast portions of the Brooks Range were doomed to development. Thanks in part to their efforts, the park was created in 1980, an 8-million-acre masterpiece of visionary legislation. Fred died not knowing the crowning irony: that at the last minute his beloved lake would be cut from Gates of the Arctic and thereby denied the protection wilderness designation would have provided. The owners of pending mining and real estate claims convinced the boundary-drawers that the area was unfit for wilderness status. Today the fruits of that decision—a road, mining operations, vacation homes—spread south from the lake, vivid testimonials to Fred and Elaine's percipience.

One afternoon the Beaver returned. Inside were two passengers, Elaine and Fred's older daughter Heather and her partner Ryan Emenaker. Heather was the vanguard of the family summer-visitation party; her mother and her younger sister Dawn would be arriving in a few weeks, both for extended stays.

Heather was three years old when her father died. Elaine departed Loon Lake soon after and settled in Northern California. Heather has scant memories of her early years at the lake. She returned for short visits when she was five and nine, but it wasn't until 2000, when she was twenty-six, that she began to go back regularly and get to know the place as the home it had once been. Like her father, she is tall, wiry, erudite, strikingly earnest. She exudes purpose—understandably so, because, as it turns out, she has one. Words tumble from her, serious words. She is ready to engage anyone with a moment to spare in a lively, intense conversation about the sad state of the world and—this is what distinguishes her from your run-of-the-mill malcontent—what to do about it. She has short jet-black hair, a beautiful smile, and a cheery, utterly open manner. I felt we were friends the moment we met.

She remembers her father as "two gigantic legs."

"I was standing between them," she told Bob and me one afternoon as we sat at lake's edge tossing pebbles into the icy waters. She laughed at the memory. "I had a little hatchet and a little piece of wood, and I was chopping the wood." Another recollection was more telling. Fred had caught a fish. In its stomach, in famous fish fashion, there were little fish. In a kind of warm-up for the work she would take up two decades later, Heather sided with the little fish.

"I took them out of the fish's stomach, ran down to the lake, and tried to revive them."

Heather's life in the world beyond Loon Lake centers on issues of social justice. I got an inkling of this when I glimpsed the book she was carrying when I first saw her—Volume 2 of the autobiography of feminist-anarchist Emma Goldman. No mere petition-signer or sign-waver, Heather has stood on the front lines of some of most hotly contested political battles of our time. She has taken a lead role in the fight against World Trade Organization policies, joined permanent encampments in Northern California to forestall the logging of old-growth redwoods, and traveled to Black Mesa, Arizona, to aid the so-called Navajo grandmothers in their struggle to avoid expulsion from their land. To support herself and pay for her schooling, Heather takes employment in fields consistent with her political beliefs. She had, for example, worked in a care home for the elderly; before that, she counseled parentless teenagers who could not be placed in foster care because of legal or behavioral problems. Heather was about to enter college near her home on California's North Coast. She planned to major in women's studies and eventually work with young women on the street.

Listening to the words of this remarkable young woman, I found it impossible not to think of her parents and of their megalomaniacal goal of saving the world. Heather didn't dispute the comparison. She did, however, point out a fundamental difference between Fred and Elaine's approach to the problem and her own.

"What my parents did is probably no longer possible," she said. "I don't think I could leave the world the way they did. My soul is here at the lake, but my heart is intimately connected to the struggles of the world out there. They needed to separate themselves in order to do what they thought was right. I need to stay intimately connected, to work from within to try to keep pieces of the world intact."

Along with Fred and Elaine's utterly serious approach to life and its complications, Heather inherited their passion for the wild. Despite having been back in the Arctic for only a short time, she was thoroughly at ease there and luxuriated in her home away from home. She chopped wood like a lumberjack, usually with a blue bandana wrapped around her head. She tolerated mosquitoes without grousing, canoed boldly, spoke of blizzards and grizzlies with a fondness that amazed me.

"All the clutter of the world falls away when you're here," she said. "The lake centers you emotionally and spiritually. The world and society disappear." Heather regards Loon Lake as a refuge to which she can repair to gather strength and nerve. "It's as if this place with all its intense life and death cycles touches on the pure essence of existence. Whenever I leave I take a part of that with me. We need places like this to rejuvenate us for the trying times ahead."

One evening, Bob and I decided to invite Heather and Ryan for dinner. For the main course we turned to our huge store of freeze-dried backpacking foods. Of all the skills the serious backcountry traveler must master in order to survive in the wild, none are more critical than that suite of steps known collectively as "reconstituting the meal": choosing the aluminum foil package of desiccated comestibles that is perfect for the occasion, adding the correct amount of water, stirring and shaking with the recommended degree of robustness, and finally, keeping nearby the proper medications for treating the stomachache that is almost certain to ensue. I was fortunate to have as my partner in the preparation of the evening meal a man whose understanding of these requisites was second to none. So committed is Bob to the art of the freeze-dried meal that, years ago, he began keeping a log of his backpacking dinners, together with a pithy review of each. So, for example, on the evening of August 13, the featured dish, lasagna, was "tasty and filling but needs oregano badly." The next night, Sierra chicken was "pretty bad. How many chickens do you see in the Sierra?" A night after that, turkey tetrazzini was "best with cognac." Bob has recently instituted a rating system that involves the awarding of ice axes to each product tested, with five axes being tops. He will sometimes solicit opinions and ratings from his companions, but he reserves the right to make final judgments himself. The man, it must be said, is a brutal critic. Most meals he has sampled have garnered lowly ones and twos, with the occasional three. Bob has yet to stumble on a five-axe meal, but he remains hopeful.

On the night of the grand banquet in the Brooks Range, my partner and I decided to throw caution to the winds and head south of the border: Mountain House Mexican-Style Chicken with Rice (two axes) and Richmoor Natural High Chicken Fajitas (three axes). *Olé!* It was hard to imagine that Heather and Ryan were not vegetarians, but since we had no vegetables we decided not to ask.

Why chance spoiling the evening? Whatever their persuasion, our guests ate heartily and without complaint and did not ask to read the ingredient lists on the sides of the packages.

Early the next morning, Heather, Ryan, Bob, and I walked up a hillside a short distance from the "new" cabin, which Fred and Elaine had put up as their family began to grow. We paused in a beautiful setting overlooking the lake, the spot where Fred was interred in 1977. Heather told some stories about her dad. Then she placed a white rock on a circle of rocks that marked the site, as she does each time she visits. The rest of us followed her example. A light breeze floated by, leaving in its wake a blush of summer warmth. In that instant I believed everything Fred had told me about the Arctic—the kindness of the place, the peace it offered to anyone who cared to come and look.

I knew there would be times when I would question that presumption. After all, the benevolent garden which, during his lifetime, Fred had extolled so convincingly was, simultaneously, the plot of cold earth that took him long before his time. The North, I was beginning to understand, was neither wholly light nor completely dark; it was, rather, a little of both—bipolar, if you will. If in some sense it could be taken as a model for the condition of my mental and spiritual health, as I had gone to it believing that it could, then peace was never likely to find a permanent place in my life; but neither were anguish and despair. Like caribou circling between the trials of winter and the raptures of summer, each would come and go, ebb and flow.

On that amicable prospect overlooking Loon Lake, in that serene moment, it was light that flowed. In that moment I could join the Inuit hunter in his timeless celebration of the dawning of the great day—not ultimately a song of day and of light, but rather one of wonder and hope, of the gift that allows anyone anywhere to say, let's go there and then there, and then let's float a raft from there to there. And maybe when we arrive, we will find rest at last.

It's not easy to bury someone in the Arctic. Not far below the earth's surface lies a layer of permafrost that's nearly impenetrable. As a result, the depth of the grave usually falls somewhat short of the recommended six feet. To make up the difference, the burial party heaps rocks and dirt on from above, forming an easily recognizable mound that may rise a foot or more above the earth's surface.

Besides its shape, Fred's grave differed in one other noticeable way from what one might see in a normal, manicured cemetery. Around the periphery of the site lay the sparse groundcover and stunted growth that are typical of Arctic latitudes, but the mound itself supported a spectacular riot of foliage. Wildflowers, willow seedlings, luxuriant mosses and lichens, alder shoots, plants of a dozen varieties sprouted upward and outward in twenty different directions. I saw no orchids, but orchids would not have looked out of place on that exuberant pile of dirt and rock. Irrepressible in life, Fred remained so in death. *Welcome to the Arctic, old friend. You have come at last! Now look: Do you see how glorious it is? I told you so!*

In the great dome above, a fine day was rolling into place, a silver-blue day, a silky breeze of a day, a day that's hard to remember for anything in particular and impossible to forget. Heather and Ryan scooted off down the hill, to save the spiders, I suppose, or, God help us, the mosquitoes. Less ambitiously, Bob and I headed for the old gray canoe and an intrepid exploration of the hard-charging creek we had seen spilling from a canyon half a mile to the east. Within minutes we were willow buds on the lake, moving in easy unison with its rhythms and its melody.

The Arctic!

With each sweep of my paddle, all I could think was, *Oh, how glorious it is!*

THE FIRE AND THE ROSE

I

ONE SPRING MORNING long ago, my high school English teacher delivered a lecture on the evils of Hawthorne's New England. Besides being droll, disorganized, contemptuous of popular culture, and slightly mysterious—qualities that many in the student body interpreted as weird—Arnold Jeschke was passionate. His passion extended to many things that concerned his students: the active voice, uncluttered thinking, the importance of memorizing great poems, Shakespeare, and, most of all, the ability of great literature to mirror the world and to aid its citizens in their quest, if they were on one, to distinguish right from wrong. By the time Arnold Jeschke wrapped up his talk, I had accepted the proposition that a great darkness dwelt at the core of the human soul, and its name was Nature.

Growing into adulthood, I saw this view confirmed in many ways—by reading bestselling books by trendy preachers and old-fangled psychiatrists, by paying attention to the actions of despots, psychopaths, and my local schoolboard, by reading *The New York Times*. In my literature classes in college I learned that darkness has been a major theme in American literature from the very beginning. It sprang from the deep woods of New England, reached its earliest culmination in the works not only of Hawthorne but of Melville, Poe, and a host of lesser lights, and played on in practically every subsequent American writer worth reading: Twain, Fitzgerald, Dreiser, Steinbeck, Faulkner, the expatriates Eliot and Pound—the list went on and on. The nation of my birth was the sin and stain of Faulkner's Yoknapatawpha County, where life could be summed up, in the author's doleful words, as "this pointless chronicle."

"What are the roots that clutch, what branches grow / Out of this stony rubbish?" brooded T. S. Eliot:

> *Son of man,*
> *You cannot say, or guess, for you know only*
> *A heap of broken images, where the sun beats,*
> *And the dead tree gives no shelter, the cricket no relief,*
> *And the dry stone no sound of water.*

Had such a view been grounded in mere opinion, I might have dismissed it. But there was a logic and a consistency to the narrative, for it chronicled the effects of two relentless and eternal forces: the Eden force, which marked me and my fellow humans as inescapably evil; and the Darwin force, which consigned us inescapably evil wretches to endless mortal combat with one another in the farcical hope of obtaining a few pathetic scraps of food, the opportunity for momentary reproductive ecstasy, and one more miserable day under the sun. Authorities in an array of fields chimed in with their helpful corroborations. Economic anthropologists found natural selection behind the rise and eventual triumph of an amazing variety of seemingly unrelated institutions: blue jeans, Harvard, the New York Yankees, the Catholic Church. The ethologist Konrad Lorenz produced mountains of data suggesting that humans were innately aggressive. Friedrich Nietzsche contrived a race of godless supermen dominated by a will to power; in the years that followed, a seemingly endless parade of tyrants and dictators set about implementing his program. Sigmund Freud pretty much sealed the deal. As he saw it, we humans might as well have been alley cats, so unkempt, so vulgar, so self-obsessed were we. The only surprise was that any of us had ever had a generous or noble thought, or committed a selfless deed.

The two forces applied everywhere, across the world, presumably on Neptune and Alpha Centauri. But they acquired a particular virulence here in America, where Europeans had literally wrested a nation from a Garden of Eden through the concerted application of classic Darwinian principles. America was a perfect pristine wilderness the morning Christopher Columbus happened onto it in 1492. As decades passed, the continent ran red with blood. Countless Europeans suffered incalculable hardships subduing the garden. Along the way, they inflicted incalculable hardships on others, sacrificing millions of native peoples to the cause, enslaving and sacrificing millions more Africans. In a kind of willful projection, white Americans spoke of Africa as the Dark Continent and stigmatized the darkness of African skins. But this upending of geography fooled no one. The subjugators knew where the dark continent lay, and they accepted its shadowy nature as natural and inevitable.

On the newly humbled land, a great and powerful nation rose up. War and conquest continued. Fortunes were made and lost. Winners and losers were selected out, the former always at the expense of the latter. Not everyone was happy about this necessary trade-off, but that was the way the world worked, and one had to—well, *adapt.*

For anyone with normal eyes and ears, the dark view of the human soul made a lot of sense. Our planet was clearly a brutal place, and it seemed to be getting only more so. And yet, it was in some ways odd that so many educated Americans should have embraced this distressing picture. For running alongside it, or perhaps perpendicular to it, was another equally accessible view, a picture of hope and light. If it didn't explain much on a global scale, it was what one observed much of the time in one's everyday life, at the scale of the workplace and the grocery store, the high school basketball game and the backyard barbecue. Most people behaved civilly toward one another most of the time. Friends and colleagues labored good-naturedly side-by-side and went out for beers after work. Children were, for the most part, sources of joy and wonder to their parents. The acts they committed were sometimes thoughtless or mischievous, but they were never evil. For every cheerless story by Nathaniel Hawthorne in the local library, there was a radiant, inspiring poem by Walt Whitman to weigh against it.

Just as oddly, one found, if one looked closely enough, that some of the same people who stood ready to lead us into the fearful night were simultaneously prepared to guide us out the other side into dazzling morning. The innately aggressive Konrad Lorenz turned out to be a gentle man who adopted a duck, which rode around on his shoulder as though he were a lily pond. The despairing T. S. Eliot revealed in his maturity, in *Little Gidding*, that he had been wrong:

> *And all shall be well and*
> *All manner of thing shall be well*
> *When the tongues of flame are in-folded*
> *Into the crowned knot of fire*
> *And the fire and the rose are one.*

As for the hopeless pessimist William Faulkner, here are his most widely quoted words, spoken when he accepted the 1950 Nobel Prize for Literature: "I decline to accept the end of man," said the authority who gave us Yoknapatawpha County and the

Snopes family. "I believe that man will not simply endure: He will prevail."

Nor was my own situation notably lamentable. Certainly I had my share of troubles, but generally I was safe, happy, healthy, well fed, gainfully employed, and even loved by a few generous souls. It might have seemed curious, then, had I stopped to think about it, that I should continue to believe in the great darkness.

~

II

ONE NIGHT, CAMPED alone under a starless sky amid the black precipitous forests of Yosemite National Park, I had an encounter that changed forever my view of Nature.

It was late October. I was thirty miles north of John Muir's famous valley, in a steep-sided canyon that had been hewn from the western slope of the Sierra Nevada by a stream that, at that late moment of a grievously dry year, had been reduced to a trickle. The land was empty, exhausted—waiting, it seemed, for the deliverance of winter snows.

There are times when it is possible to discern upon the landscape near-perfect reflections of one's own moods and patterns, and this was one of them. A mirror rises up, inviting the passerby to pause and to peer inside. At such times, nature is seen in its most compelling and affirming guise. Deeply in love, a backcountry wanderer stumbles upon a field of Indian paintbrush and shooting stars, a landscape humming in bumblebees and ardent fragrances; despondent, another trudges over endless acres of deadfalls and gutted earth. Both glimpse the logic and continuity of creation; both sense, if they are open to such things, their right to exist, their firmly rooted places in the world.

Someone had done me a great wrong. We had argued and I had walked out and climbed into my car and driven two hundred miles so that I could be alone in the woods. Now, in the third day of my withdrawal, miles from the nearest road, I hiked steadily northward into ever more desolate mountain country. Late in the afternoon I found a spot of land that suited my mood. I parked my backpack by a rock and resolved to stay awhile.

I knew that there was a pertinent history to this canyon. Probably it explained why I had been drawn there. A century and a half earlier, an unlucky party of trappers under the leadership of a mountain man named Joe Walker had been pinned down somewhere near here in deep snow, at exactly this time of year. Walker and his men floundered for days, faltering eastward toward the hoped-for salvation of California's Central Valley. Starving, they shot and ate their horses one by one. That was the last straw. Cold, snow, hunger—those they could handle. But shooting their horses? Their hearts were shattered.

I knew that Walker had passed my way and I was cheered by that knowledge. Before bedding down, I built a small fire. In the shadows that marched across a polished rock face at the edge of my camp, I made out the flickering form of a tall man in a heavy overcoat. Shoulders hunched, head hanging, he trudged along in stony silence, leading a train of weary horses through the snow.

I understood vaguely that I was preparing for something— or perhaps I was being prepared. Earlier in the day I had had a strange experience, one that seemed to set the tone for what was to come. A few miles from my stopping place, as I made my way up the canyon, I crested a rise and came upon a party of six men meditating beside a dry creek bed. Apparently they belonged to an order of monks. They were outfitted in maroon robes, deployed in a half circle, perched in lotus position. Deep in prayer, their eyes closed, they took no notice of my arrival.

I understood that I should move on but I was drawn to the scene, so I stopped for a few minutes to observe. Perhaps twenty yards from the supplicants I sat on a crumbling log and snacked on peanuts and raisins. Although we were in thick forest, the six had found a spot where a wide blanket of sunlight spread softly across the ground. In its warmth they prayed. I marveled at them, still as fawns hiding in tall grass. From my observation post I saw not a twitch of an eye during all the time I was there. I don't recall ever seeing people who seemed so comfortable with landscape, so at one with it.

Now, hours later, it was I who meditated, on the crimson flames of my little fire. The normal, not-quite-identifiable sounds of the night forest fiddled in counterpoint to the crackling of the coals. I lay on bare ground a few yards from a stand of towering firs. The tops of the trees leapt upward into black, implacable sky. In a nearby trough ran a narrow rivulet, the only water I had found all day. Late in the year, as the withered countryside awaited the redemptive snows of winter, water was a precious commodity in these parts. I knew that other creatures in the neighborhood would be attracted to this spot no less than I, and that I should not be surprised to receive visitations from some of them during the night.

The treetops stirred in a sudden billow of chill wind. The disturbance drifted to the ground like a night fog and spread across my campsite. I snuggled down in my sleeping bag. I had left my tent at home. In my newly chosen digs I lay exposed to trees and sky, with only a bivouac sac to protect my bag and provide a modicum of additional warmth.

I flicked on my flashlight and took a final look around. Then I doused the light, turned onto my side, and in a blackness of spirit and mind drifted off to sleep.

∿

THERE IS A *sound in the darkness. There is a sound in the darkness. There is a sound in the darkness and then a sound and then a sound again, and then the darkness becomes half-sleep and then it sounds in my half-sleep and then it sounds again and I come awake, and then I hear it, the sound in the darkness, and then I feel it, and I hear the sound and I feel the sound and I know that there is something making the sound and that there is something making the feel, and it is beside me and it is before me and it is upon me. And I open my eyes and I see the head and I see the eyes and I smell the breath and I see the bear and she is upon me, she is upon me, she is at my legs and my stomach, my heart is stopped, she is at my head groaning in my ear, she is at my head groaning in my ear, she is laying her head upon mine and groaning in my ear, she is laying her head and my heart is stopped, she is laying her head upon mine, she is turning me, she is beside me and upon me, she is groaning in my ear, and I am okay, she is laying her head and pressing her head and groaning in my ear and I am okay, and for a long time this is happening, this laying her head and groaning in my ear, and I do not understand but I am okay and I do not struggle and I do not resist, I allow her to lay her head and to groan in my ear and to be upon me and to turn me and to turn me and to lay her head and to groan in my ear.*

And this happens for a long time, this laying her head and groaning in my ear, and I am okay. And she goes away and I am okay and then she returns and she lays her head and groans in my ear, and I am not afraid, I am exhilarated, I have had her head lying on my head, I have her groan sounding in my ear, and I am exhilarated.

And soon I am asleep, and then it is dawn and I am awake again and I am okay.

~⁔

III

SHE LOLLED ON a spot of grass, on the far side of the campsite. Idly gazing about, she took in the thin mist that browsed among the firs and the pines, then the man in his sleeping bag, then the slow mackerel sky. Occasionally she cast an eye on her cub, which was up a tree trying vainly to reach my food bag. The young one was lithe and precocious, the mother fat, fit, and confident— well-prepared for winter, it appeared to me, for another year of adventure on the far Yosemite.

Not long after sunrise, the two wandered away. Soon after that, I was headed down-country on the dusty, juniper-scented trail that twisted back to my car.

Our days are filled with events great and small. Most we soon forget; a few become touchstones to which we return again and again. The details remain the same, but the shape and significance may change, and with them our interpretation of the world.

For many years I had a pretty good bear story. At gatherings around campfires, among company when an astonishment was called for, I dusted off my tale, amused my listeners for a few minutes, then placed my trifle back on the shelf.

But not long ago, at a moment when the world seemed a particularly dark place, when nine African Americans had been slaughtered during Bible study in a church in South Carolina, and two children crucified in eastern Syria for not fasting properly during Ramadan, and thousands in eastern Congo tortured and murdered—

Not long ago, I recalled that distant evening in the cathedral forests of the High Sierra. What I remembered was different from the story I had told down through the years. What I remembered was this: *One night my heart was troubled. A bear lay down beside me. When she saw that I was dismayed, she offered me warmth and goodwill. When she saw that I was afraid, she uttered a promise of reconciliation and peace. A barrier was breached, a light ignited. I awoke to a new world of possibility and hope.*

DECRESCENDO

Long ago, in Kentucky, I, a boy, stood
By a dirt road, in first dark, and heard
The great geese hoot northward.
I could not see them, there being no moon
And the stars sparse. I heard them.
—ROBERT PENN WARREN, "TELL ME A STORY"

Toward sundown, as a cold, wind-driven January afternoon hastened to a close in the ancient flat-topped mountains of north-central Colorado, the snow cloud that had gripped the upper ramparts of Castle Peak for most of the day drew away and I caught my first clear glimpse of the summit rocks. In that revealing moment I remembered the howl of Old Lefty. It was a shock to recollect that unearthly sound, because I had never heard the howl of a wild wolf before—certainly not the howl of Old Lefty, one of the last wild wolves in the Colorado Rockies, who by the time I was born had been dead twenty years. But I remembered it clearly, the way you remember the rhythm of a childhood verse, or the cadence of your father's voice, or the energy of a long-lost Benny Goodman record . . . hollow, floating, ghostly, slowly rising, cracking, then settling in somewhere far above your head, white-hot, the color of fever. The howl an old Pennsylvania trapper once likened to the sound of a dozen train whistles, and Grizzly Adams, in a more conventional rendering, called a horrible noise, the most hateful a man alone in the wilderness at night can hear.

I was standing in a snowy garden of sagebrush when I remembered the call. Above me, deep organ tones of twilight caromed off the rocky turrets that gave the peak its name. In 1921, with a suitcase full of Number 4½ Newhouse traps under his arm and a .30-30 on his shoulder, government hunter Bert Hegewa came out from Denver on an urgent mission for the United States Biological Survey. Somewhere near here, at about this time of year—courting season, high howling season—he imposed officially sanctioned silence on the clamorous slopes of Castle Peak. With that, wolves were effaced forever from Castle Peak, from the White River National Forest, from all the great Rockies of this majestic quarter of Colorado.

Or so people thought. Yet the feverish cry stayed on. Sixty-eight years later, on a wolf hunt of my own, I heard it again, soaring high above the mountain, clear as a sky-gram of snow geese. Silence is long but memory is longer, and even the forgetful have flashbacks.

~

SOUND IS A wave. Unlike light waves, which can traverse empty space, a sound wave requires a medium—a solid, a liquid, or a gas—if it is to travel. As the wave moves, the particles of the medium vibrate along the axis of the direction of travel, alternately bunching together and separating. The number of bunches, or cycles, that pass a given point in one second is the frequency of the wave. Human ears can hear frequencies from a low of about 16 cycles per second—a little below the lowest note on a piano—to a high of about 20,000, a nearly inaudible hissing or rasping sound. It is natural to imagine that if we cannot sense something it must not exist, but the bounteousness of sound provides a good palliative to that conceit. One creature's silence may be another's serenade. Bats are expert composers of ultrasonic waves, their shouts and whispers reaching frequencies of 120,000 cycles per second. Listen some evening to a spirited gathering of bats and you may wonder what all the fuss is about; the bulk of their chatter will be lost to your ears, pitched far beyond the range of your hearing.

Wolves, on the other hand, because they can hear at least partway into this confab, might prick up their ears. To you, a quiet evening on Castle Peak; to a wolf, pandemonium.

How an ear that has never heard the howl of a wolf can remember it has not been determined. The Sioux prophet Black Elk gave us one possible explanation. "I did not have to remember these things," he said of the particulars of the great vision he had received sixty years earlier. "They have remembered themselves all these years."

Then, too, there are people who seem to be born with sounds in their heads—those with perfect pitch, for example, who can sing any musical note at will by calling it up from the complete library of tones they carry around in their minds. Where they collected these handy melodies, none of them can explain. Perhaps precision-tuned pitch pipes are included among the toys that our proud genes can select for us as baby gifts, along with silver spoons, green thumbs, and the rest. Perhaps wolf howls are the same—bright packages from the Pleistocene, memories of nights when the howl of a wolf was a signal to sleep lightly and draw closer to the flames.

The cause is uncertain, but not the effect: Toward sundown on a frosty January afternoon, it is possible to stand on a silent mountainside that has not known the song of a wolf for sixty-eight years and to hear it again, sharply, like a pandemonium of bats.

∾

THE INTENSITY OF a sound is a function of the amplitude of the sound wave. At each end of the spectrum of intensity there is a celebrant in nature. The ocean is loud; the desert is quiet. The ocean inspires sermons and symphonies; the desert, contemplation and introspection.

The mountain traveler encounters both extremes and everything in between. A mountain is thunder and sunrise, waterfall and hoarfrost, thrush song and juniper. A visitor to the high country is rocked continually from one end of the curve to the other. On the north slope of Castle Peak I tracked a rabbit upward through the snow for the better part of an hour; I stopped when the scream of the wind, a sure counterpoise to the silent tracks, told me I had gone high enough. A mountain broadcasts in full-dimensional stereo, and every wavelength has something to say.

I had set out on Lefty's trail at sunup that morning, driving north from Interstate 70 on a country road that ambled along beside the Colorado River into a broad valley cleaving two sections of the White River National Forest. Where the road tunneled through shadow, islands of black cinder-ice corrugated the surface. But despite the season, the wide floodplain of the river was mostly bare of snow, and the Colorado itself, just a peppy stream in this early chapter of its travels, had opened a confident course through the ice. Angling up from the river to the east were the lower ramparts of Castle Peak, mile-wide buttresses splintered by dark, nasty-looking gullies. The rock was pink and sorrel and shattered, stacked crazily like overdue library books, dotted with piñon and cedar. Here on the outskirts of the Rockies the land felt dusty and sunbaked, even in winter. The valley moved with a slow, primordial pulse, a rhythm of giant ferns and dinosaurs.

For more than a century this has been cattle country, and any hunt for wolves here must include a hunt for ranchers. In a hundred miles of wandering on rocky roads encircling Castle Peak

I found just one man who remembered wolves. He was eighty-four. For most of his life he had run cattle in the valley, as his father had before him. Wolves were gone by the time he took up the trade. Nevertheless, mention of this ancient nemesis, after the slaughterhouse perhaps the most efficient killer of cattle and sheep, brought no faraway look to his eyes. He hadn't seen wolves in seventy years and that wasn't a day too long. I asked him about Old Lefty, and he said he remembered a renegade wolf and valley ranchers hiring a trapper to clear it out, probably while he was still a teenager. But when I asked him if he remembered the wolf's howl, he shook his head.

I saw that if I was going to find Lefty I'd have to do it on my own, so around noon I parked the car in a grove of cedar where the dirt road turns left toward McCoy, packed a lunch, and took off cross-country toward the summit of Castle Peak. My plan was to spend the afternoon paying my respects, exploring the bluffs and ravines Lefty had known so well, perhaps turning up a relic of his twelve years on the mountain. But it wasn't long after leaving the car that I'd forgotten my plan and was prowling after rabbit tracks, listening to the wind.

~

SILENCE IS NOT "nothing." Only a person who is permanently and totally unconscious hears nothing; to the rest of us, silence communicates content and evokes an emotional response. Think of the pregnant pause, the calm before the storm, the eloquence of Harpo Marx, the working silence of a Quaker meeting, the shouting silence of a Beckett play. Look at Edvard Munch's *Scream*, and listen. Think of what Jack Benny could do with silence, the most lethal weapon in his considerable comedic arsenal. Think of the music the audience hears in John Cage's notorious *4' 33"*, as the players sit through the piece without lifting their instruments.

Think of the knockout physical power of silence. Mathematics writer Martin Gardner reported that once, as a practical joke on the conductor of a symphony orchestra, the members of the orchestra agreed to fall silent in the middle of a strident composition. At the prearranged moment the musicians abruptly stopped playing, and the conductor fell off the podium.

Silence can have less violent but equally remarkable physical effects. During the silence of meditation, people's hearts slow and their blood pressure drops. In the Sudan, the Mabaans have perfected a method of hunting that is based on complete silence; as a result, the noise level of their everyday speech has dropped so low that it is practically inaudible to outsiders. Mabaans move softly, as gracefully as dancers, and are said to conduct themselves in a composed and amiable manner. When they hunt, they can hear animals no one else knows to be there.

∼

THE SOUND OF America was wild, and it was ear-rending. Listen:

Pelicans, ditzy wing-slappers, rising by the hundreds like a clatter of pots and pans over the river islands of places we know today as Kansas and Nebraska. Parakeets, shrieking flocks of them, in Virginia, Tennessee, and the Carolinas, tame, darting, pint-size rainbows swarming inches from the fingertips. Turkeys jabbering, jammed so thickly into trees along the river banks of Arkansas, Missouri, and Oklahoma that travelers told of turkey trees and likened the birds to apples. Whooping cranes tall as trombones, tooting their five-foot windpipes across Louisiana, Iowa, New Jersey, and Maryland. Trumpeter swans, elegant thirty-pound jazz bands, blaring down the Ohio and the Mississippi and south to the Gulf. Ivory-billed woodpeckers, monstrous wild-eyed things, red-crested, hard-hatted, jackhammering the forests of Georgia, South Carolina, Florida, and Alabama.

Plovers and curlews, shrill-crying, roaming the Atlantic like storm clouds, pounding the mainland of Massachusetts, Rhode Island, Connecticut, and New York. And for 9 million years, sand-hill cranes, too high to be seen, too clamorous to go unheard, passing over Nebraska, over the Southwest and the Midwest, over all the Atlantic states.

The living wind—the words are Aldo Leopold's—of passenger pigeons. Six miles off, a flock had as good as arrived: The wind shifted, the horizon purred. Then a roar and a blacking out of the sun for hours and sometimes days as the birds flew by. John James Audubon, that master statistician, estimated 300 million birds per hour in one passing flock. Such a throng didn't nest, it besieged several hundred square miles of trees, took them over like paratroopers. At night the sound of their gargantuan bickering made the forest crackle and hum as though it were afire.

Walruses, fat and bossy, fussy as bankers, bleating dawn to dusk on the rocky shores of Maine and Massachusetts. Prairie dogs, squat and sassy, jabbering from Kansas to the Gulf of Mexico, a five-hundred-mile-long salute to small talk. Screeching squirrels by the tens of thousands, migrating across the plains in dense, relentless columns. At a river, at the Missouri or the Platte, the first brigade would plunge in and drown; the second would take to the backs of the first and race across. Gold-coated, deep-throated jaguars, gliding through Tennessee, Arkansas, Oklahoma, and New Mexico. Bighorns cracking heads from Canada to Mexico, grizzlies bawling in every corner of the West, mountain lions hissing and screaming in Rhode Island, in Delaware.

Bison herds of ten thousand in Kentucky. On the plains the total ran to 30 or 40 million. Large herds measured twenty-five miles end to end and numbered a quarter-million animals. George Catlin likened the sound of unseen bison to that of distant thunder. Meriwether Lewis wrote of the continuous roar of hundreds of males battling at once during mating season—a trampling and bellowing audible six miles away.

And everywhere, in Vermont and Utah, in Iowa and Nevada, in the Dakotas, Pennsylvania, Wisconsin, Oregon, and West Virginia, on the plains, in the mountains, on the tundra and in the desert, the haunting, floating cry of the animals whose range exceeded all others: the resonant, scintillating, mournful howling of wolves.

∼

FOR SEVERAL HOURS I improvised a raggedy theme-and-variations that wandered generally upward along the north and west slopes of Castle Peak. Unlike the forbidding fourteen-thousand-foot peak of the same name near Aspen, Lefty's Castle is a home, a gentle and welcoming place, the kind of mountain that even in January invites you to come up and stay awhile. The theme for the day was Lefty, but since I wasn't sure how to elaborate it, I let the variations discover themselves. For a time I followed the rabbit tracks, which bounded along before me as breezily and expertly as Arthur Murray dance prints. Suddenly they disappeared into thin air.

Houdini, this bunny. How did he do it? Midway across an acre of cottony snow the confident prints, racing smartly for the far edge, simply up and ended.

I knelt to inspect the evidence, silent but certainly not mute. Maybe he forgot something, executed a flying 180, and scampered home in the original tracks. But the positioning of the toes told me otherwise: This was a one-way street. Searching the gray sky to the west, I spotted a red-tailed hawk barrel-rolling high over the valley of the Colorado. I'd been told that those fellows sometimes tackle rabbits. Hypothesis: Frisky Peter was not Houdini at all, but hare-brained Icarus.

Abandoned by my faithful guide, I momentarily felt lost. I looked toward the top of the mountain and heard the wind whistling a

not-so-silent warning to stay below. The chill summit rocks disappeared beneath a restless cloud. About me the aroma of sage, until
now a lively companion on my travels, went bitter and cheerless.

I turned and adjusted my focus thirty miles, to Dome Peak,
white and spectacular on the horizon. Suddenly I thought of my
friend Art. We climbed together for a decade, traversed a hundred
slopes like this one to reach the soaring summit routes we favored.
We were first on the airy crest of Mount Russell one spring, the
year his brother died of cancer. On that dizzy, snowbound eminence I saw him kneel, slip the notebook from the summit canister,
and write, "This one's for Jim." We joked about the Himalaya and
the Far North, and I promised him that one day, before too long, I
would phone him and say, "Let's go." And that would mean it was
time for us to take a deep breath and head for Nepal.

He walked me off the Grand Teton the day I quit, the day I
decided that twenty years was enough, that, because I was afraid,
I must never tie a rope around my waist again. He took me to
his tent on the Lower Saddle, in a disturbing and disorienting
amber light. In the hush of the mountains, we talked for an entire
afternoon about my shame and heartbreak, and about a new and
unanticipated disorder: the deadly emptiness I felt. Art helped me
through the ordeal as we had often helped each other over a difficult section of a climb.

To my surprise, he told me of his own fears, the quaking knees
at the tough spots, the midnight premonitions that the next mountain would be his last. I went home to a new life without climbing.
He continued, but not for long. A few months later, on a route called
"Ordeal" on Discovery Wall at Pinnacles National Monument in
California, his waist harness somehow became disengaged from
the rope. He fell a hundred feet to his death.

I couldn't join my friends when they carried the tiny package
of ashes to Mount Moran in the Tetons, because it would have

violated my vow. But a few days later in the shining High Sierra I scrambled to the top of amiable Shepherd Crest, a mountain designed for the new me, and there, alone on a grand, million-mile afternoon, I spoke the words of Psalm 121: "I will lift up mine eyes unto the hills, from whence cometh my help"; then I knelt, slipped the notebook from the canister, and penciled in my gift: "This one's for Art."

～

IN THE LATE afternoon, bumblebee-sized snowflakes began darting on the wind. A sudden gust hurtled out of Bull Gulch and caught me on the open slope just below Castle Creek Ponds. I stopped and pulled on my mittens. This was as high as I would go today, not much over nine thousand feet, still two thousand below the summit. I had thought of going to the top, but the summit cloud had deterred me and, perhaps semi-deliberately, I had dawdled too long on my errands. Today the top of Castle Peak seemed a poor idea for someone alone.

But I was not alone. A hundred feet higher and a few degrees to my right, an almost imperceptible flutter in the sagebrush caught my eye. A lithe doe, her gossipy tail twittering, moved out of a shadow, paused, then sprang effortlessly up the slope as though carried by the breeze. She stopped and tilted her nose upward. I could see her twitching flanks, the thin puffs of smoke at her nostrils. We both came swiftly to attention, and I wondered what she perceived in the silence of the snowfall.

She sprang again. I gasped in surprise as behind her a graceful, unexpected parade bounded into view: a second zigzagging in her hoofprints, then a third and a fourth and a fifth. In a handsome line the quintet danced along the ridgeline above me, blithe captives of an unheard song.

~

WE CAN SAY with some confidence that prior to 1850 there must have been several thousand wolves in Colorado. True country squires, they had an easy time of it, feeding on a seemingly inexhaustible supply of bison, pronghorn, deer, and other natural prey with which they shared the mountains and the plains.

In 1858 the balance that had obtained for thousands of years began to totter. In the fall of that year, a teamster turned loose a few old oxen in the eastern part of the state, assuming the animals would starve over the winter. Instead they happened onto rich winter grass. The following spring the oxen turned up fat and healthy.

A few years later a settler named Sam Hartsel confirmed the discovery. He drove a hundred head of shorthorn cattle into the high mountain park west of Colorado Springs and there found hardy grasses flourishing year-round. At precisely the moment when less imaginative entrepreneurs were pouring into Colorado in search of prosaic silver and gold, cowmen hit a motherlode of far greater and more lasting importance to the state's economy. Sam Hartsel struck grass, and the rush was on to graze the Rockies.

To justify clearing the land for settlement, we turned to the myths that had served us faithfully on each step of the march west. Duty and destiny stood foremost—vindications since Plymouth. Then there were more finely tuned romances, each with its own local slant. The myth of the evil wolf, for example, a favorite since Aesop, found a ready home in Colorado. By 1870, stock tales of "cruel," "ruthless," and "bloodthirsty" wolves that preferred steak to all other meat were staples of Colorado folklore.

But to excuse the massacre of prairie dogs, bison, bighorn sheep, and other docile creatures, animals even the most messianic booster couldn't tag as evil, we required more upbeat delusions.

We turned to two American classics: the myths of the mighty hunter and of the people who loved the land.

The first had its genesis in eighteenth-century Kentucky: Daniel Boone in buckskin—brave, crafty, persevering, the wily natural man alone against the beasts of the forest. After the Civil War we added a grand and irrefutable subtext to the basic narrative, one obedient to the new god: technology. We might wince at shooting raccoons and porcupines, but the hallowed names of Winchester, Springfield, Sharps, Henry, Spencer, and a host of other distinguished arms manufacturers quickly relieved us of our pesky misgivings. After all, their products gleamed with American ingenuity, which was heaven-sent. Besides, those wondrous engines—breech-loaders, magazine loaders, telescopic sights, smokeless powder, all manner of poisons and traps—were handsome, well-made, practical, efficient. We'd be fools not to use them!

Every region had its own local Buffalo Bill, a hero who cleared the woods of one pest or another. The inheritance of these mighty hunters exalted them; technology made them divine.

It was, as I say, a myth. The hunters who cleared America of wildlife during the nineteenth century did very little hunting, and they did not need to be particularly brave, since the greatest danger most of them faced during their tramps in the woods was that their rifles might explode in their faces or they might swallow some of their own poison. The great American hunt for wild animals was more like a lazy swing on the front porch with a mint julep by your side. Pigeon hunters kindled sulfur fires under the trees of nesting passenger pigeons. The fumes rose up; the birds plopped dead onto the ground. Those that flew away before succumbing to the fumes slammed into nets or phalanxes of swinging poles wielded by the fire builders, who then picked up the downed birds and crushed their heads with pincers.

On the plains, bison hunters perfected the still-hunt. Standing in place, the hunter first hunted for a bison—not much of a challenge since, in all likelihood, he was facing several thousand of the animals languidly munching on prairie grass. Having selected his target, he next hunted for the choicest spot on thirty square feet of stationary bison hide at which to aim his bullet. After firing, he waited patiently while other bison gathered around the dead animal in curiosity, then hunted for the choicest spot at which to aim on each of them.

When the animal did not come to the hunter, the hunter hunted not for the animal but for a clever place to hide his traps and his poisons. Traps were riskier, since a trapped animal could escape by chewing off its snared limb. Poison quickly became the weapon of choice for hunters during the land-clearing decades of the last century (and, indeed, remains so for state and federal hunters today). Unlike the trap, which provided an out for any animal gutsy or crazed enough to mutilate itself, poison left nothing to chance. Poison carried the cachet of authority, of the final word. Poison was *democratic*—that was what moved the heart. Strychnine, the most popular, in notably hideous fashion killed not only the animal that consumed it but every animal that fed on the newly created carcass, and on their carcasses, and so on down the line. Not only wolves and coyotes, the principal targets, but eagles, hawks, owls, skunks, woodchucks, prairie dogs, squirrels, dogs, cats, horses, goats, and occasionally children consumed strychnine on the great land and died. Stanley Young, a supervisor with the U.S. Biological Survey who oversaw the killing of some of the last wild wolves in the West (and who was, paradoxically, one of the first persons to take a scientific interest in the wolf), reported that no rancher ever passed a dead animal without lacing it with a liberal dose of strychnine.

Poison on the land. We arrive at the second of our great national delusions: that of the people who loved the land. To appreciate the myth fully, keep vividly before you a picture of a mass of strychnine on a grand expanse of nineteenth-century America and, around it, scores of gruesomely twitching beasts. As they convulse in their death throes, consider this people who loved the land, these pioneers rapturous before the majestic plains and mountains, these farmers and ranchers in the red sunset kneeling reverently to the ground and sifting the sweet-smelling earth between their fingers.

I do not know how to see it except as myth. The belief that we loved the land is central to our vision of ourselves as a people. Yet that treasured belief, so necessary if we were to transform the land into the subservient habitation we know today, fails entirely to square with the evidence. Certainly we loved something—the idea of the land, the promise of the land. But the land was forests, which we leveled, and topsoil, which we destroyed, and rivers, which we dammed, and streams, which we polluted, and grasses, which we burned, and swamps, which we drained, and Native Americans, whom we decimated, and wildlife, which we massacred. That is the record, and it does not sound like love.

A poison was on the land. And the poison was this: *This land will make you rich.*

~~

NINETEENTH-CENTURY LITERATURE abounds in tales of hunting adventure, much of it quite rapid:

ONE SECOND IN THE LIFE OF JOHN JAMES AUDUBON:
Weapon: rifle and one spray of buckshot
Take: seven whooping cranes

FORTY MINUTES IN THE LIFE OF THOMAS C. NIXON:
Weapon: rifle
Take: 120 bison

ONE DAY IN THE LIFE OF FRANK M. STAHL AND FRIENDS:
Weapons: rifles
Take: forty wolves

ONE DAY IN THE LIFE OF A NATCHEZ, MISSISSIPPI, HUNTER:
Weapon: rifle
Take: 750 golden plover

ONE NIGHT IN THE LIFE OF TWO KANSAS TERRITORY HUNTERS:
Weapon: strychnine
Take: sixty-four wolves

ONE DAY IN THE LIFE OF GEORGE W. BROWN:
Weapon: strychnine
Take: thirteen wolves, fifteen coyotes, forty skunks

ONE DAY IN THE LIFE OF WINDHAM THOMAS WYNDHAM-QUIN,
FOURTH EARL OF DUNSRAVEN:
Weapon: rifle
Take: 120 woodland caribou

ONE YEAR IN THE LIFE OF ROBERT PECK:
Weapon: strychnine
Take: 800 wolves

ONE YEAR IN THE LIFE OF THE RESIDENTS OF SUN CITY,
KANSAS TERRITORY:
Weapons: miscellaneous
Take: enough wolves to pave a road seventy-five yards wide
with the carcasses

EIGHTEEN MONTHS IN THE LIFE OF WILLIAM CODY:
Weapon: .50-70 Springfield Army musket
Take: 4,280 bison

THREE YEARS IN THE LIFE OF SIR ST. GEORGE GORE:
Weapon: rifle
Take: 105 bear, 1,600 elk and deer, more than 2,000 bison

By 1870, the bison, the principal prey of the wolf, was stamped-ing toward oblivion. Bison hunter William Webb estimated that, in 1871, hunters shot fifty thousand bison in Kansas and Colorado alone. Hunters sometimes took hides and tongues, but the bulk they left to rot on the plains. Webb put the amount of abandoned bison meat from these fifty thousand kills at 20 million pounds. Bison carcasses were said to line the Kansas Pacific Railroad route for two hundred miles.

The slaughter continued through the following decade, with hunters complaining that the numbers of animals at which to shoot were decreasing steadily. By 1885, hunters actually had to hunt for bison. By the turn of the century, 75 million of the animals were dead, 999,999 out of every million that had lived. A few dozen remained.

Other species had fared little better, and some worse. Grizzlies had been extirpated from 99 percent of their former range in the contiguous United States. Plover and curlew no longer filled the Atlantic sky. The turkey trees were gone, as were the clattering pelicans of Kansas and Nebraska, the walruses of New England, the jaguars of Tennessee, Arkansas, Oklahoma, and New Mexico, the mountain lions of Delaware and Rhode Island. Sandhill cranes, whooping cranes, and trumpeter swans hung on by a thread (the number of whooping cranes that John Audubon killed with one shot represented one-third of the number of whooping cranes alive in 1941). The megalopolis of prairie dogs had disappeared. Brigades of squirrels no longer migrated over the plains. The magnitude of the disaster is impossible to comprehend, but in *Of Wolves and Men*, Barry Lopez's magnificent biography of the wolf, he puts as carefully calculated a number on it as we are ever likely to get. From 1850 to 1900, he estimates, some 500 million creatures were killed in the United States. Perhaps it is enough to say that by the turn of the century, the raucous cry of the American wilderness had been reduced to a gravelly, consumptive whisper.

A few species—Eastern elk, Labrador duck, sea mink—had disappeared altogether. But most held on into the new century. Then the amazing completeness of the rout, and the irreversibility, became blindingly manifest. Merriam's elk winked out in 1906, Badlands bighorn in 1910, Louisiana parakeets in 1912, Carolina parakeets in 1914, Wisconsin cougars and California grizzly bears in 1925, ivory-billed woodpeckers, probably, in 1946. The last passenger pigeon, a female named Martha, died in the Cincinnati Zoo in 1914.

As their traditional prey disappeared, wolves turned their attention to domestic stock. For a short time they prospered. But as cattle and sheep losses mounted through the latter decades of the nineteenth century, ranchers and local governments committed themselves to the total eradication of wolves. With bounties as incentives, with rifles, traps, and poisons as their tools, hunters set upon the wolf with a ferocity unmatched in the annals of a notably ferocious war, one rooted not in annoyance, the charge against species that were merely in the way, or contempt, the curse on the ridiculous bison, but in hatred and rage. Barry Lopez estimates the harvest at between 1 and 2 million wolves. By 1915, when the federal government chipped in with $125,000 to clear wolves from federal lands, including the national parks, only a handful of renegades remained in the lower forty-eight states.

~

IN THE RELATIVELY empty region of the night sky between the head and the right foreleg of the constellation identified by ancient peoples as the winged horse Pegasus, there shines a star very much like our Sun, known to astronomers as IK Pegasi A. It is about one hundred and fifty light years from Earth, which means that a beam of light setting out from IK Pegasi A will rocket through the frozen darkness of interstellar space for about one hundred and fifty years before touching down on this planet.

It works both ways. One hundred fifty years after an event unfolds on Earth, the optical record of that event will arrive in the vicinity of IK Pegasi A. Thus, sometime in the next few years, snoopy astronomers on a lush blue-green planet that we might imagine to be orbiting the star at a safe and civilized distance can turn their telescopes on Earth and watch as Thomas C. Nixon kills one hundred and twenty bison in forty minutes; not long after that, they can take in the nightlong dispatching of sixty-four wolves by poisoning, courtesy of two Kansas Territory hunters, and a few months later the one-day slaughter of one hundred and twenty woodland caribou by Windham Thomas Wyndham-Quin, Fourth Earl of Dunsraven.

The views, then, from deep space are spectacular. Not so the music. Because space is a vacuum, the silence of the cosmos is complete and unbreakable. (A few reclusive hydrogen and helium atoms do pop up out there every once in a while, but not enough to carry a tune.) Were someone to go for a float with me out near IK Pegasi A and turn to me to comment on the lovely view—perhaps the curious new perspective on the Milky Way, or the handsome grain on the stock of Lord Dunsraven's rifle—I wouldn't hear the remark. Were my companion to shout, I wouldn't hear. Were my friend, in frustration at my failure to respond, to line up ten cement mixers, a hundred jumbo jets, and a thousand rock concerts (or, more to the point, 1 or 2 million wolves) and set them all howling at once, I would hear nothing. We are not considering a variation on the old paradox of the tree falling silently in the forest, which depends on an absence of ears; here there are ears but essentially zero gabby particles vibrating in a medium to transmit the sound.

It is not sufficient to call this silence. Unlike the pregnant pause, the silence of Harpo Marx, or the calm before the storm, this is a consummate silence, a silence without dreams, a silence known only to the unconscious. Here in the emptiness of the northern sky we have discovered our ideal listening post, where we can sit back, kick off our shoes, and tune in to the immaculate voice of extinction.

ON ITS NIGHTLY rounds sometime in 1913, a four-year-old male gray wolf, the alpha wolf of one of the last wild packs in Colorado, stepped into a steel trap concealed in a clump of sagebrush somewhere on Castle Peak. The trap sprang, snaring the wolf by the left front leg. The wolf, which by all accounts appears to have been an unusually determined animal, chewed its own flesh and bone through to the core, and some hours or days later it rejoined its pack. A rancher checking the trap afterward found the wolf's severed left forefoot.

The stub of the wounded leg soon healed and, with what ranchers in the Castle Peak region began to understand as premeditated malice, the pack resumed its nightly business. The lead wolf learned to run on three legs, lowering the fourth to the ground only when leaping an obstacle in its path. Every stockman in Eagle County learned to recognize the unmistakable signature. It soon became more than a set of prints: It became a symbol of revenge. Ranchers found it, or thought they found it, in the mess of tracks surrounding every freshly killed sheep or steer. They believed that the wolf marked its kills with its personal stamp, like a serial killer.

Castle Peak was made a minefield of traps and poison pellets. But somehow the killing went on. For some reason, traps and poisons had no effect on the pack's depredations. Perhaps, as one of the last, the lead wolf was one of the fittest—a wolf capable of learning a lesson from the 1913 disaster, an animal of uncommon vigilance and discrimination.

A remarkable animal, yes, but not the mythic beast that came into being. Before long, local legend had elevated the hobbled wolf from three-legged leader of the pack to phantom killer, a supernatural beast striking in the dead of night, impervious to man's pathetic weapons. During the eight years following the loss of its foot, the wolf was blamed for the deaths of 384 head of livestock in the Castle Peak region. By 1921, when local ranchers threw in the towel and called for help from the federal government, the legend of Old Lefty, the smartest, cussedest, most black-hearted wolf anyone in these parts had ever come up against, was in full flower.

Help arrived in the person of Bert Hegewa. He moved into a one-room cabin near the mouth of Bull Gulch on Castle Peak early in January 1921. Like most members of the mop-up team employed by the U.S. Biological Survey, Hegewa was an anomaly, a hunter who really knew how to hunt. He chalked up an impressive record against the wily and tenacious wolves he stalked. A month earlier he had killed all the members of a resolute pack near Pagoda Springs; during the previous year, another dozen renegades. After finishing his business with Lefty, he would kill a wolf called Unaweep on the Uncompahgre Plateau near the Utah border, and after that Bigfoot, a wolf that had acquired a chilling reputation as "the terror of the Lane Country."

In *The Last Stand of the Pack*, a 1929 work in which survey supervisor Stanley Young documented the agency's work in stamping out the last pockets of wolf resistance, Young left us a picture of Bert Hegewa: about thirty years of age, of medium height, bearded, with tousled, tawny hair and premature crow's feet around blue eyes. Hegewa went about in a red-and-black-checked woodsman's shirt and corduroy pants, and he carried a .30-30 rifle. Young dedicated his book to Hegewa and the other hunters of the survey:

> *They are the heirs of the Mountain Men. They are the follow-*
> *ers of the last frontiers. They are the friends of all animals;*
> *the compassionate, regretful executioners of animal renegades*
> *when such outlaws must die that other wildlings may live.*
>
> *On far trails, wind swept, snow blanketed, hail pelted, on*
> *trails where frost bites or sun bakes, on trails where danger*
> *stalks with them as a close companion, these determined men*
> *carry on the tradition of the organization to which they belong.*
> *They get their wolf!*

Hegewa spent his days exploring the wide slopes and shattered ravines of Castle Peak. Although the mountain is only 11,275 feet in height, it is massive and complex, encompassing well over sixty square miles of convoluted terrain above the eight-thousand-foot level. In two weeks of trying, the hunter found not a trace of Lefty and his band.

One morning near mid-month, he awoke to a blizzard raging on the summit of the mountain. Against the advice of a cowboy with whom he shared the cabin, Hegewa took off on skis. He toured the mountain, staying below the storm throughout the day. Once again he came up empty-handed.

Then, toward sunset, just as he was about to head for home, he spotted faint animal tracks in the snow. The tracks led him up a draw and over a ridge, into a thicket of mountain mahogany. Hegewa followed, crossing a meadow, then skiing into a stand of yellow pine. There, out of the wind, the faint marks became clear, and Hegewa found what he had been looking for: the fresh signature of a wolf running on three legs. The hunter guessed that the track was less than an hour old.

Night was falling and the blizzard had moved lower on the mountain. In a strong wind and heavy snowfall, Hegewa set out in pursuit of the wolf. Dusk found him on the south side of the mountain, climbing toward the center of the storm. At tree line the track leveled off, then descended into the shelter of the forest. Hegewa stayed with it till finally, in last light, he lost the trail.

But he had good reason to congratulate himself, for he had found the pack's main runway on the mountain. Now in full darkness, too far from the cabin to return in safety, he thrashed through the trees until he located a spruce with an inviting undercover of snow. He unlatched his skis, then, perhaps momentarily warmed by a glow of keen satisfaction, burrowed under the snow and prepared to spend a cold night out.

∽

SIXTY-EIGHT YEARS LATER, in an easier cold on a high vantage ground somewhere on Castle Peak, I danced from one foot to the other in a waggish effort to stay warm. Twilight lay softly on the mountain, bringing a transitory peace, like tower chimes. I peered down snowy slopes into the valley of the ebony Colorado. Wide fields crisscrossed by streams and fences glimmered in the half-light. Within them cattle stood and shuddered, anticipating the terrors of the night. Closer by, the deer grew still and rabbits turned to stone. The silent world was wolf country tonight.

I moved to the edge of a gulch, a shadowy rent in the mountainside tumbling ever wider toward the distant river. A wall of massive frost-hewn blocks shored up one side, its lengths and widths so masterfully rendered that for a moment I thought the wall was human-built.

I warmed at the thought. Then I peered down to the jumbled floor of the gulch falling into darkness and felt a chill. Suddenly I understood how far I had come to reach this place.

I had meant to be in Glenwood Springs by now. But at sunset the sky had cleared, the wind had died, and a perfect quiet crept in over the mountainside. It was a peace too rare to squander. I had no food or flashlight or extra clothing, but no matter; I would stay on awhile, tune in to the sound of night on Castle Peak.

I looked at the sky, wide open now, harbinger of an arctic night. The first star flicked on and then the second, and soon the entire show. By snowlight I contoured east in search of a suitable listening post among the huddled sage. In the silvery light the yellow-green plants looked luminous, the mountainside shone with the luster of satin.

Existence, preached Vladimir Nabokov, is but a brief crack of light between two eternities of darkness. In his enchanting autobiography, *Speak, Memory*, Nabokov tells the story of a young man of his acquaintance, a chronophobic Nabokov calls him, who saw home movies that had been taken a few weeks before his birth. The beloved house, his mother waving from an upstairs window, especially the empty baby carriage awaiting his arrival: These familiar sights possessed an existence that somehow excluded the man's own, and they threw him into a panic. Nabokov writes that the man felt as if in the reverse course of events, his very bones had disintegrated. In that terrifying moment he witnessed the perfect silence of deep space.

The daredevil in me is envious. But, denied prenatal docudramas and interstellar joyrides, where am I to turn for such diversion? Perhaps to Aldo Leopold, who recommends "thinking like a mountain." Leopold knew well the cry of the wild wolf, a cry that he says stirred the emotions of every living thing that heard it—the deer and the pine, the coyote, the rancher, and the hunter; perhaps, he adds, many a dead thing as well. "Only the mountain," he writes, "has lived long enough to listen objectively to the howl of a wolf."

In his youth Leopold never passed up a chance to kill a wolf. Once when he and some friends were eating lunch on a high rim-rock, they spotted a female wolf and her pups playing below. In a second the men were firing into the pack.

> *When our rifles were empty, the old wolf was down, and a pup was dragging a leg into impassable slide-rocks. We reached the old wolf in time to watch a fierce green fire dying in her eyes. I realized then, and have known ever since, that there was something new to me in those eyes—something known only to her and to the mountain. I was young then, and full of trigger-itch; I thought that because fewer wolves meant more deer, that no wolves would mean hunters' paradise. But after seeing the green fire die, I sensed that neither the wolf nor the mountain agreed with such a view.*

The death of fire in the wolf's eyes was the birth of fire in Leopold, a fire to hear a wolf in a way that does not come naturally to living things: not with the apprehension of the deer, the hatred of the rancher, or the feverishness of the hunter, but with the time-honored objectivity of a mountain. An objectivity that, as I see it, is a silence that is endless and respectful and soulful, a deep-space silence that signifies nothing more troublesome than a willing acceptance of the universe. The baby carriage is not empty; it contains us all. Leopold ends by suggesting that it is the mountain's objectivity that is behind Thoreau's observation that "in Wildness is the preservation of the World." "Perhaps," Leopold writes, "this is the hidden meaning in the howl of the wolf, long known among mountains, but seldom perceived among men."

In the star-studded night on my sloping field of snow, my search for Lefty became a search for the mountain itself.

~

NOT EVEN A night out without a sleeping bag could discourage the remarkable Bert Hegewa. In the morning he crawled out from under his spruce, shook himself off, and booby-trapped the wolf trail.

The first day he caught a coyote. When he inspected the area the following morning, he discovered fresh wolf prints fifty feet from the main runway. The pack had come through, all right, but at the last moment had veered to avoid the coyote, which had come through first.

Hegewa booby-trapped the detour. That night the pack returned and again took the cutoff. Running in the lead, Lefty leapt a branch that Hegewa had placed strategically in the trail. When the wolf came down, he landed in not one but two of Hegewa's traps.

The traps were not staked to the ground, so Lefty could still travel, but only with difficulty. Each trap weighed more than five pounds; moreover, heavy drag hooks raked along behind them as the wolf moved, impeding his progress and leaving deep furrows in the snow to mark his route. Somewhere one of the hooks jammed in an obstruction in the path. As Hegewa discovered later, the wolf pulled with such power that he straightened the drag hook and broke free. When a second hook caught in a clump of sagebrush, however, Lefty hadn't the strength to pull out. It was there that Hegewa and the cowboy found him in the morning.

Stanley Young describes the wolf as huge, bedraggled, red-eyed, and enraged. The cowboy roped him around the neck and pulled tight, stretching the animal away from the captured drag hook. Hegewa cut a branch from an aspen tree and laid it over Lefty's shoulders, pinning the wolf to the ground. With the animal battling beneath him, he eased himself out onto the branch, one knee on Lefty's abdomen, the other on his neck. Gingerly he slipped a noose over the wildly snapping jaws and clamped them shut. Then he hog-tied the animal so that it was unable to move.

There was no honor to a fallen leader in what came next. Hegewa wrapped a collar around Lefty's neck, chained him to a stake, and surrounded him with traps. Then he and the cowboy returned to the cabin, leaving the wolf behind as live bait for the other members of the pack.

That night and for several nights afterward, the pack returned. Three more wolves fell into Hegewa's traps. The others, if there were others, abandoned the mountain. Ranchers reported that the wolf tracks to be seen on Castle Peak grew fainter over the next few months and disappeared with the first spring rains. Fresh tracks were never seen again.

Young scrupulously avoids mentioning the actual death of Lefty. We learn only that Hegewa brought in a bottle of the wolf's scent, his pelt, and his head, the latter to be mounted as a trophy, open-jawed and snarling. The carcass Hegewa left on the mountain for scavengers.

A few weeks after Hegewa departed, local stockmen wrote to the Biological Survey in Denver thanking the agency for the hunter's services:

> *It is a big relief to us to know that "Old Lefty" is a thing of the past—for his track on the range meant he was back and on the job of cattle killing once again. We breathe a sigh of keen satisfaction, and fully realize the capture of "Old Lefty" was truly a job for you Government men who study out these things and apply methods no ordinary amateur can touch.*

A few scattered pockets of resistance remained in the far corners of the state. Conflicting reports put the date of the final eradication of wolves from Colorado at 1935 and 1941. A 1938 report states that two wolves were seen that year in Colorado's national forests. A Monte Vista taxidermist claimed that a wolf was killed in Conejos County in 1943. In 1967 two old and no doubt nostalgia-drunk bounty hunters reported that they saw a wolf near Parlin, but no one believed them.

SPECIES	LAST SEEN
Kenai Peninsula Wolf	1910
Newfoundland Wolf	1911
Banks Island Wolf	1920
Florida Red Wolf	1925
Great Plains Wolf	1926
Mogollon Mountains Wolf	1934
Cascade Mountains Wolf	1940
Northern Rocky Mountains Wolf	1941
Texas Gray Wolf	1942
Texas Red Wolf	1970
Southern Rocky Mountains Wolf	1970

Genetic data suggests that some four hundred thousand gray wolves may once have roamed the region now known as the lower forty-eight states. At the beginning of 2016, by Humane Society estimates, the total gray wolf population in the lower forty-eight states stood at roughly 5,500, with self-sustaining populations in Montana, Wyoming, Idaho, Minnesota, Wisconsin, and Michigan. The Alaskan total was estimated at between 7,700 and 11,200.

The gray wolf received protection under the Endangered Species Act in 1974. In 2011 and 2012, ESA protection was removed for wolves inhabiting Montana, Idaho, Wyoming, Minnesota, Wisconsin, and Michigan, and parts of nine other states. Following the removal of protection, the six named states instituted wolf-hunting seasons. Depending on the jurisdiction, a variety of methods besides hunting with firearms is now permitted, including trapping, snaring, night hunting, use of electronic calls, and use of legally salvaged wildlife as bait. Wolf hunting has never been illegal in Alaska, where some 15 percent of the wolf population are killed annually. Aerial hunting by helicopter is permitted on an irregular basis, depending on the strength of public outcry against the practice.

Small, protected populations of Mexican gray and red wolves are found in several Southern states, where efforts by the U.S. Fish and Wildlife Service to establish self-sustaining populations have so far proven unsuccessful.

> *A photograph of jaguars*
> *An elk head on a wall*
> *A monument to petrels*
> *Skins of mink and fox*
> *Petroglyphs of bison*
> *Memories of whales*
> *Pigeons in museums*
> *Weathervanes of roosters*
> *Clouds resembling dolphins*
> *A pack of stars called Lupus*

I never found Old Lefty. The howl that I heard toward sunset was an auditory illusion, a symptom of the high mountain madness that sometimes afflicts the lonely and the hopeful. What I did find, as I settled to my observation post among the sage, and the night wore on, and the cold air pressed in around me, was a flawless spinning of the gears, of the night and the cold, of the earth, the sage, the snow, the air, the mountain, and the star-jammed sky—a reliable clockwork that, for a few moments at least, seemed to number me among its busily twirling wheels. I had been monitoring the flashing lights of Orion, that irrepressible peacock, when it came to me that I wanted to feel the cold, really feel it, as I had never felt it before. Without further thought I peeled off my mittens, my wool cap, and my coat, and tossed them at my side. Then I stood as calmly as I could (I froze, we might say) and waited. I was sure that something curious was going to happen.

The night air coiled around me, tightened its grip, and penetrated my skin, and the warmth of my body drained away. But, strangely, I felt no discomfort, no urge to shiver or tighten down on my muscles. I stood tranquilly, my arms at my sides, my face turned toward the sky. The cold swelled within me. I closed my eyes and listened. Not a sound broke the icebound calm, not an atom danced in the rock-still air. I was afloat in the deepest silence I had ever known, a silence black and bottomless and perfect. It evoked in me a feeling that was unfamiliar and gratifying, a sense that I had discovered something I had fervently believed in but, until that moment, had never experienced as truth.

Soon the feeling passed and the quiet lifted, and I began to shiver violently. I opened my eyes and knelt to retrieve my wrappings. Quickly I zipped up my coat, pulled on my mittens, and tugged my cap down over my ears.

It was late. I had a long hike ahead of me to reach my car, and it was time to get moving.

I looked east, where the tip of the crescent moon was a dot of light on the horizon. The sky was clear and would soon be bright; the air was calm. It was a good night to travel a mountain.

I took my pack in my hand and started down the slope. After a few steps I stopped. Something seemed wrong. I could feel the black hulk of Castle Peak behind me, and, higher up, the topmost rocks perched in the distant sky.

I hesitated only a moment. Then I turned, pulled my pack over my shoulders, and headed for the top of the mountain.

This one's for Lefty.

PILGRIMAGE TO TSOODZIŁ

FROM *MOUNTAINS OF THE GREAT BLUE DREAM*

This I may say is the first time I have been at church in California.
—JOHN MUIR, OF HIS ASCENT OF CATHEDRAL PEAK

I

BENNIE SILVERSMITH: "MY hair is long, to represent rain. When you see rain beyond the horizon it looks like hair hanging down from the sky. Sometimes when I wash my hair it gets very wild, and then it looks like a great storm."

Turning his head, Silversmith indicates the knot at the back, a fat barrel of jet-black hair wrapped in a thick white cord. This slightly exaggerated gesture—the slow twist of the neck, the modestly bowed head framed by an open palm—has an operatic quality about it. I take it as a warning to stay alert, to watch for symbol and portent. Silversmith seems to be saying, "If you believe that hair is hair, my friend, you are in for a big surprise."

"My hair knot represents the medicine bundle that our forefathers used in the healing ceremonies. Inside the medicine bundle was dirt from each of the sacred mountains. The cord I use to tie the knot is a lightning bolt, or a rainbow, or sunshine."

Bennie Silversmith is a Navajo medicine man, a towering, broad-shouldered figure who, despite his relative youth, is known among his people for power and wisdom. Seated opposite me in his office in Window Rock, Arizona, he is a commanding presence;

this is due partly to his sheer physical size, partly to the gravity with which he addresses any subject. He is outfitted in a dusty-rose down vest, blue flannel shirt, and modish tinted glasses that seem slightly out of place on the head that can so convincingly entertain a medicine bundle.

I have come to Window Rock, capital of the Navajo nation, to talk about mountains with this embodiment of lightning bolt and rainbow and sunshine. On this serene April afternoon, it is sunshine that lies gently on the red-rock countryside—an exploratory, gray-tinged light still stiff from the hard days of winter. Not far from us stands the great Window Rock, an immense wall of sandstone bored through by a hole large enough to admit a small asteroid. It is a stomach-turning exercise to stand beneath the red wall, as I did earlier in the day, and to peer up into the blue kaleidoscope and contemplate the awful size of the thing, but little more so than to consider even the least-celebrated vista (dry gulches strewn with down-and-out monoliths; entire longitudes of red on red on red) in this many-wondered land of the Navajo, an endless playground for the eye. For the casual spectator it is dangerous country, dangerous to the heart and to the lungs; aerobically unfit sightseers have been known to perish on the spot. In spring, when the light is tentative and the wind irritable, the land gives an unmistakable sense of movement, of proceeding to its ancient summer quarters as though it were inspired. You ride the land, foot to the floor, and you feel its heartbeat beneath you. This heartbeat resonates in Bennie Silversmith and empowers him to perform his medicine, which he does with exceeding skill, as I am soon to find out.

I have come seeking the counsel of this Navajo religious leader because I wish to visit one of the sacred mountains of his people. Like most of the world's religions (Christianity and Judaism are notable exceptions), that of the Navajo regards as holy certain high places on the earth and believes them to be inhabited by God. Silversmith's people recognize six sacred mountains. Spread over a wide area of New Mexico, Arizona, and Colorado, they mark the boundaries of the tribal homeland. Each plays an important role in the Navajo creation story and in the daily lives of traditional-minded members of the tribe. So deeply rooted is the belief that these sacred peaks are the limit of the land that some Navajo refuse to travel beyond them.

In response to a question, Silversmith describes the sacred mountains to me one by one: Dook'o'oooslid, the mountain of abalone . . . Sisnaajini, the mountain adorned with white shell . . . Tsoodził, the mountain of blue-green turquoise . . . Dibé Nitsaa, the mountain adorned with jet . . . Dzil Na'oodilii, the mountain dressed in precious fabrics . . . Ch'ool'i'i, the mountain draped in sacred jewels. "The sacred mountains are our strength," he tells me, visibly savoring the Navajo word for "strength" before translating it for me. Several times during our conversation, Silversmith repeats the word and the context: "From the sacred mountains we get our strength."

He speaks in a slow, meandering cadence, the rhythm of a wide, deep-running river. I choose the metaphor deliberately, to suggest the nature-oriented syntax that characterizes much of his speech: An old woman's white hair is like snow, her skin like parched summer earth. Silversmith's face remains impassive as he talks, a demeanor I take at first to denote solemnity. I quickly learn that it can also mean just the opposite. After he has described his thick head of hair as rain hanging down from the sky, I point to the beloved bald spot on the top of my head, as if to lament the poverty of the comparison.

Silversmith stares at the circle of pink for a moment. Then, deadpan, he announces in a grave voice, "Sun . . . peeping . . . through . . . clouds." At this I laugh out loud, and the least suggestion of a smile, like the curve of the crescent moon, crosses his lips.

Silversmith's frequent references to the things of the natural world and the confidence with which he invests them with religious content and purpose reveal a conviction of God's presence in nature that I envy. My prolonged contact with mountains and wilderness has shown me that what he believes is true, yet because I was raised a Christian, because I carry in me the traces of several thousand years of Judeo-Christian tradition, I cannot fully believe in what I have discovered. When I try, my skin begins to prickle and old sermons rattle in my bones. My family attended church once a week and sought God in Heaven. The man who took his church in the woods was a deserter and a heathen, and lazy to boot. (It required strength and stamina to survive church, especially our Episcopal church, with its exhausting Olympiad of ups and downs.) My mother and father were quite liberal on most religious matters and not much attracted to fire and brimstone, yet on one thing they were unwaveringly conservative and fiery: Trees were for climbing; church was for God.

For most of my life I have taken my church in the woods, though never without a nagging suspicion that what I was doing was destined to have dreadful consequences for me somewhere down the line. From time to time I return to the Episcopal church out of a sense of duty and confusion, and probably fear. Dilatorily I have dipped my toe into the freezing waters of alien religions, most organized, a few quite the opposite. Following every baptism, I return to the woods, where, God help me, I find a kingdom that seems to be spiritual, a power that seems to be infinite, and a glory that seems to be God.

Like a blind man who has learned of the stars, I inhabit a limbo between darkness and light. I continue to be amazed and embarrassed when I encounter a fellow pantheist on a trail somewhere, a fallen Lutheran or defrocked Catholic praying piously to the fir trees or babbling over a sunset he or she reports as heavenly. In unguarded moments I do it myself, and I hear the cant in every word. It's one thing to change opinions, points of view, or political parties; it's quite another to exchange old traditions for new ones. My tradition, handed down from Genesis, teaches that nature is corrupt and that humans have dominion over it for use in glorifying the Creator. My discovery is that nature is sacred and that it is nonsensical to claim dominion over such a thing, for to do so is to claim dominion over God. I wish I could bear witness to this revealed truth with the conviction of a Bennie Silversmith. Regrettably, my gospel is too recently learned for me to preach it with self-assurance. Like the good news of electricity, moving pictures, and ATMs, it is gospel that still leaves me blinking my eyes.

For many Christians and Jews who have begun to see the tragic consequences of the Genesis myth—dominion gone berserk—the American Indian is emerging as a figure worthy of esteem and emulation, offering to the Euroamerican "a mystical sense of the place of the human and other living things," in the words of historian and philosopher Thomas Berry. "This is a difficult thing for us since we long ago lost our capacity for being present to the earth and its living forms in a mutually enhancing manner." For right-thinking Christians and Jews, the earth is object: visible, tangible, dead. "Subjective communion" with our planet, Berry suggests, is something we can learn, or relearn, from Native Americans.

Such communion is manifest in the words and manner of my informant as he describes Tsoodził, the sacred mountain I wish to visit. It is a female mountain, Silversmith says in a voice that is warm and deferential. It is a water mountain—his hand undulates in imitation of a wave. "It is a mountain," he says gratefully, "that was put here to enable the Navajo to be fruitful in life." How different from the mountains of the Bible—320 of them in the concordance that I checked, 95 percent of which are "a," "the," "this," "that," or "some" mountain. Not one is described as beautiful or even mildly attractive. A few are "holy," "great," or "goodly," but only because God has momentarily put in an appearance there. In a single verse Jeremiah gives us a "destroying" mountain and a "burnt" mountain, which is about the closest anyone comes to dignifying a peak with a personalized description, albeit a grumpy one.

The precise location of several of the sacred mountains is a subject of debate among Navajos. Not so Tsoodził, the sacred mountain of the south, firmly fixed in northwestern New Mexico and visible from vantage points eighty miles away. One of my reasons for calling on Silversmith is to ask him how I can approach the mountain in a way that will not be offensive to his people. This is a matter of the utmost urgency, because disrespect for and violation of Native American sacred places, long commonplace, have become epidemic in recent years. Countless Native American religious sites have been destroyed to make way for roads, dams, housing subdivisions, and other developments. Mountain climbers, to their huge discredit, have been among the most arrogant trespassers on religious rights. Because of the importance of several sacred mountains highly coveted by climbers, some tribes have closed those peaks to climbing. Shiprock on the Navajo reservation in New Mexico is perhaps the prime example. Nevertheless, a few climbers have ignored these bans and conducted clandestine ascents of the forbidden mountains. The superiority of the climber's purpose, apparently, outweighs any niggling and tiresome objections of the people on whose lands these prizes are located.

Several decades ago, Tsoodził itself was slated for development as a ski resort. But Pueblo Indians, who also attach religious significance to the peak, joined the Navajo in protest, and the proposal was defeated. Lumbering and mining operations continued on the mountain unabated.

"If you go, you must have a purpose," Silversmith tells me with great seriousness. "Remember that going to a mountain is like going to a man's house. You wouldn't go to a man's house without a purpose. And while you were there, you wouldn't be disrespectful or take something that wasn't yours."

He outlines some specific instructions. I am to tell the mountain my purpose in coming. I am to bless myself, say prayers, sing songs, and make an offering. Finally, he gives me a warning.

"The Spirit sent a bear to protect the mountain and bolted the mountain down to Mother Earth with lightning." Thus the danger I will face: "You may go where you want on the mountain except to the very top. It is forbidden to go to the top. The top of the mountain is guarded by the bear and the lightning bolt." It is no doubt symptomatic of my unshakable view of myself as an intruder that in the days leading up to my visit to Tsoodził, these two, the bear and the lightning bolt, will come to dominate my thoughts.

As I prepare to leave, Silversmith mentions some similarities between Navajo and Christian traditions. Each has twelve Holy People. Each has a great flood. Each has a First Man, and a First Woman who commits a major indiscretion (Navajo First Woman sleeps with Turquoise Boy, an act which, like Eve's pilfering of the fruit, has lasting and unpleasant consequences). In Silversmith's view, the similarities are not coincidental.

"Everybody talks about God in his own way. Each of us has a different name for God." Suddenly he slips into parable. "It's like a man with many children. Each child has a different way of saying 'father.' One child says Dad, another says Poppa. But no matter how many different names the children have for him, there is only one father. And the father loves all of his children the same."

Outside under a dome of blue borne by six sacred mountains, I return to Window Rock for another look into its extravagant skylight. The earth pauses for breath, then catches a breeze and resumes its roll toward summer. Nearby a Navajo child plays in the shade of a ponderosa, watched over by his mother in traditional costume. The boy is beautiful, but it is well not to stare; many Navajo believe there is peril in the eyes of a stranger.

But no such proscription holds for the boy. He looks at me and laughs, evidently at my beard. "Look, Mama," he cries out. "It's like grass!"

~~~

II

A FEW WEEKS earlier I had had an intuition that I should visit Tsoodził. I had been trying to write a story about Native Americans and had lost my way. Not knowing where to turn next, I had laid the story aside with a vague intention of taking it up again at a later time.

But it wouldn't leave me alone. One afternoon I took a nap, and as I was coming out of it, plying those pleasantly lapping waters that guard the boundary between sleep and wakefulness, I heard myself asking a silent question: *What shall I do?* And something—not a voice but a fully formed realization—came to me: *Go to Tsoodził.* I had had such premonitions before and had learned to trust them. Like an unexpected letter from an old friend, they arrived with an air of mystery and excitement and faint foreboding, and they always delivered. This one was to be no exception; indeed, it heralded one of the strangest and most unforgettable experiences of my life.

Now on an April morning of black clouds and gusty winds I drove over the northern New Mexico highlands toward the mountain. It seemed a properly somber setting for attending a sacred mountain, if Tsoodził really was sacred; perhaps I had been too much conditioned by the Hollywood religious epics of my youth—*The Robe, The Ten Commandments,* and the rest—in which God always seemed to postpone his appearance until the countryside had been duly softened by a holy gully-washer. Till now the deluge had held off, but the sky appeared ready to open at any moment. I made up my mind that in the event of a downpour I would drive to a suitable viewpoint for at least a gander at the mountain in liturgical garb before I returned home. As I wound my way among mesas growing darker and more menacing by the minute, I took that to be the likely order for the day.

Thirty miles from the peak I rounded a corner and felt a surge of excitement at the sudden appearance of Tsoodził on the skyline before me. An ancient volcano just over eleven thousand feet in height, Tsoodził has managed through the eons to maintain the classical lines of its youth: smooth, symmetric, gradually rising through deep forests to a conical snow-covered summit. Unlike mountains formed by uplift and folding, Tsoodził stands alone, unobstructed by intervening foothills. Studying it now, I thought how natural it is that mountains should be regarded as sacred. In the cluttered world of topographical ups and downs, they stand head and shoulders above the rest. The eye is drawn to them. Borges wrote that everywhere on Earth all plains are the same but no two hills are alike. Who but a Nebraskan would disagree? Reaching the top of such an eminence is an ordeal, like creeping to Lourdes on your knees. And then the summit, zealously guarded by lightning bolts and bears. Surely this is the home of the gods!

I turned north onto National Forest land. The road exited the bleak altiplano and inched upward into a mixed forest of ponderosa pine and white, bare-limbed aspen. In early spring the aspen looked chilly without their manic cha-cha leaves. At intervals I came upon bombed-out slopes where loggers had snatched acres of trees at a swipe. Here was the opposing view of Tsoodził: the unholy mountain as object, storehouse of riches, servant to the people. On Tsoodził plunder included pumice, coal, and uranium to fuel nuclear weapons. Imagine Chartres with broken windows, Saint Peter's with a mineshaft drilled through the chancel, the

Wailing Wall tumbled for molybdenum. I was pleased to see that on this day, at least, the engines of sacrilege would be idle. With rain threatening, no one was clear-snatching trees today. As I drove higher on a dead-end road, I grew more and more certain that my pilgrimage to Tsoodził was to be a solitary one.

The paved road turned to dirt. A curious glow illuminated the forest ahead. I slowed and squinted through the windshield. I was startled to see a narrow column of sunlight slanting down on the mountainside ahead. As I entered the brightness, the sky above me cleared to a spotless blue. The clearing appeared so quickly it reminded me of a window opening in the solid overcast. I thought: *How odd and how fortunate.*

The spotlight followed me up the mountain. Several miles farther along and perhaps two thousand feet below the summit, rounded islands of old snow began appearing among the trees. Higher still, one island joined the next, and soon the character of the landscape had changed completely. The mixed groundcover had turned to white, whole hillsides of evergreens were leaning in the wind, and snow banners were spinning from the treetops. To my delight I saw that I had rediscovered winter.

Several inches of fresh powder lay on the road, unmarked by footprints or tire tracks. I drove on a short distance. Then, below a steep, icy grade that my spinning wheels were unable to negotiate, I pulled off the road and parked.

During the drive up the mountain I had promised myself that I would be cautious, and now was the time to begin: to consider alternatives, to measure the wind, to devise a careful plan for the hours ahead. A lone man with a small car on a snowy dead-end road in inclement weather at ten thousand feet on a wild mountain in resurrected winter—let's be sensible about this!

But being sensible never entered my mind. I was so staggered by the snow, the trees, the whole razzle-dazzle, that I practically flew through the car door. Outside in shirtsleeves I stood shivering in the chill air, scanning a mountainside that looked endless in its towering trees. By now the friendly window above me seemed a natural feature of my surroundings, and I ceased to be aware that it could close as quickly as it had opened. I pulled on my down jacket and retrieved my rucksack from the trunk of the car. Judging that I would be on top of the mountain in under two hours, I tossed out everything but a snack, a bottle of water, mittens, and a hat. I checked the zippered compartment at the top of the pack to be sure that it contained the offerings I had brought for the mountain. Then I locked the car and in a choppy wind headed up the road.

～

THE WAY LED upward along a shelf between a steep hillside and a deep ravine carved by a mountain brook. The hillside looked intriguing, so, impulsively, I abandoned the road and took to the sloping forest, a dimly lit cathedral of Engelmann spruce heady with the fragrance of evergreen.

The new angle punched me at once in the chest. I stopped to catch my breath. Then, at a slower pace, I resumed the climb. I heard the crunch of my boots kicking rhythmically into the snow, and I heard the sound of my voice singing:

Mountain of beauty,
Mountain of trees,
Mountain of snowfall,
Mountain of rocks . . .

I felt foolish at first, and fraudulent. Singing to a mountain isn't my way, and what is more dishonest than a dishonest pilgrim? But Bennie Silversmith had directed me to sing and so I sang, in the same cooperative spirit that had once led me to don a yar-mulke, equally self-consciously, at the wedding of a Jewish friend. In both instances, as a designated Episcopalian, I felt embarrassed but at the same time liberated, suspending judgment and trusting in the genius of another.

> *Mountain of blue sky,*
> *Mountain of swallows.*

I sang about what I saw, seeking out new sights to inspire the lyrics of my song. In doing so I tuned in to the shadowy under-world of the mountain I might have missed had not the hard rules of lyric writing demanded that I stay alert.

> *Mountain of gray moss,*
> *Mountain of mouse tracks.*

Great music, I suspect, is written at sea level. The higher I climbed and the more breathless I became, the less tuneful was my song. Somewhere in the midst of this rapidly deteriorating musical comedy, I realized I had forsaken melody altogether. I was no longer singing—I was chanting.

In a small clearing among the trees I paused for rest. As I sipped from my water bottle, I felt the Navajo's remaining instructions nagging at me. I procrastinated. At last, buckling under, I spoke a short prayer, aiming, in the manner of a grievously near-sighted archer, to bless myself and my journey. Frighteningly exposed, unprotected by worshippers in surrounding pews, I groped for words. As I explained my purpose in coming here, perhaps to God's very bosom, I heard the bare, pathetic empti-ness of my prayer. "Make me worthy of—what . . . I came—I've come here because I feel, well, drawn somehow . . . I'm trying to write this—thing, and I thought, maybe—anyway, help me . . ."

The words hurt. I cringed, fretted that someone might have heard me speak.

∿

THE WINDOW IN the sky slammed shut. The light that had lit the way winked out. A pointed wind, newly bitter, stole into the clearing. I looked up the slope and saw an overturned trainload of fog spilling down the mountain; as if seeking me out, it parted to envelope me. The suddenly disaffected trees receded into nebulous gray.

I didn't think of turning back. On the contrary, my desire to continue only sharpened. As I climbed higher, the fog grew thicker, the snow deeper and softer. I began sinking in to my calves, then my knees. I knew I could not continue for long, for I was fast becoming exhausted. Yet I plunged in, fought for breath, stepped up, plunged in, fought for breath. As I was approaching the limit of my endurance, Bennie Silversmith's words suddenly came to me, reminding me of the mountain's ultimate gift. Scarcely realizing what I was doing, I began to chant anew:

> *Mountain of beauty,*
> *I need your strength.*

It was a plea for something I could not supply myself and without which I could not go on. Dimly I imagined that my only hope lay in a revitalized set of leg muscles, little realizing that the true source of strength was the mountain itself.

I kicked into the snow. My boot penetrated an inch or two and stopped. I blinked. I stepped up and felt a solid layer of snow grab hold beneath me. I took another step. The result was the same: Instead of plunging in to the knee, I again hit bottom at once. Feeling relief immediately, I stood up on a solid, secure snow cover of perfect consistency—hard enough to support me, and just soft enough to crack at the surface to provide purchase and, equally important, to form discernible footprints which, when the time came, I could follow through the fog back to my car.

I was too tired to be amazed, but I did register a clear understanding that I was not alone on this venture. I remained confident of my safety but not unapprehensive. And as I climbed higher, further extended with each step, I occasionally glanced back to be certain that the indispensable footprints, my lifeline to safety, were visible behind me.

> *Mountain of firm snow,*
> *Mountain of clear tracks . . .*

In his discussion of mysticism in *The Varieties of Religious Experience*, William James concludes that mystical states add a "supersensuous" meaning to the ordinary outward data of consciousness. "Facts already objectively before us fall into a new expressiveness and make a new connection with our active life." Through most of the day I was aware that I had crossed an invisible line between the intelligible and the transcendent, and that what had begun as an ordinary hike up a mountain had become a spiritual experience. Extraordinary coincidence could explain most of what happened, but not my clear perception that coincidence explained none of it. In James's notion of the supersensuous quality of mystical states I find a perfect explanation for the change that came over me as I climbed higher and higher into the fog toward the summit of Tsoodził. My awareness of physical discomfort vanished. I climbed effortlessly, with no need for rest. Entering a state of acute sensual awareness, I heard in the ethereal silence an allusiveness—something conversing with me—and saw what was going on behind the fog, and I tasted and smelled the air and understood it as an extension of myself rather than something separate. Coincidence or accident or lightheadedness might be proposed to explain some of this. Yet how shabby and inadequate these rationalizations seem when measured against the Navajo explanation for what I experienced: Tsoodził is sacred.

At some point I moved out of the forest onto an open, treeless slope. Here fog and snow blended, creating a dizzying continuum of white. Nowhere did shadows render clues to distances or depths. Up, down, left, right—all were the same. Ahead I could see perhaps fifteen feet; behind, dimly, my two or three most recent footprints. The world was shapeless. I seemed to be afloat.

My only fear—a curious but, under the circumstances, quite well-founded one—was that I might stumble accidentally onto the top of the mountain. In my reverie I had not forgotten the medicine man's warning against climbing to the summit of Tsoodził. So limited now was the visibility that it seemed possible I could take a step on the gradually declining slope and find I had no more steps to take. I began moving one step at a time: up a foot, stop, stare into the fog to be certain there was more mountain up there somewhere, then up another foot.

The tension was exhilarating. The mountaineer in me badly wanted the summit, yet I firmly believed that were I to reach the top, I would suffer some terrible calamity. The trick, as always, was to come as close as possible to the line without stepping over it.

For some minutes I inched myself higher, savoring every moment. Finally I came to a spot where a short, steep slope rose up beside me into the fog. It topped out beyond sight at what I knew intuitively was the highest point of the mountain. It was there that I stopped, certain I had gone as high as I dared. And it was there, as I paused for my first breath in many minutes, that I clearly and unmistakably heard the roar of the bear standing on the summit of Tsoodził.

The sound came out of the fog, perhaps thirty feet above me. It was loud and full-throated, and it terrified me. I had no doubt about the source of the sound. Standing there weak-kneed and probably too white-faced to have been distinguished from my surroundings, I sputtered to myself, "Jesus Christ, there's a bear up there!"

A moment of silence. Then, a few yards to my left, a hail of rocks came crashing down the mountain. Despite my distress, I felt certain that the rocks posed no danger to me. I watched as one by one they bounded harmlessly past me and disappeared into the fog below.

I held my breath, half expecting to hear a deep voice calling out my name. But the mountaintop again grew silent, and the momentary fear I had felt passed as quickly as the volley of rocks.

I knelt in the snow. From my pack I removed the offerings I had brought for the mountain: a small silver coin and a sliver of wood, a homecoming of sorts, a step toward putting the mountain together again. I said a word of thanks for the privilege of coming to this place and prayed for a safe descent to my car. Then, purely on impulse, I asked for a sign.

Like climbing past an overhanging roof—a dangerous and utterly committing act—asking for a sign sets one on an irreversible course, laying open the possibility of shattering, irreconcilable failure. Should the sign fail to appear, the object of one's supplication is revealed as a false god. There is no denying it, no explaining it away as a mistake or a failure in communication. Only once before had I done such a thing, and I had immediately been rewarded. Now, near the bare summit of a mountain dangerously deficient in potential sign material, I did it again. Done in the right spirit, I think, this is not a calling of God's bluff but, rather, an act of prodigious faith. *Of course*, one says with supreme confidence and surely not wishing to be disappointed: *God will deliver.* I said my piece, then stood and began preparing calmly for my descent.

A moment later it began to snow. From out of the fog above me came an onslaught of great white marvelous flakes, feather-light, blizzard-thick. There were no warning shots, no genteel messenger flakes announcing what was to come. It wasn't pouring snow and then it was. I accepted this sudden storm quite happily. When I realized it was self-induced, I laughed.

And then, of course, I realized my dilemma. I glanced down at the first of the footprints leading off the mountain. Already it was partially filled with snow. In a sudden panic I threw my pack over my shoulder and jumped off down the slope. I descended sideways, scanning the terrain beyond my lower foot for the reassuring shadow of the footprint below. The imbroglio of white, the already confusing fog and ground cover now complicated by a downfall of snow: My head spun. Each footprint seemed harder to spot than the one before. I started moving faster and more carelessly, watching helplessly as the sharply etched prints of my ascent began rounding and filling, sinking inexorably into the snow cover.

My glasses fogged up. Cursing, I stopped. With a corner of my handkerchief I attempted to remedy the problem, succeeding brilliantly in compounding it instead: Now I was looking out on an immaculately white world coated with an obscuring film of moisture.

My heart sank. The zeal and certainty that had brought me this far vanished. I knew I would never outrun the snow. Even had I been able to, I knew from experience that racing pell-mell down a mountain is a sure prescription for disaster. Standing on that bare slope carpeted in featureless white, robbed of the footprints I had counted on to show me the way home, I began to wonder if I might not be in something of a jam.

I swore again and registered a long moment of foreboding. Dutifully but without much conviction, I began hammering out a plan. And then suddenly, as abruptly as the snow had begun to fall, I felt myself growing calm and confident again. Not because of the plan, which had gone nowhere. But as the snow poured down and the route dropped off below me as bewilderingly as ever, I realized that the solution to my problem lay not in seizing control of the mountain—my instinctive reaction on most occasions of high drama—but in allowing the mountain to seize control of me. To put it another way: It was necessary for me only to trust.

This method of saving one's skin is not covered in most mountaineering manuals, nor is it the one I would normally recommend. But normality had disappeared, and trusting somehow seemed right.

My fear passed at once. Gazing about, I grasped what an extraordinary moment it was. Then, slowly and calmly, I began moving down the slope. I had no clear idea of where I was going, but I understood what I needed to do. A few steps into my descent, I began to sing:

> *Mountain of beauty,*
> *I need your strength.*

Once only. As the final word departed my lips, the snow stopped. The fog lifted. The window above me flew open, revealing its circle of impeccable blue.

I found nothing peculiar in any of this. Quite the contrary, what happened seemed as natural as the perfect spring day I enjoyed during the pleasant stroll back to my car.

~

ONLY ONE OF Bennie Silversmith's prophecies, if that is what they were, remained to be fulfilled. Some friends to whom I have told this story insist that because what happened next did not happen on the summit of Tsoodził, where it was foretold, I reveal a zealot's blindness by including it in the story. They say that I am fitting the evidence to the theory rather than the other way around.

They are right. Because I believe that the experience I have described was in some way a religious one intended to reveal the sacredness of Tsoodził, I have . . . not bent the evidence to fit the theory, but allowed metaphor to creep into my tale. When the Navajo said "top of the mountain," I maintain, he may have had in mind a wider meaning than the one we customarily understand. This was perfectly consistent with his practice throughout our conversation. He may even have meant that part of the mountain where the dirt road joined the pavement, where later that day in a light rain under dark skies I drove somewhat dazedly down the mountain.

The high desert lay before me, and beyond that the valley of the Rio Grande and home. I had been thinking about my waking dream of a few weeks before, and now, on the summit of the mountain, I spoke aloud: "Grant me the strength to write my story well." And from out of the darkness there came a light. It was brilliant, silver-white, and arrow-straight. It was a bolt of lightning that nearly tore the roof off the car. Simultaneously a deafening clap of thunder resounded in my ear.

The following morning I took up my story with renewed purpose and finished it not long after.

III

IT WAS PARADISE where they were born. There, creation was good, the trees were pleasant to the sight, the water was pure, and it nourished the garden that was their home. The name of the garden was Eden, a word that meant "delight" . . . the Garden of Delight. And God gave them dominion over the fish of the sea and the fowl of the air and every living thing that was in the garden. But they did not realize their good fortune and they did not understand the nature of consequences, and they sinned. And because of their sin they were sent out of the garden into a cursed wilderness choked with thistles and thorns. And he was condemned to a hard life and an early grave, and she to bearing her young in sorrow. And paradise was lost and man and woman debased and nature corrupted. So it was, and so His followers, Christians and Jews, believed.

A powerful and haunting story, one that usefully explains much about our world and its inhabitants. And one that, like all creation myths, is full of holes. If Eden was created perfect, how then did it contain evil? Ah, well, you see . . . And for the truly pedantic there is the problem of the rib: If God snatched one from Adam to make Eve, why are men and women accoutered equally in ribs?

And the major hole: If God's creation was so good, why did He place it in the hands of certifiably sinful humans, thereby sowing it with the seeds of its own destruction? Why did He put these demonstrably irresponsible creatures in charge of the Cedars of Lebanon, the Rhine River, Glen Canyon, the green hills of Kentucky, passenger pigeons, elephants, Love Canal, the air over Los Angeles, the late, lamented fish in the lakes of the Adirondacks—these glories of His creation—to do with as they willed?

It's hard to believe that God intended any of this. And as the destructive consequences of the Genesis myth have become increasingly apparent during these opening years of the twenty-first century, a few theologians have begun a crash search for a new reading of the sacred texts, one that might preserve the faith without destroying the earth. Matthew Fox, the Dominican scholar, has achieved a considerable following among liberal Christians for his reinterpretation of much of Judeo-Christian tradition. While acknowledging that the nature-is-corrupt doctrine has dominated thought and action through the centuries, Fox insists that the true spirit of Western religion is ecological. It is a spirit that respects God's creation, recognizes our deep connections with it, and takes joy from this gift that is indeed sacred. Fox numbers among the proponents of this view Abraham, David, Jesus, Saint Benedict, Saint Thomas Aquinas, and a host of other big names, all of whom have somehow been drowned out by the Huns and Vandals of the faith.

Like most religious debates, this one promises to be endless. For a floundering Christian like myself, one casting about for a permutation of Christianity that is responsible to the exigencies of the modern world without being faithless to the traditions of the ancient, there is much to be gained, I think, in abandoning all hope that a fresh look at Genesis will magically turn up a previously unrecognized *Walden.* Instead, ask why that text's undeniably anti-nature bias came to be incorporated into it in the first place. When contrasted with the inspiration for the nature-celebrating creation myths of the American Indian, such an approach, I believe, can lead Christians and Jews to a deeper and more respectful understanding of the beliefs and religious practices of the vast majority of Native American tribes that honor nature, and at the same time cast a new light on vexatious Genesis, one that will allow its veneration without being blind to its shortcomings.

At the farthest reaches of their cultural memories, thorns and thistles haunted the writers of the opening pages of the Bible. And for good reason: Thorns and thistles defined the land of their ancestors, the land where their traditions were born. In time it would be called the Fertile Crescent, the birthplace of Western civilization. A narrow semicircular plain, it began in the country we know today as Iraq and followed the courses of the Tigris and Euphrates rivers north and west into Syria, before curving south through Lebanon, Jordan, and Israel. But before 15,000 B.C., during those eons of scorching sun and hot winds when the observing mind inferred from its surroundings the truths it would package as myth, the crescent was an unkind land. It supported few plants and animals, and never in dependable supply. Drought was a never-ending curse. Here began the horror of wilderness that we read in the Bible, and the notion of water as God's greatest gift. To the hunter/gatherers who scratched out a living from this desolation, these prototypes of the disgraced Adam and Eve, land was never bountiful; in its natural state, it was harsh and unmerciful. All of them must have felt that if the land were ever to be generous, it would have to be changed.

It was necessity, then, not God, that granted these people dominion over creation. The reclamation began with the animals. They could not have been better placed: pigs, goats, sheep, cattle, all wild, all rapidly domesticated to serve their self-appointed masters. (How essential the cooperation of chance: Had they been lions and tigers, the revolution might never have begun.) By 6,000 B.C.— five thousand years before Genesis—the hunter-gatherers had put down roots. By genius or by accident, some brave Prometheus among them had stolen a law of nature. Now in place of thorns and thistles stood fields of hardy, totally unnatural species of grain. Hybrids, better than the real stuff, fashioned by the hand of man.

To those who had accomplished this human miracle, the sight of the recreated landscape must have stirred not only the heart but the imagination. Soon, instead of consuming the entire harvest, these enterprising architects of change, now farmers, began saving some of it, replanting it for later use. Daniel Zohart of Hebrew University has suggested intriguingly that this step may represent the first instance of humans working against nature for their own benefit.

A seed was planted. The great harvest of the millennium brought forth not only newly created grains but the earth-shattering realization that the thorns could be defeated, nature controlled, happiness and peace of mind wrenched from the wicked land. By 5000 B.C.—four thousand years before Genesis—the farmers of the increasingly fertile crescent had discovered irrigation and turned it successfully against the infernal drought. By 4000 B.C. they were plundering the forests of the Zagros Mountains for wood to burn in their smelting furnaces. By 3500 B.C. the first battle of the wilderness was over. The once wretched plain was now green and generous, and the land was called Babylonia. There farmers tended wide fields of domesticated grains fed by reservoirs and irrigation canals. From herds of docile stock quartered just beyond their doorsteps they collected milk, meat, wool, and other valuable products. Some they used themselves; the rest they sold in the marketplaces of Uruk, Ur, and Nippur, vital cities of twenty thousand inhabitants that had arisen out of the cruel soil of the crescent. The grand march of Western civilization had begun. Thanks be to God!

Hardly. All of this was possible, the land had become productive, *because humans had made it so.* God admitted as much. In the Babylonian creation story, Marduk, the chief god, cultivates a plot of ground. To water it, he constructs an irrigation canal. To drain it, he digs a trench. In their wisdom, the Babylonians granted Marduk dominion over the land.

The Hebrews trace their ancestry back to this metasphere, to the city of Ur, to a people who seized control over creation. During his long wanderings, Abraham traversed the entire crescent, beginning in Ur, migrating up the Euphrates to Syria and then down to Canaan. The events of the first eleven chapters of Genesis, first recorded between 900 and 600 B.C., correspond in time to the half-millennium that began to unfold in Babylonia about 2900 B.C., some one thousand years after Ur and Uruk were founded. Who can be surprised that the stories that inspired the myth of the garden portrayed nature as accursed and humans as the masters of creation? Who can wonder that the God of the Hebrews was not to be found in the land? The land was abominable! To the authors of Genesis it was axiomatic that only by controlling nature could a people survive, raise families, serve God—even invent writing and parchment upon which to record their story of creation. It was thorns and thistles that led to Ur and what came after: a civilization that could understand the land in its natural state not as the home of God but as the dwelling-place of despair.

For the ancient peoples of North America the land was generous, and their creation stories reflect that fact. Wild game was abundant. In most places, water was plentiful. In the forests and on the plains, edible plants grew naturally and in profusion. There was no need for these people to plant fields, herd cattle, plunder forests, or dig canals, and, indeed, they did almost none of this. Of animals, they domesticated only the dog and the turkey; of plants, just three: maize, squash, and one type of bean. (Tomatoes, peppers, and potatoes originated in Central and South America.) Unlike the inhabitants of the Fertile Crescent, Native Americans never discovered the wheel, the lever, the wedge, the screw, the smelting of metal, or phonetic writing; they developed almost nothing that is regarded by Euroamerican authorities as emblematic of civilization.

And why should they have? They lived in paradise. Through some accident of truly cosmic proportions, they had not been expelled from the garden. For these dwellers of the sacred land, Eden was not a lost dream. It was home.

. . . and it was good. And God said, Let the earth bring forth aspens and oaks and cottonwoods and prickly cactus and columbines and snapdragons and mockingbirds that sing in the golden light of dawn. And let there be blue lakes and emerald valleys and verdant plains and red-rock canyons and deserts the color of rainbows. And let the rivers teem with trout and the plains with bison and antelope, and let the trees hang heavy with apples and plums and pears and all manner of fruit. And let the streams run clear and the rain fall cool and the wind blow sweet with the aroma of all that is in My garden.

*And let there be mountains tall and shining, and let them
have pines and cedars to adorn them, and deer and eagles to
make their homes upon them, and granite walls and ridges to
impart them with majesty. And let the people gaze upon the
mountains and be joyful and know that I am there. For I shall
dwell upon the mountaintops forever.*

In so blessed a land, it is unimaginable that Native Americans
should not have found God in the rocks and in the trees and on
the high peaks. Their myths confirmed God's presence in creation, ratifying their sacred relationship with the earth as Judeo-
Christian myth did not. That the prehistoric inhabitants of this
land never evolved a scrupulous concept of private land ownership,
investment property, or mortgage interest payments has been
cited by some authorities as further proof of the poverty of Native
American culture. Understood as a natural consequence of a people's belief in the sacredness of the land, these omissions seem no
more surprising or uncivilized than the capitalist revolution that
occurred in Babylonia around 2300 B.C., when private ownership of
land was recognized for the first time. Babylonians could buy land
without buying God, a business transaction that was not possible
in North America.

Not, at least, until the disciples of an alien tradition arrived
with their hymnals and their crinoline and their distantly wrought
understanding of the economy of the world. They imposed their
order on the new land, an act of grotesque sophistry, for myth is of
a place: Here were not thorns and thistles; here was a powerful and
giving land. It was inevitable that their failure to understand this
would have tragic and perhaps irreversible consequences.

It would be foolish to argue that Genesis is wrong; on the contrary, it faithfully and wisely bears witness to the traditions of
its time and place. Christians and Jews who love nature need to

recognize this and to respect the integrity of the story. It documents the truth of the land of their faraway beginnings.

But not the truth of America. It would be well for those of us who are new to this place to listen at last to the stories and observe the ways of the continent's indigenous peoples, whose traditions sprang from the land and who have one incontrovertible boast that Christians and Jews cannot make: They were not expelled from the garden. Surely that is an achievement that merits our awe and our respect. Euroamericans do not need to become Native Americans in order to see the propriety of yielding to the original inhabitants of this land their sacred places and returning those taken from them. Nor to open our eyes to the entire world of nature, not only the shining mountains and stormy oceans, which are easy to see, but the nature in our backyards, which is not. With that we may begin finding God in unaccustomed places: in the ravaged tenements of the sacred inner cities, in the foul waters of the sacred streams and rivers, in the stinking soils of the sacred hazardous waste dumps. Tsoodził, the mountain of blue-green turquoise, is everywhere. We may be thankful to recognize this at last and to know that some of the garden remains. Now let us watch over it and tend it with care. Having lost paradise once, surely we do not want to lose it again.

LANDSCAPE OF THE SETTLED HEART

FROM *MOUNTAINS OF THE GREAT BLUE DREAM*

Rise free from care before dawn, and seek adventures. Let the noon find thee by other lakes, and the night overtake thee everywhere at home.
—HENRY DAVID THOREAU, *WALDEN*

One of the many oddities about the sport of mountaineering is that although it is practiced by few and is unintelligible to most non-practitioners, it possesses an iconography that is universally known and appreciated. Who does not understand the symbolism of the ice axe, that canny product of human ingenuity that allows the climber to overcome obstinate nature, or the rope, the umbilical cord through which the life spirit of one climber passes to the other? What tradition has not employed *ascent* as a metaphor for passage to a more godlike plane, or to a state of perfect self-actualization where the soul is purified, the mind released, the epic journey completed?

Most widely recognized of all must be the symbol of the mountain itself, variously seen as the unreachable, the inscrutable, the fearful, or the obstacle to be overcome. Thanks to George Leigh Mallory's famous explanation for his, to the non-climber, baffling compulsion to climb, the mountain has entered the public consciousness, too, as a symbol of that which justifies itself. The not altogether happy result of Mallory's achievement is that it is a rare week that passes when one does not hear some cheerful prose-lyte singing the praises of mud wrestling or beekeeping, or endure a commercial promoting something otherwise utterly unpromot-able, like psychic dentistry, *because it is there!*

A rich lexicon of symbols, yet one that is incomplete, for some-how it overlooks that emblem of mountaineering which, better than any other, clearly and concisely expresses the climber's mys-terious attachment to the high peaks. I sometimes find, perched atop a mountain, that my gaze is drawn not only outward and upward but downward too, in search not of sweeping panoramas of snowy peaks but of the tiny, brightly colored tent where the day's long and hopeful journey began. Usually it is obscured by trees or rocks or some other intervening obstacle, but occasionally I can pick it out at the edge of the forest or in the midst of a sprawling glacier: the crown jewel in a sparkling tiara of snow. When I spot it I invariably let out a shout. Unless they are otherwise occupied, my companions usually scramble to my side and follow my point-ing finger until they, too, see the tent standing far below. A bit wistfully we gaze in silence. To think—we've come all that way! The sight is always a mixed blessing, for along with its heartening glimpse of the end of the road, it lays out a disquieting view of the road itself and of the hazards we must overcome before our travels are over.

For most of the years that I played this game, I regarded it as nothing more than a pleasant mountaintop diversion. But on an eye-opening climb in the northern Purcell Range of British Columbia, for the first time I saw the search as more than a game, the object of the search more than a tent. With my friend Kai Wiedman I had flown to Calgary and rented a car for a drive over the Canadian Rockies and down the western slope into the valley of the Columbia River. There we picked up a rough and dusty road that we bumped along for the next several hours, carefree as Mister J. Thaddeus Toad on a madcap Sunday afternoon outing. Our destination was a remote area of wondrous needlelike peaks called the Bugaboos.

Although it is one of the most spectacular mountain regions anywhere, the Bugaboos are little visited by tourists, which makes them all the more alluring to climbers. Not only is the road rough, dusty, and unimproved by shopping malls, it leads—according to most canons of opinion—nowhere. At road's end lies no alternative but to continue by foot along an arduous backpacking trail that ascends the valley of the Bugaboo Glacier, eventually via ladders on the walls, into a vertical Plutonian wilderness offering the visitor but a single conceivable means of entertainment: mountain climbing. The Bugaboos seem to have been created for mountaineers alone, a grand gift of skyscraping spires rising straight out of perpetual snow: Colorado with solitude, Yosemite Valley with ice, paradise with clean granite walls.

At the edge of the final trees, we pitched our tent and, having done so, underwent that transformation of mind that marks any extended sojourn in the mountains: As the days passed and we settled in to our ever more congenial surroundings, climbing seemed less and less like sport and more and more like what we did in life. Each morning we rose well before dawn, threw down a cold breakfast, and ventured out into the hostile, pitiless world. Each night, chastened, grouchy, and sore, but enormously pleased with ourselves, we trudged back to camp as though we'd just survived a hard day at the office. Jokes over the back fence with neighbors, too much Yukon Jack in a green plastic cup, Pasta Something for dinner, then early to bed to catch a few winks before starting in all over again. In the Bugaboos we led a rigorously circumscribed existence in an abode of unconditional acceptance. I knew my place (mountains by day, blue tent by night), and that knowledge instilled in me a feeling of utter contentment.

One morning we set out to climb the west ridge of a striking pyramid of pearly granite called Pigeon Spire. It's an easy climb by Bugaboo standards, which is not to say that it's deficient in lovely places from which to fall. For a modestly skilled climber like myself, ever ready to oblige at such places, the ridge offered a perfect climb—challenging but well within my capabilities, airy but with plenty of handles to grab when knees began to rattle.

We climbed gamely, toasted our blunders and indiscretions as though they were virtues, hooted camp songs into the wind. The views on both sides of the narrow ridge were magnificent, the rock beneath us firm and gnarly as a peach pit. We climbed with the sun, peeping over more and more distant ridges into inviting countries beyond. I remember the sight of my friend above or below me, grinning ear to ear, ridiculing my clumsiness in the approved fashion or urging me on, and the unparalleled pleasure of working in concert with him—the exhilarating shift from real time into the timelessness of total immersion in a task.

Several hours out, we topped the first and lowest of the spire's three summits. We took a short break, then descended a ramp to the base of a steep wall that rose toward the mountain's middle peak. From a distance the wall looked hard. After procrastinating suitably I stepped up, slipped around a corner, and to my great relief happened onto a surprise crack that led easily upward. My pleasure at finding the crack, however, was short-lived. Moments after exiting at the top I came upon a fiercely exposed skyway, the sight of which made my head swim. Horizontal, perhaps fifteen feet in length and a few inches in width, it offered little margin for error.

At sea level, as they say, an acrophobiac could handle it blindfolded. Observing the smiling glacier beckoning far below on either side of my proposed route, I eschewed the blindfold, choosing instead eyes as big as fried eggs. My final act before embarking was to shout my last will and testament down to Kai, leaving him, as I recall, all of my remaining dried apricots. Then I took a deep breath and scampered across. To my amazement I arrived on the far side in one piece.

Kai soon joined me, bringing the troubling news that halfway across the knife-edge he had been unable to stifle a gigantic yawn. We traversed the middle summit, then descended a groove to the base of the final tower. Here Kai took the lead. After dropping down and around to the left, he mounted a short face to a horizontal crack in the wall. Jamming his fingers into the crack, he eased his way along the base of the tower till he reached an easy gully leading upward. That was the end of the difficulties. Five minutes later we were stretched out in the sun on the tiny knob at the top of the spire.

With the uncertainties of the ascent behind us, we enjoyed our well-earned rewards: rest, satisfaction, small talk, and a gleaming panorama of peaks and glaciers few have been privileged to see. I felt happy, at peace in the company of mountains. Then, as if not quite finished with summit business, I allowed my gaze to slip downward . . . over the edge, down the sweeping wall of rock, down the crazily tumbling glacier, into the trees—

I saw it clearly, a tiny blue dot at the limit of my sight. Impulsively I let out a whoop. Suddenly, peering down from my giddy perch in the sky, I understood for the first time that here at my side was not friend but family, that what we were doing was not climbing but living; and, most of all, that the tiny blue dot waiting for us so staunchly and faithfully at the end of the day was not a tent at all, not even shelter or refuge or safety. It was our home.

∽

AMERICANS ARE A rootless bunch. Half a millennium after Columbus, those of us whose ancestors were not native to these shores still suffer from what the Polish Nobel laureate Czesław Miłosz, himself freshly uprooted to the United States, labels darkly "the immutable violence of new beginnings." We endure this violence in manifold ways, but never more destructively than in our relationship with the earth beneath us, this newfound land whose contours, textures, and ageless truths remain alien to us even today. Restless by destiny, lighting out for the next territory and then the one beyond, we fail to achieve perfect intimacy with any quarter of the land. The imprint we leave behind us is not one of kindly use, as Wendell Berry would have it, but of uprooted trees and tire tracks. Like the irresolute suitor who grows edgy at the prospect of commitment, we move on, as yet incapable of Gary Snyder's "radical act" of living in one place for the rest of our lives. The U.S. Census Bureau estimates that the average American moves about twelve times in his or her lifetime. My own journey so far has included twenty-nine apartments and houses in thirteen cities and seven states. Tirelessly we plod from block to block, from city to city, searching not for a plot of land to tend and to love but for escape, better jobs, warmer climates, higher pay, lower property taxes.

But not, I think, for homes. The distinction between rootlessness and homelessness is important but one that we commonly gloss over. As a result, we anguish more over our supposed homelessness than we need to. "Roots," a popular magazine emblazons on its front cover: "A restless nation searches for a place to call home." Restless we are, and bereft of permanent habitations, but, as nomads have always known, neither bears in the slightest on the search for home. Home, after all, is a stillness of the heart, not the feet. It is no less likely to be found on a speeding train than in a charming Cape Cod with a white picket fence. I have known people who moved practically annually who were comfortably at home the moment they entered their new dwelling for the first time; with few exceptions, the mountaineers that I know have this capacity. Rootless they may be, but, as most of them have discovered soon after they began climbing, home is where the tent is: a movable feast celebrated anew each time they return to the mountains.

In *The Denial of Death*, Ernest Becker argued that the compelling force in our lives is the urge to be heroes. Society is a "symbolic action system," a kind of dead-serious amusement park with Ferris wheels that spin out of control and roller coasters that scare the daylights out of us and shooting galleries that parade impossible choices before our eyes, all so that we may be surrounded with glittering opportunities to act heroically. We participate in the system in order to earn a feeling of "cosmic specialness" by carving out places for ourselves in nature.

Becker did not connect this impulse with the search for home, but I think that he might have, for his phrase "carving out a place in nature" describes better than any I know the means for settling the heart. Mountaineers do it by climbing the hills and discovering a terrain that accepts them unconditionally, one where they know they belong. Others find it at the ocean, beside prairie lakes, in city parks, or in backyard gardens. When circumstances prevent travel or obscure the earth, a simple window box planted with chrysanthemums will serve. The place that we seek may be fixed, like that window box, but more commonly it is a broad pattern of landscape, an accident of personal geography like Mary Austin's deserts and Rachel Carson's sea, where the power of nature is manifest and the earth says, *Here you are welcome.*

Robert Coles, that tireless observer of humankind, tells us of the poor Appalachian woman who placed her child on the ground before her and began rocking him with her bare feet. "This is your land," she said to the boy, "and it's about time you started getting to know it." That woman had a home, and so, we can be sure, did her child. Her deep sense of her place in nature transcended possessions, cultural boundaries, and physical setting; somehow she had learned to see herself as part of the scenery, allowing her to achieve what Frederick Turner identifies as "that surest of realities: the human spirit and its dark necessity to realize itself through body and place."

Having found our places, we return to them again and again. For many years I imagined that this pattern continued for the remainder of our lives, but an exchange of letters with Fritiof Fryxell disabused me of that quaint idea. One of America's great pioneer mountaineers, Fryxell made his mark during the 1920s and '30s, the mad-inventor period in American mountaineering, the era of clothesline ropes, hobnail boots, and seat-of-the-pants improvisation, when a young and ambitious climber could wander into practically any range of mountains and there find dozens of untouched walls and virgin summits on which he (it was always a he) could make a name for himself. Fryxell made his name in Wyoming's Grand Tetons, where he compiled a brilliant record of first ascents. Several of his routes are now regarded as classics.

Having climbed often in the Tetons, including more than a dozen of Fryxell's routes, I had often wondered what it must have been like to have known the range when it was young, when each bootstep took one higher into unexplored terrain. So when I learned that Fryxell, then in his eighties, was living in Illinois, I wrote him a fan letter. I wanted to thank him for opening the way to duffers like me, and I hoped to coax him into spinning a few yarns about the old days. But I had a more charitable purpose in writing, too: I was sure that Fryxell must be miserable in Illinois (highest point, Charles Mound, elevation 1,235 feet). In those grim horizontal surroundings, surely he would be elated to hear from someone, *anyone*, with news from the high country.

A few weeks later I received a generous and self-effacing reply. Fryxell thanked me for my blandishments and allowed that he was "plain lucky" to have found himself in the Tetons "when so much needed to be done." He wrote fondly but not sentimentally about those distant times. About his consignment to Illinois he evinced no note of bitterness or regret. Through this and through a later letter I learned something I had not guessed—I who had assumed that a mountaineer could not live without mountains: Fryxell was content in level Illinois not because mountains lived in his memory, although they did; but far more significantly, because they lived in his reality. Having long ago found his place in nature, he could never again be apart from it. Fryxell needed no mountains beckoning at his doorstep. It was enough for him simply to know that mountains exist. Armed with that knowledge, he would always be among them.

~

IT SHOULD BE obvious that if the search for home is an endeavor to integrate oneself with nature, it may or may not have something to do with family, hearth, security, or any of the other attributes we traditionally associate with home, and it may have nothing at all to do with houses. Somehow we have got it exactly backwards. We speak of the homeless, whom we should properly call the houseless, for many of those afflicted souls are blessedly settled of heart and as content with their single, ever-changing square foot of planet as the millionaire is with his thousands. These people do not need homes; they need houses. To call them houseless, however, makes all too plain not only the problem but, worse, the solution—and, even more bothersome, the implication of us, the houseful, in both. Perhaps this explains our preference for "homeless," a formulation that conveniently loses problem, solution, and implication in the timeless mysteries of home.

As for others of us, in our drive to be heroes we spend our early adult years collecting down payments for houses which, if we secure them, we spend our middle years stocking with families, hearths, security systems, and the rest. If that is the end of it, we are likely to be surprised and embittered in our old age to discover that it is *we* who are homeless, that far from acquiring cosmic specialness, we have achieved a crippling sameness, and that a terrifying malaise stalks us into the darkness ahead. How terrible to contemplate our failures, how baffling and enraging to observe the contented smile on the face of the poor woman of far Appalachia so masterfully rocking her child on the warm earth before her.

Perhaps it seems that I am only trying to say that Earth is our home. Certainly I am happy to claim that currently fashionable address as my own, though for the same reason that I dislike the term *homeless*, I would like to see Earth advocates begin advertising their client as our house. That might bring our pious sentiments down to earth, so to speak, and suggest the kind of practical solutions our current dilemma demands: Clean up your room! Tend the garden! Fix the roof!

Nevertheless, while our planetary address may be Earth, who among us is capable of finding peace on each acre of that sprawling estate? The view of our house from space may be stunning, but the place in nature that we seek must be sculpted on a more intimate, more human scale. During the last years of his life, Joseph Pulitzer lived on New York City's East 73rd Street in an Italian Renaissance mansion containing sixty rooms, forty-five of which he never visited. Pulitzer might properly have been chided for his colossal wastefulness, but it is easy to sympathize with his plight: His digs, like ours, were simply too large. For all our grand ideas and preposterous schemes, most of us take our greatest pleasures from our smallest ones. "The idea that everybody wants to be president of the United States or have a million dollars is simply not the case," John Berryman once told an interviewer. "Most people want to go down to the corner and have a glass of beer." Whether Joseph Pulitzer found happiness in his mostly unexplored Italian Renaissance mansion I don't know. I hope he at least found a shady corner of his garden with an olive tree and an allure he could not explain, a place to which he was drawn as some are drawn to the mountains and some are drawn to the sea. One that spoke to him as a friend, heart to heart, filling him with longing when he was absent and serenity when he was home.

In our grand earthly mansion, we all seek comfortable rooms of our own.

∽

THE JOURNEY HOME begins when we learn to distinguish one place from another and find that some stir our imaginations more than others. Geographer Yi-Fu Tuan has coined a term for this journey: topophilia, the proclivity to grow attached to a particular landscape. Since we know that cats have their favorite chairs and horses their preferred corners of the corral, we can be sure that topophilia is a characteristic we share with other living creatures. What is surprising is just how many, and how far down the ladder of life this tendency occurs. Somehow attachment to place has proven its selective value almost from the beginning of evolutionary time.

Consider the tiny planarian worm, a resident of seashore and swamp for some 600 million years. One of the simplest forms of life on Earth, the planarian enjoys neither brain, digestive system, circulation system, nor, except on occasions so rare they must surely have acquired among members of the species the status of Christmas, sex. To gather its news of the world, to think, worry, appreciate, and plan, the planarian relies on a single pair of nerves connected by two ganglia.

That is it, about a trillionth or so of what each of us can turn to the same purpose. Given these modest gifts, the planarian must have a level of awareness scarcely higher than that of the matchbox or the spoon. Yet in ways no one can fathom, the little creature can learn, remember, choose sensibly, and, most important for our purposes, exhibit topophilia. Planarians prefer to eat in places they know well—comfy places, homey places. Offered food in a strange location, they'll take twice as long to begin eating as will their cousins on familiar ground. Give them an opportunity to know a spot, to stretch out and learn the lay of the land, and they'll quickly grow attached to it, taking their meals there as apparently contentedly as you or I might in our favorite chair at the dining room table. It's pleasant to speculate that planarians may have a rudimentary understanding of home, and that home would live forever in their hearts, if only they had hearts.

For those of us who are higher on the ladder of life, the task of finding our preferred landscapes is correspondingly more complicated, requiring the application of several of our improvements over the resourceful worm. As closely as I can tell, my own journey of discovery began when I was about four years old, soon after our family moved to a century-old house on two acres of land in the lush, slightly rumpled Pennsylvania countryside south of Lake Erie. It's a region of wooded hills, family farms, and winters that strike like earthquakes. Half the year, it seemed, we spent buried under the rubble, the other half digging out and getting ready for the next shock. The hills are lovely and the farms earnest, well-tended affairs, but it is those winters that give the area its character. Because of them, even in summer a gray pall hangs over the countryside, and a look of endless exhaustion.

During the nineteenth century our house served as a landmark for weary travelers plying the dusty road between Erie and Pittsburgh. For a time a large fountain had stood in the front yard.

Passersby often stopped there to refresh themselves and their horses. The house became known as the Fountain House. If the fountain had disappeared long before we moved in, the house nevertheless became an important waystation for me, and a wellspring of revelation.

Having lived my entire four years in the nearby city of Meadville, it seemed to me that in emigrating to the country we had removed to a foreign land, and an exotic one at that. The road to the house was still unpaved when we arrived in 1947. Behind the garage there was an outhouse, which I remember vividly for its festoons of merry flypaper dangling from the ceiling like party banners. We had walnut trees, wild and very prickly raspberry and blackberry bushes, and six apple trees that produced shiny green apples capable of bringing on a stomachache within thirty seconds. Just beyond the walnut trees I put in a small garden and soon discovered a talent for radishes, which eventually became my sole crop. My brother raised Angora rabbits, magnificent, enterprising creatures that tended to escape several times a week. A single failing prevented them from making permanent getaways: gluttony. They could always be found not far away in my little garden, munching radishes.

In such a place it was inevitable that I would begin a search, albeit an unconscious one, for a harmonious contour and texture of land. Just beyond our property there was a hill which, to my inexperienced eye, looked enormous. It was covered with pine trees. One day, probably not long after I moved to the country, several neighborhood children and I entered this vest-pocket forest for the first time, and my journey of discovery began. I remember that I was afraid of the place, but at the same time awed by it and drawn to it. Standing at the edge of the wood, peering into the shadows within, I believed I was about to encounter dangers and powers greater than any I had ever faced. Then I took a bold step, probably my first such, and stole in among the crowding trees. I was certain that what I was doing was forbidden.

As the days passed, we children began playing regularly in what we now called "the pines." I continued to be afraid of this dimly lit woodland, but my fear was of a quite acceptable variety. It sprang, surprisingly, not from trepidations over unseen evils but from those feelings of wonder and awe that had drawn me into the pines to begin with.

That fear was only one of the place's attractions. The pines felt wholly different from the rest of the world. No matter how warm or bright or bustling the day beyond, inside it was always cool and dark and hushed. The air was permeated with a moist odor of decay, which I loved, and underfoot, in the thick carpet of rusty pine needles, I discovered the pleasure of making my mark and establishing a link between myself and these tall, mysterious trees. In the pines I learned direction and connection. I learned to find my way.

Some things could not be explained. Sometimes we came upon trails through the duff that we had not constructed. The conviction arose that a bear lived in the woods and that it might have carved the routes. To my knowledge, none of us ever saw the bear, but at our ages, mercifully, reality was only incidentally a product of the senses.

The final mystery was one that did not seem so at the time but, as the years have passed, has by its nature and its longevity grown to be the greatest mystery of all. It is one not of sight or sound but of resonance, an echo of a seemingly undistinguished moment in time. Why that moment continues to reverberate within me when a billion others do not, why even six decades after it crept past me feather-light in the forest it recalls itself with the urgency of death, I do not know. There is almost nothing to it. Perhaps five years old, I am standing alone, the straight, rough trunk of a pine tree rising to my left. It is dark and silent in the forest and I feel completely at peace. I look toward the brow of the hill. Above, dapples of blue sky drift downward through the treetops.

What incomprehensible force could have seized that prosaic moment and sealed it upon me with such ferocity? Powered not by tornado or flashing comet but by the simple majesty of pines, it created an image of unfading eloquence, one which, I believe, has helped to determine the direction of my life.

In winter, mighty storms swept down from Ontario and buried the country in snow. The bare hillside beside the pines became a sled-riding course famed throughout the neighborhood. Each afternoon, long trains of Flexible Flyers flew down the slope, five or ten sleds in tandem, one practically atop the next. One day some daredevil among us discovered that by climbing higher and beginning his run in the pines, he could achieve a velocity that induced screams in spectators. As those of us who emulated his feat quickly found out, this was not a stunt for the fainthearted. At the halfway point the sledder had to pull off an almost impossible maneuver, a hard left onto the old path at terrible speed. Any miscalculation, any failure of nerve or of will, and both sled and rider were doomed. Across the path they sailed, over the icy lip on the far side, and upside-down into the raspberry bushes.

But success . . . Success was the delicious alternative, and its slim likelihood made the risk of failure incontestably worth taking. Success put us on the old run at a blinding rate, sent us rocketing down the slope, slicing the bitter wind, leaping the nasty bump at the bottom, tearing past the apple trees, past the outhouse, past the terrified Angora rabbits, into the backyard of the Fountain House, and finally, crying from laughter, smack dab onto a patch of ground that during the tender summer days to follow would become, briefly, the world's largest radish garden. What a triumph it was, and what a joy, to absorb the power of the pines at the top of the hill and make it all the way home!

We moved to another town when I was seven, and I didn't see the pines again for many years. When I returned I was amazed, and disappointed, to see how small the area was—perhaps an acre or two of trees in all, on a hillside that rose gently to a height little greater than that of the house. From the backyard of the Fountain House, a short distance away, the pines were scarcely noticeable.

And yet it was the pines I was most eager to see. However insignificant my miniature forest may have appeared to others, in me it inspired the same feelings of fear and of awe that it always had. Not many years later, I began seeking out other and deeper forests, as if in a fever, first in New England, later throughout the American West; simultaneously I began exploring peaks and passes and have continued to do so ever since. When emptiness fills my chest, a climb into the country of forests and mountains is a journey of rediscovery and a coming home. Gathered once more into an embrace of circling trees, I plant my feet in the rich under-growth and search for the dappled sky.

ᴀCKNOWLEDGMENTS

This book documents many years of adventure and traverses many square miles of terrain. As I've dreamed up, planned, and attempted journeys great and small, not always successfully (like my plan to hike fifty miles on my fiftieth birthday, an odyssey that ended at the two-mile mark with a sprained ankle), two generous souls have stood by me steadfastly and with unfailing good cheer: my wonderful and wildly accomplished wife Carol and my wise and multitalented son Jake. To both I say thank you, bless you, I couldn't have done it without you.

This work reunites me, happily, with Jack Shoemaker, founder, with William Turnbull, of the celebrated North Point Press, which published my first collection, *Mountains of the Great Blue Dream*. I'm grateful to Jack for finding me again, and to the gifted staff with whom he has surrounded himself, including Wah-Ming Chang, Megan Fishmann, Deborah Kenmore, Jennifer Alton, Nick Gomez-Hall, and Joe Goodale. The assistance of my brilliant copy editor Oriana Leckert was indispensable.

I'm fortunate to reside in beautiful and thriving northwestern Nevada, where a robust community of writers, poets, artists, dancers, musicians, and actors understands art precisely as struggle, provides indispensable support for its members, and carries out its necessary work unimpeded by the demands of fame and conformity that impinge in other more storied locales. Special thanks to Father Jeff Paul and the kind and generous people of St. Peter's

Episcopal Church in Carson City for fostering vision and strength among its members, and for providing help and comfort to those in need, regardless of their colors, conditions, belief systems, or political affiliations; to June Joplin, for fifteen years my friend and fellow performer in our Great American Songbook duo "Me and Bobby McGee"; and to members of the Carson City Rotary Club and especially Barbara D'Anneo, who, though I am not a member of the club, have for ten years granted me the privilege of providing music for their gatherings, and who in 2016 named me a Paul Harris Fellow.

My deep thanks to three mountaineering legends: Allen Steck, Dr. Richard Long, and John Evans, for sharing recollections of their ascent of Mount Logan's Hummingbird Ridge with me. The story of that climb is recounted in "Intruders on a Lifeless Ridge." Along with conversations and email exchanges with the three, the written accounts of the climb by Steck and Evans that appeared in the 1966 volume of the *American Alpine Journal* were invaluable in helping me to put the story together. I've used quotes from those accounts with the permission of the *American Alpine Journal*. For the story of the 1925 ascent of Mount Logan, I'm indebted to Paddy Sherman and his exhaustively researched history of great climbs on major Canadian peaks, *Cloud Walkers* (St. Martin's Press, 1965).

I'm grateful to Elaine, Heather, and Dawn Meader for permission to tell part of their Arctic story in the chapters from my book *Arctic Circle* that are reprinted here. At their request I've changed the names of certain geographical features that are central to their story and to mine.

Lastly, a long overdue nod to Mr. Bernstein, a teaching assistant in a required course called General Education A, which I was subjected to my freshman year in college. In the margins of my first writing assignment (I still have it), he wrote many discouraging words, none more so than these: "You invoke Socrates as an authority, without any precision. You give the impression that you needed a famous name at this point to back up some vague thinking on your part." He was right, of course; I had no idea what I was thinking. The challenge of discovering what it was—that indescribable quest that T. S. Eliot called "a raid on the inarticulate"—is one that has occupied me for a long time. I would never have known it existed were it not for Mr. Bernstein, and I'm grateful to him for setting me on a path to find it.

More on my journeys and speculations can be found on my website, www.robertleonardreid.com.

~

"To Live One's Life" first appeared in *Touchstone* (January, 2000).

"West, to the Future" first appeared in *Wild Nevada: Testimonies on Behalf of the Desert* (University of Nevada Press, 2005) and was reprinted in *Literary Nevada: Writings From the Silver State* (University of Nevada Press, 2008).

"Rebuilding the Clouds," "Journeys Through Space and Time," and "A Shelter in the Sky" first appeared in *America, New Mexico* (The University of Arizona Press, 1998).

"The Condor's Last Flight" first appeared in *The Progressive* (February, 1981).

"A Poem, Gathering in My Mind" first appeared in *From Exploration to Conservation: Picturing the Sierra Nevada*, under the title "The Writer's Eye: Moments of Seeing in the Literature of the Sierra Nevada" (Nevada Museum of Art and the Wilderness Society, 1998).

"To Feel the Earth Turn," "Honeymoon Blues," "Very Close to Everywhere," "Travels With Lucky," "The Porcupine in Winter," and "A Vow Fulfilled" first appeared in *Arctic Circle* (David R. Godine, 2010).

"Decrescendo," "Pilgrimage to Tsoodził," and "Landscape of the Settled Heart" first appeared in *Mountains of the Great Blue Dream* (North Point Press, 1991) and were reprinted in editions of the same title (Harper Perennial, 1992, and University of New Mexico Press, 1998) and under the title *The Great Blue Dream* (Hutchinson, 1992).